# What the Classics Did for Islam

To my beautiful and clever daughter
Sophie Regina

# What the Classics Did for Islam

Peter E. Pormann

polity

First published in 2027 by Polity Press Ltd.

Polity Press Ltd.
65 Bridge Street
Cambridge CB2 1UR, UK

Polity Press Ltd.
111 River Street
Hoboken, NJ 07030, USA



ISBN-13: 978-1-5095-7352-3
ISBN-13: 978-1-5095-7353-0 (pb)

A catalogue record for this book is available from the British Library.

Library of Congress Control Number: 2026936851

Typeset in 11.5 on 14pt EB Garamond
by Cheshire Typesetting Ltd, Cuddington, Cheshire
Printed and bound by CPI Group (UK) Ltd, Croydon



For further information on Polity, visit our website:
politybooks.com

# Contents

# Introduction

Islamic cultural and religious identity is one of the most contested topics in the modern world. Hardly a day goes by in which we do not hear about Muslims in conflict with 'the West', although many of them live in 'the West' and have long sought an accommodation with 'western' culture. At the same time, right-wing movements across Europe and the Americas ardently affirm the need to protect 'western culture' from Islamic influences. In all this, however, we often forget the shared heritage that unites the Abrahamic religions: Judaism, Christianity, and Islam have all been profoundly influenced by the classical tradition, each in its own way.[1] Although we sometimes hear about a fundamental rejection of 'knowledge of Greek' or 'Greek wisdom' (חָכְמַת יְוָנִית) in Judaism, on closer inspection one finds numerous Greek terms and concepts in the Talmud and the Mishnah, and some of the most prominent Jewish thinkers (such as Maimonides, c. 1135–1204) were steeped in Greek philosophy, theology, and medicine. The foundational Christian text, the New Testament, was written in Greek, and Greek was certainly the dominant language in the early church, even if Latin later replaced it in the West.

The new series that this book inaugurates puts the question: what did the classics do for X? Yet, to be humorous for a minute, asking what the classics did for Islam is a bit like the scene in Monty Python's *Life of Brian* (dir. Terry Jones, 1979) where Reg, played by John Cleese, asks his fellow People's Front of Judea (PFJ) members: 'All right, but apart from the sanitation, the medicine, education, wine, public order, irrigation, roads, a fresh water system, and public health, what have the Romans ever done for us?' For classics had an enormous influence on virtually all aspects of Islamic religion and culture. And when I say 'classics' here, I refer in particular to Greek culture, with which Islam was in close contact from its inception. For the Roman Empire had effectively split into two, East Rome and West Rome, Greek being the dominant language in the East and Latin in the West, although for some topics such as law Latin remained central throughout the Roman world.

The Greek heritage encompasses not just the works by elite Greek writers such as Homer, Hippocrates, Plato, Aristotle, Euclid, and Ptolemy but also of those written in the common language (*koinē*), for example the Greek translation of the Old Testament known as the Septuagint, the New Testament, popular hagiography, the Alexander romance, and many early Christian texts. Moreover, although my focus will be on written evidence, oral transmission undoubtedly played an important role. This heritage then shaped collectively the philosophical, theological, and literary discourse among Muslims, who eagerly read, dispassionately discussed, but also hotly contested these texts from the eighth to the twenty-first century.

Greek culture was not confined to Europe but was 'without borders', as Casper C. de Jonge recently put it.[2] Or, to quote Cicero (106–43 BC), 'Greek literature is read in nearly every nation under heaven' (*Graeca leguntur in omnibus fere gentibus*), so that Greek authors came from Africa, Asia and Europe alike.[3] Greek literature was influenced by the surrounding cultures, not least those of ancient Mesopotamia.[4] And with the conquests of Alexander the Great Greek culture extended all the way to India and beyond; after all, one of the roughly twenty Alexandrias that he founded is Alexandria in Arachosia – a city in modern Afghanistan whose ruins are now known as Old Kandahar.

This book tells the story of the encounter between Graeco-Roman culture and Arabo-Islamic thought. It argues that Islam, both as a religion and as a culture, is as much heir to the classical tradition as is our so-called West. Islam was born in a highly Hellenised world, and the different aspects of Islamic religion all show signs of the encounter between the two cultures. This is true for Islamic law, as it is for the theological debates that developed in later times: Islamic speculative theology, called *kalām*, is inconceivable without Greek philosophy, which is also at the origin of *falsafa*, of philosophy in Arabic. As one prominent scholar put it, 'human and historical Islam is arguably almost as Neo-Platonic as it is Muḥammadan'.[5] Moreover, mathematics, physics, alchemy, biology, medicine, astronomy, astrology, the occult sciences, geography, music, and engineering all drew heavily on Greek sources. Greek popular literature such as the Alexander romance enjoyed an enormous popularity, and in modern times, Greek tragedies and comedies were performed on the Arab stage to great acclaim. In other words, there is hardly any area of Islamic culture and religion that has not been profoundly influenced by the classical heritage.

In the past, scholars talked of a sequence of civilisations, of torchbearers who passed the wisdom of one culture to the next. In this way, the human intellectual history becomes a sort of relay race. This idea goes hand in hand with that of the rise and fall of empires. So, for instance, in his monumental *History of Arabic Literature* (*Geschichte der Arabischen Literatur*) – 'literature' here referring to anything written in Arabic, including the sciences, medicine, philosophy, and so on – the famous German semiticist Carl Brockelmann (1868–1956) labelled the period after the fall of Baghdad in 1258 as one of 'decline' (*Niedergang*).[6] The torch of knowledge was passing from Muslims to Christians, who had begun to translate many philosophical and medical works from Arabic into Latin. Likewise, many Arab and Muslim scholars themselves adopted this discourse about decline in the nineteenth and twentieth centuries.[7]

Yet, although the metaphors of torchbearers and decline and fall are quite attractive, they do not reflect the reality on the ground. For instance, over the last thirty years, the chorus of voices rejecting the idea that the Muslim civilisation declined after a presumed classical age that ended in the twelfth century grew steadily, and few experts still adhere to it.[8] To put it differently: just because many core texts in medicine, philosophy, and the sciences were translated from Arabic into Latin from the eleventh century onwards, it does not mean that research and scholarship ceased in the Islamic world.

Likewise, we should abandon the model of knowledge passing from one civilisation to the next, as the historical situation is far more complex. James Montgomery has therefore proposed a new model, that of cross-pollination, where civilisations influence each other mutually and where the process of knowledge generation is not a one-way street leading to the present.[9] To give just one salient example here, in the Introduction: a number of important medical texts were not translated just from Greek into Arabic but also from Arabic into Greek, for example a work *On Smallpox and Measles* by Abū Bakr Muḥammad ibn Zakarīyāʾ al-Rāzī (d. 925) and a medical encyclopaedia entitled *Sustenance of the Travel and Food for the Sedentary* by Ibn al-Ǧazzār (d. 980). Therefore the cultural encounters described here were neither linear nor one-sided.

To be sure, when different cultures meet, there can also be friction. The great Arab author and polymath al-Ǧāḥiẓ (c. 776–869), for instance, lived through a century when most of the available Greek literature was rendered into Arabic and the Arabic language changed significantly as a result. He himself was well versed in this translated literature and drew on authors such as Plato and Aristotle when writing his *Book of Animals*.[10] He was also extremely critical of the cultural and linguistic change that occurred as a result of these translations, and sometimes became nostalgic for a return to a purer Arabic tongue. Staunch Ḥanbalī zealots such as Ibn Ṭaymīya (1263–1328) took issue with the speculative theology and its practitioners and were critical of Greek influences.[11] One of the pioneers of European Islamic studies, Ignaz Goldziher (1850–1921), even proclaimed that 'Islamic orthodoxy' was hostile to the Greek scholarly tradition.[12] In the twentieth century we find Egyptian intellectuals such as Ṭāhā Ḥusayn (1889–1973) and Louis 'Awaḍ (1915–90), who promoted the study of the classics, being heavily criticised by conservative and Islamist thinkers. And nobody can forget how the Islamic State in Iraq and Syria, known by its acronyms ISIS and 'Daesh', destroyed the temples and monuments in the city of Palmyra; or, more recently, how it murdered and maimed Jews celebrating Hanukkah on Bondi Beach.

Yet, despite these tensions, for the most part Islam embraced the classical legacy; and this engagement continues today. For instance, the 'philosopher of the Arabs', al-Kindī (c. 801–73), who was the first firmly to establish philosophical enquiry in Arabic, adhered to the Neoplatonism of Late Antiquity. Likewise, the Brethren of Purity, a kind of secret society in ninth- and tenth-century Baṣra, engaged in Neoplatonic pursuits and espoused many Greek mystical traditions such as Neo-Pythagoreanism; one scholar even called its representatives 'the Pythagoreans of Islam'.[13] Especially in the Shiite milieus, these doctrines were highly influential, and this explains in part why Ayatollah Khomeini [Rūḥullāh Ḫumaynī] (1900–1989), the founder of the Iranian Islamic Republic, was so fond of Plato as to model some of its institutions on the *Republic*. In tenth-century Baghdad a new Aristotelian school emerged, associated with philosophers such as al-Fārābī (c. 870–951). But whether it be al-Kindī, in the Neoplatonic tradition, or philosophers such as Averroes [Ibn Rušd] (1126–98), a fervent Aristotelian from Muslim Spain, they did not perceive a conflict between revealed religion and philosophy: in their view both arrive at the same truth, albeit by different means.

It is important to note, though, that Islam engaged with the Greek tradition not only at the level of religion but much more generally as well. Already in pre-Islamic poetry and the Qur'ān we find Greek loan words, and the Arabic language in general is heavily influenced by Graeco-Arabic translations. Language and literature go together here. Many Greek expressions, metaphors and images pervade Arabic poetry; one example is the proverbial 'to write on water' (εἰς ὕδωρ γράφειν), first documented in Sophocles (c. 496–406 BC), which appears in Arabic in many variations across the centuries.[14] The most famous one today is the end of Fairouz's lyrical song, based on a poem by Ǧibrān Ḫalīl Ǧibrān ([Kahlil Gibran] 1883–1931), 'Give me the flute and sing' (أعطِني النايَ وَغَنِّ), which ends with the verse: 'men are but lines written yet only on water' (إنَّما النّاسُ سُطورٌ كُتِبَت لَكِن في الماء).

Homer was recited in ninth-century Baghdad and twentieth-century Cairo; *Oedipus King* was adapted in at least five different Arabic versions, all performed on the Arab stage; and Aristophanes' play *Lysistrata* was rewritten and set in Baghdad by the Egyptian playwright Lenin al-Ramlī (1945–2020) as part of a global protest movement against the US-led invasion of Iraq in 2003. The two most prominent twentieth-century Arab poets, the Iraqi Badr Šākir al-Sayyāb (1926–64) and the Palestinian Maḥmūd Darwīš (1941–2008), both engaged with Greek mythology in their lyrical output. The classics department at Cairo University has hundreds of students of Greek and Latin. And even today, in an article titled 'Teaching Plato in Palestine', a prominent philosopher asks the question 'Can philosophy save the Middle East?' and is able to answer it in the affirmative.[15]

The following seven chapters will take the reader on a journey through the history of Islam and its various encounters with the classical tradition; but when one goes on a voyage, one also has to decide what one wants to see. As the influence of this tradition is not just ubiquitous but also profound, I had to choose. I did not just want to tick a long list of great achievements that you, the reader, barely have time to appreciate, let alone comprehend.

But I also wanted to furnish you with a good sense of the breadth of the impact that classics had on Islam. In other words, giving a comprehensive account of this influence would amount to describing how Islam evolved and developed over the course of 1,400 years. This is far too ambitious a task. The present book will therefore rather tell my story – the story of how Muslims engaged with the Greek past – through a series of vignettes that can illustrate the different aspects of this encounter. But in each case I shall provide some wider context to these vignettes and also quote additional literature, so that readers may easily explore those aspects that are more summarily discussed here.

The focus will be on the Islamic heartlands of Egypt, the Arabian Peninsula and the Fertile Crescent, as well as on Arabic sources – not just because of the proclivities of the author but also because developments there were often paradigmatic and shaped attitudes in other Islamic cultures. This said, as with the thematic choices, I will endeavour to provide a few striking examples of how non-Arab Muslims, for instance in Persia or further east, tackled the classical legacy in their own languages. In temporal terms, the examples range from the pre-Islamic period until the twenty-first century; yet, of necessity, not all centuries are given equal attention. If, for instance, I touch only briefly on the seventeeth, eighteenth, and nineteenth centuries, this does not imply that there is less engagement with the classical tradition, but merely that certain periods have attracted less scholarly attention than others.

# 1

# Islam Is Born in a Hellenised World

In order to understand how the classical tradition influenced Islam, we first have to ask ourselves what we mean by 'Islam'. It is possible to answer this question in a variety of ways.[1] For instance, most people will understand it together with Christianity and Judaism, as one of the three great monotheistic (or Abrahamic) religions, practised by hundreds of millions of worshippers worldwide. In the literal Arabic sense, *islām* means 'submission (to God)', and this is why Goethe was able to say in his *East-Western Diwan*: *Wenn Islam Gott ergeben heiſst, im Islam leben und sterben wir alle!* ('If "Islam" means "being submitted to God", then we all live and die in Islam').[2] In the modern world we find many different varieties of Islam, just as there are numerous Christian denominations. Some Muslims, for instance, drink alcohol and do not fast during Ramadan; and by this I do not mean individuals who are exempt for health reasons or who simply do not follow the injunction of their religious community, but Muslims such as the Ismailis, who do not believe that you have to fast during Ramadan, an article of faith that is fundamental to the majority of Muslims.[3]

To determine what the right doctrine is, Muslims turn to a number of sources of authority, the most important ones being the Qur'ān, the Muslim Holy Writ; the Ḥadīṯ, the utterances of the Prophet Muḥammad; and the Sunna, the record of the Prophet's behaviour and actions. And this is where our story begins. According to traditional accounts, the Prophet Muḥammad was born around 570 and lived most of his life in Mecca on the Arabian Peninsula. He received the Qur'ān from the archangel Gabriel (Ǧibrā'īl), over a period that ran from about 610 to his death in 632. In other words, Islam was born in Late Antiquity, in a world influenced by Greek culture and marked by the conflict between the Byzantine and the Sasanian Empires.[4] Greek and Persian, respectively, dominated elite culture in that part of the world, and for the first two generations of the Umayyad Empire the administration operated in these languages. It was only with the reforms of the caliph ʿAbd al-Malik, around the year 700, that Arabic replaced Greek in the West and Persian in the East.

## Pre-Islamic Arabia

Greek culture and language, however, impacted not just on elite culture. We find Greek terms also in the Bedouin poetry of the pre-Islamic and early Islamic times. Take the example of the famous poet al-Burayq ibn ʿIyād (early seventh century). In one of his odes, he boasts about his exploits as a warrior and describes in graphic detail the carnage that he inflicted:

> Many a wailing woman whose voice is shrill
> have I sent away, when the Mirzam [a star] rose,
> who wailed, while probing the wound so that her palm
> and wrist disappeared [in the wound],
> [the wound] of a man, whose head is bent
> and whose wounds exhale blood,
> [a woman] who separated his joints with a probe
> as the comb separates the hair hanging down.[5]

The woman, desperate to save her man, tries to set his joints with a probe, and this probe is called *mīl* in Arabic, a word borrowed from the Greek word *mḗlē* for 'probe'. Thus we find a Greek loan word already in early Arabic poetry. We do not need to wait for the Graeco-Arabic translation movement to see the impact of the Greek language on Arabic; it starts from the earliest days.

We do find not just Greek terms in Arabic but also Latin ones. Perhaps the most striking example comes from the 'Opening Sūra' (*al-Fātiḥa*), which serves as the most popular and most widely recited prayer in Islam; it ends as follows:

إِهْدِنَا ٱلصِّرَاطَ ٱلْمُسْتَقِيم
صِرَاطَ ٱلَّذِينَ أَنْعَمْتَ عَلَيْهِمْ غَيْرِ ٱلْمَغْضُوبِ عَلَيْهِمْ وَلَا ٱلضَّالِّين

Guide us on the right path,
the path of those on whom you bestowed favours, not those against whom one is angry, nor those who go astray.[6]

The word for the right 'path' is *ṣirāṭ*. It comes from the Latin (*uia*) *strata*, meaning 'paved way', and is etymologically related to the English word 'street'.

Generally, people in the Roman Empire were also governed through the legal framework of Roman law, as studied and interpreted in the law schools of Alexandria, Beirut, and Constantinople – to name three prominent centres. Likewise, even those living outside the eastern frontiers of the empire, as many Arabs did, witnessed, and were at times subjected to, this legal framework in action. It is still a major point of debate to what extent Roman law influenced Islamic law. Patricia Crone argued persuasively that it was not so much the legal framework of Roman law in the abstract that had an impact on Islamic jurisprudence, but rather local (or 'provincial') practices that were in force in the territories later conquered by the Muslims.[7] She makes this argument for the patronage system in Islamic law (called *walāʾ*), but the influence can best be illustrated through a concrete example. In Islam, a system of market inspection (*ḥisba*) developed where the market inspector (*muḥtasib*, *ṣāḥib*/*ʿāmil al-sūq*) upholds the rules of fair trade and roots out various kinds of fraud and misselling. The Greeks had a very similar system, and the market inspector in their world was called *logistḗs* or *agorānómos*. Crone contended that the term *muḥtasib*, literally 'reckoner' or 'calculator', is indirectly derived from *logistḗs* and has the same literal meaning, just as *ṣāḥib*/*ʿāmil al-sūq* is indirectly derived from *agorānómos*, which literally means 'overseer of the market'.[8]

Moreover, Juan Cole has advanced the idea that Roman law had a clear impact on how certain subjects are treated in the Qurʾān.[9] One example is the penalty prescribed for adultery. In the Qurʾān, this crime is not punished by death; this reflects the influence of Roman rather than Jewish law.[10] It is only after the eighth century that jurists sideline the Qurʾānic injunctions and advocate capital punishment.

In pre-Islamic Arabia, Eastern Roman rulers often clashed with local Arab tribes, although they could also become allies later on. For instance, the church historian Sozomen (first half of fifth century) recalls how a general who fought on the Roman side had to flee as Mania, the female ruler of the Arab tribe, offered overwhelming resistance. Sozomen then concludes that 'many of those living there remember these events even nowadays, and among the Arabs, they are [told] in songs'.[11] This mention of songs (*ōidaí*) appears to be the first literary evidence for the recital of poetry among Arabs.[12]

The most famous Arab allies of Byzantium were the Ġassānids or Banū Ġassān, a tribe that came to be within the confines of the Byzantine Empire, embraced Christianity, and concluded a treaty (*foedus*) with Byzantium around 490. At first they paid tribute to Byzantium, but then around 502 they gained the status of official allies (called *súmmachoi* in Greek) and provided important military forces to the Byzantine army. Until the Muslim conquests from the 620s onwards, they fought at Byzantium's side, notably against the Sasanian Empire. They adhered to the doctrine of the Syriac monophysite church, professing that Christ has only one (divine) nature and not two (human and divine), as was the doctrine in the Byzantine Orthodox Church. The followers of this church are sometimes called Jacobites, after Jacob Baradaeus, who was ordained bishop around 540.[13] Of course, not all Arabs in pre-Islamic times fought on the side of Byzantium, and others, such as the Laḫmids, opposed the Ġassānids. But this just goes to show that even in pre-Islamic Arabia tribes forged shifting political alliances and dealt with Byzantine envoys and ambassadors on a regular basis. Even in the area of warfare we find continuities between the Graeco-Roman and the Arab traditions, the Arabs excelling especially in infantry archery.[14] In fact the Qurayš – the most prominent tribe in Mecca and the one to which the Prophet Muḥammad belonged – may well have supplied the Byzantine army with leather goods.[15]

## The Emergence of Islam

We know, then, that Islam emerged in a strongly Hellenised world; but how it emerged is, unfortunately, much less certain. The reason for this is that, apart from the Qur'ān itself, most of our sources for the earliest Islamic history are based on stories told to explain and illustrate the Qur'ān and collected a century and a half after the events, or even later.[16] Over the past fifty years, revisionist-minded Islamicists have doubted the traditional account of Islam's early history and replaced it with different narratives. Here is not the place to fight this battle or argue for one approach or another. But it is worth recalling, for instance, that in his book *Muhammad and the Believers: At the Origins of Islam* the scholar Fred M. Donner claimed that until the reign of the caliph ʿAbd al-Malik (685–705) the Muslim community was one of believers in the oneness of God and included Christians, Jews, and Zoroastrians and that Muḥammad was not yet seen as prophet or as a figure central to the movement; this only happened later, after 692.[17]

We should not forget that Jews and Christians often used Greek as their language: the Hebrew Bible, what Christians call the 'Old Testament', had been translated into Greek, reportedly by six translators from each of the twelve tribes of Israel: this is why it is known as the Septuagint, the translation of the 'Seventy', with the number of translators rounded down from 6 × 12 = 72. The New Testament is entirely written in Greek, and it was first and foremost in this language that Christianity spread, even if Aramaic was the main spoken language in Palestine and the Levant. So, when we find similar stories or people in the Bible and the Qur'ān, this may well point, again, to Greek influence, even if other translations such as the Peshitta, the main ancient Syriac version of the Bible, also played a role. Abraham (Ibrāhīm), Isaac (Isḥāq), Jacob (Ya'qūb), Joseph (Yūsuf), Moses (Mūsā), David (Dāwūd), Jesus ('Īsā), and Mary (Maryam), to name just a few, all appear in the Qur'ān, and Joseph and Mary even have entire suras named after them.[18]

To illustrate the overlap between stories told in Muslim, Christian, and Jewish scriptures, I would just like to highlight three examples: the tale of Joseph and his brothers; the birth and death of Jesus; and the story of the Seven Sleepers of Ephesus. The Joseph sura (*sūrat Yūsuf*) tells of Joseph as a small boy having a dream in which eleven stars, together with the sun and the moon, prostrate themselves before him. His brothers plot against him and eventually get permission from their father Jacob to take Joseph outside, where they secretly throw him into a well. When they return to their father, they show him a shirt stained with 'false' blood and tell him that a wolf has devoured Joseph. But travellers find Joseph in the well and sell him into slavery to a high-ranking Egyptian official. Joseph is of extreme beauty, and the official's wife tries to seduce him. Although he does not succumb to her charms, he is still imprisoned, because she falsely accuses him. In gaol, he meets two fellow inmates and interprets their dreams: one will live, but the other will die. The first inmate is freed and remembers Joseph years later, when the king has a dream in which he sees seven fat cows and seven lean ones, together with seven green ears of corn and seven dry ones. The king's advisors cannot interpret the dream, so the former inmate suggests calling on Joseph. Joseph rightly explains the dream as predicting seven prosperous and seven lean years, and advises storing the harvest, so that there are provisions that can be eaten during the lean years. As a result of his correct interpretation, Joseph rose to power in Egypt, and later on his brothers came to him to buy supplies. He asked them to bring their youngest brother with them the next time they come. Their father, however, was reluctant to let them leave with his youngest son, because (so he thought) he had already lost one and did not want to lose a second. Joseph employed a ruse to get his youngest brother sent to prison, and the brothers returned to Jacob, who sent them back to get their imprisoned brother. When they pleaded with Joseph, he reminded them of their crime against him; then they realised who he was and he forgave them. Finally Joseph's father, his mother, and all his brothers came to Egypt to meet him. As he sat on his throne, the initial dream prophecy was fulfilled: the sun and the moon – his father and mother – together with the eleven stars, his eleven brothers, prostrated themselves before him.

This is obviously a short summary of the Qur'ānic narrative and leaves out a lot of details, but it easily shows many connections with the story of Joseph as told in the Bible (Genesis 37–50): the initial dream, the jealous brothers plotting against Joseph, the wife of the Egyptian official (Potiphar, the captain of the pharaoh's guard in the biblical account) trying to seduce him, the dream of the pharaoh (called 'king' (*malik*) in the Qur'ān), the seven abundant and seven lean years, Joseph's rise to power, his father's visit to Egypt and his eventual reconciliation with the brothers – all these elements appear in both accounts. And lest we forget, the Hebrew scripture was at least partly known and read in Byzantium in its Greek translation, the Septuagint, although the Syriac version, the Peshitta, also played a role.

Jesus is mentioned in various places in the Qur'ān.[19] For instance, Jesus' conception and birth are narrated in the Mary

Sura (Sūrat Maryam) (Qur'ān 19:9–34). Mary is a virgin and the archangel Gabriel visits her in the form of a beautiful man. He declares that she will give birth to a son, who is going to be a prophet. She then departs and gives birth under a palm tree, where God provides her with food and drink. When she returns with her infant son, the people are shocked and assume that she has committed 'a monstrous thing'. Yet Jesus speaks despite his young age and reveals that he is a prophet. He is kind to his mother, showing by implication how all others should be.

Elsewhere we learn of Jesus saying: 'I shall create for you from clay in the shape of a bird, and breathe into it, and it shall be a bird, by God's leave; I shall cure the blind and the leper; and I shall make the dead live, by God's leave' (أَنّي أَخْلُقُ لَكُم مِنَ الطِّينِ كَهَيْئَةِ ٱلْطَّير فَأَنْفُخُ فِيهِ فَيَكُونُ طَيْراً بِإِذْنِ اللهِ وَأُبْرِئُ ٱلْأَكْمَهَ وَٱلْأَبْرَصَ وَأُحيي المَوْتَى بِإِذْنِ اللهِ) (Qur'ān 3:49). Another verse denies Jesus' crucifixion: 'They say "we have killed the Messiah [*al-Masīḥ*], Jesus, son of Mary, the messenger of God." Yet they did not kill him, nor did they crucify him, but it was made to appear [so] to them' (وَقَوْلِهِمْ إِنَّا قَتَلْنَا ٱلْمَسِيحَ عِيسَى ٱبْنَ مَرْيَمَ رَسُولَ ٱللهِ وَمَا قَتَلُوهُ وَمَا صَلَبُوهُ وَلَٰكِن شُبِّهَ لَهُمْ). All this shows that in the Qur'ān there is clear knowledge of Jesus as he is described in the New Testament. The story of breathing life into a clay bird does not come from the Bible, but from the Infancy Gospel of Thomas. This is a text retelling Jesus' childhood, but it is not recognised as authentic by the church; hence it belongs in the apocryphal writings. Importantly, though, Jesus is presented as a prophet, not as God's son; he is not God himself, and is therefore called 'Jesus, son of Mary' ('Īsā ibn Maryam).

Finally, the story of the Seven Sleepers of Ephesus probably goes back to a lost fifth-century Greek source, and our earliest extensive version is told by Jacob of Serugh (c. 452–521), a theologian and prominent poet writing in Syriac.[20] During his reign (249–51), the Roman Emperor Decius decrees that the inhabitants of Ephesus ought to perform a pagan sacrifice. Some Christian children of prominent citizens flee and hide in a cave to avoid engaging in this pagan worship. God makes them fall asleep and protects the entrance of the cave. Decius' henchmen cannot find the children and abandon the search. Then, some three hundred years later, the entrance to the cave breaks open when a builder quarries for materials. As the light falls upon the children, they awake and send out one of their number, Iamblichus, to buy bread with some of the money they have in their pockets. Iamblichus arrives at Ephesus and is astonished to find Christian crosses over the city gates. After some back and forth, the children all come to the city and realise that paganism has been replaced by Christianity. Later, Emperor Theodosius (presumably Theodosius the Great, although the chronology is wrong, as he reigned from 364 to 378) comes to Ephesus and greets the children. They declare that God made them sleep in order to show that the resurrection is possible, and soon afterwards they fall asleep again, this time forever.

In the Sura of the Cave (Sūrat al-kahf) (Qur'ān 18:9–26), the story of the sleepers is retold, but in a much abridged and more enigmatic way. Young people, perhaps three, five, or seven, see that their contemporaries worship other deities beside God, and they isolate themselves from these pagans by hiding in a cave together with their dog. There they sleep for 309 years; then they awake and send one of their number to go into the city to buy provisions with silver coins. The purpose of this sign, this wondrous story, is 'to let them know that God's promise is true' (لِيَعْلَمُوا أَنَّ وَعْدَ اللهِ حَقٌّ). Again, we can immediately see the similarities between the two tales, except that many details – about Ephesus, Decius, Theodosius, Iamblichus, and so on – are missing from the Qur'ānic narrative. And yet it is clearly the same story that we find in the Qur'ān and the lost Greek source.

As already stated, one can find many other parallels between the Jewish, Christian, and Muslim scriptures. Because of these many similarities, some scholars have gone so far as to see the Qur'ān as a Late Antique text and argued that it can best be explained against the background of Judaeo-Christian scripture.[21] Angelika Neuwirth is particularly interested in the literary form of the Qur'ān and has argued that it shares certain features not only with pre-Islamic poetry but also with other hymnal traditions, such as that of the Psalms. For her, the Qur'ān emerged from this Late Antique milieu, which is not a historical period so much as an 'epistemic space'. The Qur'ān emerges, as it were, in dialogue with its surrounding cultures, and this is not a one-way process. Investigating the structure of the Qur'ān and its literary devices allows us to understand how it was formed; but, in turn, the Qur'ān can also tell us something about Late Antiquity.

Neuwirth's views can perhaps best be illustrated by an example. We have just seen that Jesus features in the Qur'ān. Given the central importance of Jesus to Christianity, one might wonder why the Qur'ān does not devote more space to this figure, especially since his divinity is denied – as is, by implication, the doctrine of the trinity, that is, the doctrine that God is three: Father, Son, and Holy Ghost. The reason is that Muḥammad's community had already accepted Jesus as a prophet rather than the son of God. In other words, the relative scarcity of occurrences of Jesus' name allows us to infer what debates were animating the community at the time.

Neuwirth's is just one, albeit highly influential, interpretation of how the Qur'ān was formed, and I could have quoted many other scholars who plough this growing and increasingly politicised field. But my purpose here is to explore the importance of classical culture for Islam. Therefore an interim conclusion must be that Islam as a religion and Arabic as a language developed in a Hellenised world, and the traces of their encounter with Greek culture can be found in the Muslim holy writ itself. And, although religion was a crucial aspect of society in early Islamic history, there is much more to the culture, as the example of a hunting lodge called Quṣayr 'Amrā can show.

## Case Study: Quṣayr ʿAmrā between Greek Art and Arabic Poetry

Situated in modern Jordan, some 40 miles east of the capital Amman, Quṣayr ʿAmrā was originally a large complex of buildings, of which the main relic today is a bath house. It was probably built by the heir apparent and future Umayyad caliph, al-Walīd II (709–44; r. 743–4), and is remarkable in that it preserves a large amount of the original frescoes. Garth Fowden produced a comprehensive study of its visual art and also interpreted one fresco, found in the changing room (apodyterium), in a highly interesting way, which illustrates well how Greek art could be transformed and linked to Arabic poetry.[22] The fresco, situated in an arched aperture over a door, shows a man on the left and a winged boy hovering to his right. In the foreground we see what appears to be a person in a shroud. The man's pose seems pensive and his head is somewhat inclined to his left, perhaps as he glances at the shrouded figure. The composition resembles that of other images, which show a sleeping Ariadne in the foreground as she is being discovered by the god Dionysus. She had been abandoned by Theseus on the island of Naxos after helping him to kill the Minotaur and escape from his labyrinth on Crete. In these images we see Dionysus to the left, glancing at the half-naked Ariadne. In the background on the right there hovers the winged figure of Eros, the god of love, who looks at Dionysus and makes him fall in love with her.

But al-Walīd reinterpreted this image. He himself had been unlucky in that he married Saʿda, the daughter of Saʿīd, who was the great grandson of the third caliph, ʿUṯmān. Yet he later fell in love with Saʿda's sister Salmā, divorced Saʿda, and asked Saʿīd for permission to marry Salmā; but Saʿīd refused. Only when al-Walīd himself became caliph in 743 was he able to tie the knot with Salmā. Unfortunately, however, she passed away shortly after the wedding. Al-Walīd had already been recognised as an important poet, and some of his poems spoke of his longing to be united with Salmā. He continued to compose poetry after her death, and the following piece is particularly poignant:

God may bring me together with Salmā;
does God not do whatever he wants?
He brings her out and puts her on the ground
and puts her to sleep, with her dress having fallen down
He brings me and puts me on her;
then I wake her up after the judgment has been passed
He sends constant rain streaming down on us
and washes us, so that no worries remain.[23]

Al-Walīd imagines being reunited with his beloved wife. It is God who brings both her and him out; this is a clear image of resurrection. And it is He who joins them physically together. The image of rain falling on them and reviving them is again Qurʾānic, as the following quotation can illustrate (7:57): 'Then we [*sc.* God] bring water down from them [*sc.* the thick clouds], and we bring out all sorts of fruits, just as we bring out [i.e. resurrect] the dead' (فَأَنْزَلْنَا بِهِ ٱلْمَاءَ فَأَخْرَجْنَا بِهِ مِن كُلِّ ٱلثَّمَراتِ كَذٰلِكَ نُخْرِجُ ٱلْمَوْتَى).

The fresco, then, is in dialogue with this poem. Dionysus sees Ariadne, whose dress has fallen down, and the winged figure of Eros makes him succumb to her charms. Now in the fresco, al-Walīd takes the place of Dionysus, and his love for Salmā is illustrated by the winged figure. But his beloved is dead and wears a shroud rather than a dress. The image, then, evokes both loss and hope for an eventual reunion. And it is yet another poignant example of how Greek culture, here Greek art and myth, interplay with Arabic poetry and Qurʾānic imagery.

In the historiography of the late eighth and later centuries, we find the concept of a 'period of ignorance', *ǧāhilīya*, prior to the emergence of Islam. Nonetheless the inhabitants of pre-Islamic Arabia were not ignorant; they rather negotiated their affairs through a complex set of allegiances and diplomatic ties and wrote beautiful poetry that contained Greek words and concepts. The Umayyad Empire (661–750) had as its capital the city of Damascus, which had many Greek-speaking inhabitants. Paradoxically, when the ʿAbbāsids (750–1258) ousted the Umayyads and moved the capital further east, to a small village called Baghdad, which was to become a great metropolis known as the City of Peace, the engagement with Greek culture greatly intensified, as we shall see next.

# 2

# Heirs to Plato and Hippocrates

With the arrival of a new dynasty, that of the ʿAbbāsids, interest in all things Greek greatly increased, and the political and cultural elite paid good money to have the works of philosophy, science, and medicine translated into Arabic. The ʿAbbāsids removed the Umayyads around 750, in a revolution that started very much in the East; and they had particular successes in recruiting Shiite and Persian Muslims. Their black banners were a symbol for the coming of the Mahdī, the direct descendant of the Prophet: the imam – a messianic figure whose return would usher in an age of judgement and redemption. The ʿAbbāsids themselves were of Arab stock, yet their supporters were drawn from a variety of ethnicities. It is precisely this new ideology that contributed to creating a climate in which most of the Greek texts available in Late Antiquity were rendered into Arabic.

It is hard to overestimate the importance of translation for the development of cultures in general and of Muslim civilisation in particular. Many scholars continue to speak of a Graeco-Arabic 'translation movement', which designates the efforts, from the eighth to the tenth centuries, to render Greek thought into Arabic.[1] Dimitri Gutas, for instance, one of the veterans in the field, compared the translation movement to the age of Pericles and the Italian Renaissance in historical significance.[2] This movement, however, is neither homogenous nor driven by the same factors and actors; it happened at different times and in different places. Indeed, I no longer think that it is useful to talk about a 'movement' in this context. Translations from Greek into Arabic happened at various points for a variety of reasons. I therefore have argued that it makes much more sense to speak of various translation phenomena.[3] For instance, there were some early translators in the second half of the eighth century such as al-Biṭrīq ('the patriarch'), who rendered the Hippocratic *Aphorisms* and other medical texts; and al-Ḥaǧǧāǧ ibn Yūsuf ibn Maṭar translated Euclid's *Elements*, possibly in the early eighth century.[4] The two most prominent figures are undoubtedly Yaʿqūb al-Kindī (c. 801–73) and Ḥunayn ibn Isḥāq (d. 873 or 876), but they, too, moved in different circles and produced translations in different ways and for different reasons.

Before we come back to these two, it is useful to tell two stories that illustrate the close connection between Greek and Islamic culture. The first is about Alexander the Great: as he conquered Persia and other places further east, he plundered the Avestan books that he found – the ones that contain the literature of ancient Persia – and had them translated into Greek, to be put in the famous Library of Alexandria.[5] Likewise, when the School of Alexandria closed in the seventh century, a chain of transmitters brought philosophical and medical knowledge to Baghdad.[6] In this way, the works of the Greeks are really the works of the people of the East, such as the Arabs and the Persians. These two stories are apocryphal, to be sure, but, like many myths, they contain a grain of truth in that Greek culture drew heavily on the surrounding civilisations, not least those of Egypt and the Ancient Near East, and in that the teaching techniques and texts available in Late Antique Alexandria influenced what was to be translated into Arabic in Baghdad and elsewhere.

## The Beginnings of Philosophy in Arabic

Yaʿqūb al-Kindī (c. 801–73) hailed originally from Baṣra but spent most of his career in Baghdad.[7] He was known as the 'philosopher of the Arabs' for his pioneering role; and he used his considerable wealth to further philosophical enquiries. To this end, he gathered around him a number of translators, mostly Syriac-speaking Christians, to render philosophical works into Arabic. He was especially interested in Aristotle and in Neoplatonic authors such as Plotinus (c. 204–70), Porphyry (234–305), and Proclus (412–85). In his major metaphysical work, *On First Philosophy*, al-Kindī expresses the debt he owes to previous philosophical endeavours in these words:

> Aristotle, the towering figure of Greek philosophy, said: 'We must thank the fathers of those who brought some truth, since they [the fathers] were a cause for their [the sons'] being, to say nothing of the [sons], since they transmit the wisdom of the fathers, and since they have caused us to attain truth.' How fine is what he said about this! We must not be ashamed to admire the truth or to acquire it, from wherever it comes. Even if it should come from far-flung nations and foreign peoples, there is for the student of truth nothing more important than the truth, nor is the truth demeaned or diminished by the one who states or conveys it; no one is demeaned by the truth, rather all are ennobled by it.[8]

Influenced by the Greek mathematical texts that had been translated previously, al-Kindī creates what one prominent scholar has called a 'metaphysics file', and the two most important texts in it were the *Theology of Aristotle* and *Aristotle's Explanation of the Pure Good* – often known by its Latin title, *Liber de causis* (*The Book of Causes*).[9] Although these two titles attribute the respective works to Aristotle, these actually constitute translations of Neoplatonic works, namely Plotinus' *Enneads*, books 4–6, and Proclus' *Elements of Theology*. Al-Kindī commissioned

Christian translators to render these texts and then revised them himself, although we do not know how extensive his revisions were.

These translations are often modified or adapted to fit the new context.[10] For instance, where Plotinus speaks of the parts of soul according to Plato – rational, spirited, and appetitive – the translator replaces the Platonic tripartition with the Aristotelian division into vegetative, animal, and rational; or when Plotinus says that 'the One is all things and not a single one', the translator rephrases this as saying that 'the pure One is the cause of things'.[11] The first example points to an important feature of philosophy in Late Antiquity that al-Kindī continues to some extent, namely the fusion of Neoplatonic and Aristotelian doctrines.

The second example leads us to a tricky question: the relationship between revealed religion and philosophy. In Plotinus' philosophy, all things are created from the One, through emanation. The One is the creator who sustains all being. For al-Kindī, this One is the same as God, yet Islam shies away from the notion that God can be multiple; in fact its most fundamental doctrine is the assertion that God is one (*tawḥīd* in Arabic). Therefore the One cannot be 'all things', nor can it be 'nothing'; it is for this reason that the translation is subtly adapted.

As the earlier quotation indicates, for al-Kindī nothing is more important than the truth, and this truth is not multiple, but one. The Qur'ān presents the same truth as philosophy does, only in different ways. We can provide two examples from al-Kindī's philosophical output to illustrate this. He penned a treatise titled *On the Prostration of the Outermost Body*, which deals with the following verse from the Qur'ān (55:6): 'and the stars and the trees prostrate themselves' (وَٱلنَّجْمُ وَٱلشَّجَرُ يَسْجُدَانِ) before God. But what can this possibly mean? Al-Kindī offers an allegorical explanation and argues that this is an image illustrating that heaven and earth obey God. Philosophy establishes that the movement of the stars is the proximate cause for what happens in the sublunar world, but the stars themselves carry out God's bidding, which is the distal or ultimate cause. The other example concerns prophetic knowledge. God reveals things directly to the prophets, so that they have no need for philosophy or other means by which normal people arrive at the truth. Elsewhere al-Kindī explains prophetic dreams, which can foretell the truth to strong souls, whereas weaker ones require symbols and metaphors that only hint at it.

Many subsequent philosophers adhered to the idea that the same truth is expressed differently in scripture and in philosophy and that 'the many', the common people, and 'the few', the elite philosophers, gain access to it by different means. This, for instance, is the famous argument of Averroes (Ibn Rušd, 1126–98) in his *Decisive Treatise*.[12] Another philosopher who very much wanted to reconcile philosophy and revealed religion is the Neoplatonist al-ʿĀmirī (d. 992).[13] He continued the legacy of al-Kindī at a time when Aristotelians such as al-Fārābī (c. 870–951) dominated the philosophical scene in Baghdad. In chapter 3 of his major work *On the Afterlife* he provides an outline of the history of philosophy.[14] It all started with the Qurʾānic sage Luqmān, who then taught Empedocles – the first Greek philosopher according to this account. A chain of teachers and pupils follows: Pythagoras, Socrates, Plato, and Aristotle. Pythagoras in particular is said to have learnt 'from the niche of prophecy' (*miškāt al-nubūwa*). This is clearly an allusion to what is known as 'the light verse' (Qurʾān 24:35), which begins as follows: 'God is the light of Heaven and Earth. His light resembles that of a niche [*miškāt*] in which a lamp [shines]' (اللهُ نُورُ ٱلسَّمَـٰوَٰتِ وَٱلْأَرْضِ مَثَلُ نُورِهِ كَمِشْكَوٰةٍ فِيهَا مِصْبَاح). In a work titled *The Choicest Maxims and Best Sayings*, the author Mubaššir ibn Fātik (fl. 1048) attributes the following saying to Pythagoras:

> Wisdom belongs to God absolutely. The love of wisdom is connected to the love of God, most High. To love God, most High, is to carry out acts of his love. When one carries out acts of his love, one draws closer to God, and is thus saved and victorious.[15]

In this way, philosophy begins with a Qur'ānic sage, Luqmān, and the Greek sages proclaim a version of philosophy very much in keeping with Islam – as well as with Christianity and Judaism, for that matter.

Political philosophy was an important part of Greek thought, and both Plato and Aristotle penned books on this topic. Plato's *Republic* outlines a utopian state governed by a philosopher king and protected by a class of guardians. Children are raised collectively and private ownership does not exist; thus the general system could be seen as a form of what we call communism. Averroes wrote a commentary on this work, which survives only in Hebrew translation.[16] Averroes, like Plato, lived in politically turbulent times. He became a courtier in Cordoba under the Almoravid dynasty, which was ousted by the Almohads in 1145, when Averroes was only 19 years old. As a physician and a judge, he served the new dynasty until his death. His commentary on the *Republic* does not adopt the format of quoting the entire text, passage by passage, and offering an explanation of the text after each passage. Rather it summarises the main ideas and then comments on them. Take the example of women: Plato believed that women from all classes, including that of the guardians, should serve in society, training and working alongside men.[17] Averroes agrees:

> Likewise, because of the praiseworthy purity and understanding with which some women are created, it is possible that philosophers and rulers are among them. [. . .] When he [*sc.* Plato] realised that these shared things [*sc.* children, women, and property] were necessary and that women should rightly be on guard duty together with men, it seemed clearly reasonable that the guardian women would stand guard in the city or go to war, just as female dogs do together with the male dogs; it is reasonable that they [*sc.* the female guardians] share all aspects of guard duty with them [*sc.* the male guardians].[18]

Here Averroes does not just paraphrase Plato, highlighting the aspects with which he agrees, but also goes beyond him by complaining that in cultures of his own time women are not allowed to exercise their full potential.

In the next example he, again, relates the Platonic text to his own society. Plato made the point that the laws can change the character of individuals only gradually, and Averroes adds:

> when the laws are utterly corrupted, one finds that the states [of the soul] are utterly reprehensible. This is clear from our situation after forty years, demonstrated by the habits and states of [the souls of] those in power and high office. The cause for this is the regime bent on honour that had been permitted and under which they grew up. It is for this reason that the situation has become so dire at present. Among them are some who possess the virtuous character trait and are virtuous according to the religious laws, although this only happens rarely.[19]

Here Averroes clearly refers to the change in regime in 1145, some 'forty years ago', and criticises the Almohads' zeal to attain glory. More generally speaking, Averroes employs the *Republic* to formulate his own idea of 'the virtuous city'. In this he resembles al-Fārābī, who also formulated a vision of the virtuous city and on whose work he draws.[20] Moreover, in this virtuous city, the righteous rulers adhere to 'religious laws'; Averroes thus identifies Plato's philosopher king with the jurist who interprets and applies religious law, an idea that we shall encounter again at the end of chapter 5, when discussing the Iranian Republic.

## Greek Medicine Translated into Arabic

Like Averroes, many of the most prominent philosophers in the Islamic world were also physicians, and even al-Kindī wrote profusely on medical topics.[21] The most important translator of medical texts was Ḥunayn ibn Isḥāq, and we are particularly well informed about his approach to Graeco-Arabic translation as he composed an *Epistle on the Works of Galen that Were Translated [into Arabic] and Those that Were Not.*[22] Let us begin by hearing from Ḥunayn himself how he went about translating Galen from Greek into Arabic, beginning with the treatise *Sects for Beginners*:

> Before me, a man called Ibn Sahlā from Karḫ had translated it [sc. *Sects for Beginners*] into Syriac, yet he did so badly. Then I translated it, when I was a young man aged twenty or slightly older, for a physician from Ǧundaysābūr called Šīrīšūʿ ibn Quṭrub; I employed a Greek manuscript with many defects. Later, when I was about forty, my student Ḥubayš asked me to correct it, after I had collected a number of Greek manuscripts of it. I collated these manuscripts with each other, until I produced one sound version. I collated this version with the Syriac, and corrected it [*sc.* the Syriac]. I used to do this with everything I translated. A few years later, I translated it into Arabic for Abū Ǧaʿfar Muḥammad ibn Mūsā.[23]

This very dense paragraph needs unpacking. First of all, there already had been a Syriac translation of *Sects for Beginners*, prepared by an 'Ibn Sahlā from Karḫ' about whom we know nothing further. Karḫ here probably refers to Karḵā, a city in Ḫuzistān, in today's South-Western Iran. In his early twenties, Ḥunayn produced his own Syriac translation for 'a physician from Ǧundaysābūr called Šīrīšūʿ ibn Quṭrub', presumably also using the earlier translation by Ibn Sahlā together with a defective Greek manuscript. Again, we know little else about Šīrīšūʿ ibn Quṭrub, but the city of Ǧundaysābūr (as it was known in Arabic; Gondēšāpūr in Persian) was famous for its Syriac-speaking physicians and lies in Ḫuzistān, too. Over the next twenty years Ḥunayn collected more Greek manuscripts and came to be in a position to produce a much improved Greek text by collating the Greek manuscripts in his possession (that is, comparing their versions of the same text and exercising judgement as to the best variants). At the request of his pupil and nephew Ḥubayš, he then collated the improved Greek text with his Syriac version and improved the latter too, as he always did. Finally, he produced an Arabic translation for Abū Ǧaʿfar Muḥammad ibn Mūsā (d. 873), who was one of the three 'sons of Moses' (Banū Mūsā): their father, Mūsā ibn Šākir, was a notorious highwayman turned plutocrat. Ǧaʿfar, like his father and brothers, was a scholar with close connections to the courts of the caliphs.

The quotation about *Sects* teaches us a lot about how Ḥunayn worked. He often starts with existing Syriac translations, endeavours to find and collate Greek manuscripts, and frequently revises his work over the course of his career. Today most of the Syriac versions are lost to us, which makes it very difficult to ascertain what role these intermediary translations played in the process of transmission from Greek to Arabic – although there are some exceptions, to be discussed later.[24] We also notice the importance of patronage for Ḥunayn's work. It is only because he is commissioned to translate texts, be it into Syriac or into Arabic, that he undertakes these tasks; one tenth-century source talks about the extremely high remuneration he received, so money must have played some role in all this. Therefore patronage, especially that of high-ranking figures at the ʿAbbāsid court, played a crucial role in getting Galen rendered into Arabic.

This is an important point, because it can dispel two false notions about Ḥunayn's translations. First, there is a myth about al-Ma'mūn (r. 813–33) and other caliphs setting up a House of Wisdom (*Bayt al-ḥikma*) and sponsoring Ḥunayn's translation. But neither the House of Wisdom nor any of the caliphs is ever mentioned as a sponsor in Ḥunayn's *Epistle*, and therefore they are very unlikely to have played a central role in all this. Moreover, Dimitri Gutas and Kevin van Bladel thoroughly debunked the story of the House of Wisdom.[25] The second false notion is that these translations were only a Christian affair. To be sure, most translators belonged to a Christian denomination, but the sponsors who commissioned these Arabic renderings were Muslims for the most part; they had a genuine interest in Greek thought and wanted to access it. Without them most Arabic translations would never have been undertaken.[26]

Although Ḥunayn endeavoured to collect Greek manuscripts and improve the Greek text, at times he hit significant roadblocks. The case of Galen's *Commentary on Hippocrates' 'Epidemics'* illustrates both the vibrancy of the commentary genre and the difficulty in the textual transmission.[27] The *Epidemics* comprises seven books, and Galen wrote commentaries on books 1–3 and 6. Ḥunayn repeatedly tells us about the difficulties which he faced: he had access only to two manuscripts, one of which contained mere excerpts while the other was quite corrupt.[28] Moreover, in book 2, which has six parts, one part, the fifth, was missing entirely. On the basis of this sketchy evidence and by collating the two manuscripts, Ḥunayn was able to reconstruct most of the Greek text and then produced Syriac and Arabic translations, the Arabic one for Abū Ǧaʿfar Muḥammad ibn Mūsā, whom we have already met.

This Arabic translation had a profound influence on medical theory and practice in the Islamic world and beyond. Take the example of Abū Bakr Muḥammad ibn Zakarīyāʾ al-Rāzī (d. c. 925), arguably the greatest clinician of the medieval period. He was inspired by the *Epidemics* and by Galen's commentary to conduct various clinical observations that led to new discoveries.[29] In the area of medical epistemology in particular, his engagement with the *Epidemics* prompted him to test a clinical procedure by having a control group. Moreover, following the Hippocratic model, al-Rāzī compiled his own case notes, many of which were later collected and published by his students. He thus moved what one might call clinical research into a hospital environment, and his experiences there underpinned a significant part of his innovations.[30] Besides, many other medical authors drew on this Arabic translation in their own work.[31]

## A Comedy of Errors: Classicists and Their Arabic Evidence

Arabic translations of Greek texts are also extremely important to classicists who want to recover Greek sources otherwise lost or to improve extant ones.[32] But doing either is not always easy, and I would like to illustrate this statement with two stories of quixotic attempts to tackle the windmills of Graeco-Arabic studies – two comedies of errors leavened with a pinch of academic rivalry – that would probably make you laugh, were they not so tragic. One involves Galen's *Commentary on Hippocrates' 'Epidemics'*, which we have just discussed; the other concerns perhaps the most famous fragmentary text of Greek literature, Aristotle's *Poetics*.

The first tragicomical character in our cast is the Scot David Colville (c. 1581–1629), son of the laird of Cleish, Kinross-shire, brought up in the staunch tradition of the Kirk.[33] He followed his uncle, a political conspirator, and travelled to the continent shortly after James VI of Scotland ascended to the English throne in 1603. As a catholic monk, he spent ten years (1617–27) in the Escorial near Madrid, the monastery that served in part as model for the setting in Umberto Eco's *Name of the Rose*. There he had access to numerous Greek and Arabic manuscripts and copied a number of them. In particular, he collated various Arabic manuscripts of Galen's *Epidemics* commentary, focusing on those parts that were lost in Greek. He died suddenly, 'of a fever – or perhaps of the scholarly melancholy to which he had been prone . . . saying on his deathbed that scholarship and manuscripts were his only delight'.[34] Apart from being copied by someone in early nineteenth-century Paris, his *Epidemics* manuscript remained unnoticed.[35]

In the early twentieth century, the German philologist Wenkebach tried to produce a critical edition of Galen's work and spent almost half a century on this endeavour, including two world wars. As he did not know Arabic, however, he relied on a German translation of the Paris copy of Colville's manuscript and of another Arabic manuscript. The Arabic translation was based on a Syriac one, which in turn was translated from the Greek. Although Wenkebach devoted his life to the task, he often misunderstood the Arabic evidence in the German translation. It is a bit like Chinese whispers: when a text passes through so many different linguistic layers, it gets corrupted. Undaunted, Wenkebach often translated the German back into Greek – a Greek that had little (if anything) to do with the lost source, as scholars now realise.[36]

Umberto Eco's *Name of the Rose* centres on the lost second part of Aristotle's *Poetics*, which dealt with comedy. In the novel, this part is kept in the monastery's scriptorium, but deemed too dangerous for public consumption. In the end, the monastery – library and all – burns down, very much like the real Escorial in 1671, when many of the manuscripts used by Colville perished in the flames. Still, the first part of Aristotle's *Poetics*, on epic and tragic poetry, survives not just in Greek but also in a tenth-century Arabic translation made from the Syriac. The Austro-Hungarian classicist and Arabist Jaroslav Tkáč (1871–1927) devoted to this topic a doctoral dissertation that he defended at Vienna University in 1898. He then spent the rest of his life producing an edition and a Latin translation of the Arabic version. But he died suddenly, of a stroke – or was it perhaps scholarly melancholy again? Then Alfred Gudeman (1862–1942), a Munich classicist with no knowledge of Arabic (or Syriac, for that matter), published the work posthumously, in two volumes, in 1928 and 1932.[37] His Semiticist colleague Gotthelf Bergsträßer (1886–1933), however, judged it very harshly, saying . . .

> that Tkáč applied neither the required diligence and precision, nor the necessary methodological caution; that he hardly goes beyond his predecessor Margoliouth – whom he constantly criticises, even though he largely depends on him – and that serious objections can be raised against his assessment of the translation. One has to state this clearly, because A[lfred] Gudeman showered

> Tkáč's work with dithyrambic praise. How he, who is no expert in the field of Syriac and Arabic studies, felt entitled to offer such a judgment remains a mystery.[38]

One cannot but wonder what happened when the much younger Munich professor of Semitics met his older classicist colleague in the corridors of the university. Classicists had to wait for nearly another century to see significant progress in using the Arabic translation to improve the Greek source: in 2012 Leon Tarán and Dimitri Gutas produced a major new edition of the Greek text and study of the Arabic version, although Gutas, who turned 80 last year, is still working on his own edition of this Arabic version.[39]

These two tales can illustrate the vagaries of philological work and the difficulties involved in these tasks. Yet nothing is more satisfying than to recover lost texts: what would we not give to read Aristotle's thoughts on Greek comedy? Unfortunately they are not available either in the Greek original or in Arabic translation.

Tarán and Gutas' 2012 edition made great progress in using the Syriac and Arabic evidence for the improvement of the Greek text. It is for the purpose of showing the great difficulties in the way of making use of Arabic versions that I have told the story of some of these abortive attempts.

## The Sixteen Books of Galen and Sex for Beginners

Ḥunayn also makes a very interesting remark about the Galenic canon of sixteen books (a collection popularly known in his day as 'the sixteen books of Galen'). These were Galenic works that were taught in the amphitheatres of the iatrosophists – the professors of medicine – in Late Antique Alexandria. They comprise titles such as *Sects for Beginners*, *Elements according to Hippocrates*, *Pulse for Beginners*, *Mixtures*, and *Natural Faculties*. Ḥunayn says:

> These [sixteen] books are those which were exclusively read at the place of medical instruction in Alexandria. They read them in the order which I have just mentioned. They were in the habit of congregating each day to read and understand one of these textbooks, just as our fellow Christians today come together in the places of instruction known as 'schools' each day to read one of the textbooks by the Ancients.[40]

We can therefore see the continuity from Alexandria to Baghdad: the same textbooks were read in both places, and therefore it is not surprising that medicine in the Islamic tradition developed largely on the basis of Greek ideas. This is not to say that there was no innovation; of course there was.[41] But the theoretical framework of humoral pathology – the idea, first expressed in the Hippocratic *Nature of Man* and championed by Galen, that health is the balance of the four humours (blood, phlegm, yellow bile, and black bile) and disease their imbalance – underpins medicine not just in the Islamic world but also in Europe until the early modern period.[42]

Sexology, at first a medical genre, can illustrate like few others how the Greek heritage was not just adopted and adapted; it turned into a wholly original branch of literature. Jeremy Kurzyniec has recently traced this development, and it is a story worth telling.[43] In the ninth and tenth centuries, the Arabs penned more than a dozen books specifically concerned with sexology or sexual intercourse. These books are rather short, draw heavily on Greek sources, and contain a good deal of pharmacology, namely recipes that make intercourse possible by enabling men to have erections, and also more pleasant, as aphrodisiacs are part of the offerings. We have already encountered some of the authors of these manuals, for example al-Kindī and Ḥunayn ibn Isḥāq; others include Qusṭā ibn Lūqā (d. c. 912), who wrote two works on the topic, and Muḥammad ibn Zakarīyā' al-Rāzī (d. c. 925), the most accomplished clinician of the medieval period.[44]

A watershed in the development of this genre was the *Encyclopaedia of Pleasure* by the late tenth-century author ʿAlī ibn Naṣr. To the medical content and the recipes for various aphrodisiacs and stimulants, he adds raunchy poetry and racy stories, as well as advice taken from the Kama Sutra. He also quotes, quite often, from the elusive figure of 'Araṭayās, the Greek', surely a reference to the second-century medical author Aretaeus of Cappadocia. Yet, as Kurzyniec has shown, it is very unlikely that the many quotations attributed to Araṭayās, the Greek, come from Aretaeus of Cappadocia. It is much more likely that ʿAlī ibn Naṣr used this name in order to lend his work some prestige: Greek sources were highly prized, and by having more of them, the renown of the *Encyclopaedia of Pleasure* equally increases.

In any case, after ʿAlī ibn Naṣr, we see a real explosion of works on sexology that mix poetic and prose literature with the Kama Sutra and the Greek medical tradition. Even the titles of these works get more and more explicit: from the *Clever Man's Guide to Intimacy with the Beloved* and the *Perfumed Garden of Sensual Delight* to the *Old Man Regaining the Sexual Power of His Youth*. This just shows the creative engagement with the Greek heritage, which is transformed and enriched, and ultimately turned into something innovative and unprecedented.

## Astronomy and Astrology

The interaction between the Arabic and the Greek worlds extended even to the heavens. For many of our star names are derived from Arabic. One example is Betelgeuse (α Orionis), a red supergiant star in the constellation Orion. Betelgeuse is known to many as the home of Ford Prefect and Zaphod Beeblebrox, characters in Douglas Adam's *Hitchhiker's Guide to the Galaxy*. Other examples are Rigel (β Orionis) and Aldebaran (α Tauri), the latter having inspired the name of Princess Leia Organa's home world in *Star Wars*.[45] This clearly points to our indebtedness to the Arabic tradition in the field of astronomy.

The Arabs and Muslims themselves, in their turn, owe a huge debt to Claudius Ptolemy, a second-century author of seminal works on astronomy, astrology, and other scientific disciplines. Among the texts translated into Arabic we find the *Almagest* or *Mathematical Composition*, the most important astronomical work before the Renaissance; the *Four Books* or *Tetrabiblos*, largely on astrology; the *Planetary Hypotheses*, explaining the movement of the spheres; and the *Phases of the Fixed Stars* along with the *Simplification of the Sphere*, two works on the position of the stars.[46] It is hard to overestimate the importance and influence of these Arabic translations on the subsequent tradition, both in Arabic and in Latin: without them astronomy and astrology would not have flourished in the Muslim world the way they did.

Ptolemy's view of the universe was to dominate the Middle Ages, both in the East and in the West. The earth is at the centre and we live in the sublunar world, that is, the world beneath the sphere of the moon. Above this sphere come those of the planets and the sun, and then, finally, that of the fixed stars. The movement of the planets is further described by epicycles and other means of accounting for their erratic behaviour when we view them from earth. Incidentally, the Greek πλανήτηϲ (etymon of 'planet') means 'wanderer' and derives from the verb πλανᾶϲθαι ('to err', 'to wander'); it is generally translated in medieval Arabic as كَوْكَب مُتَحَيِّر ('wandering star') or just مُتَحَيِّر ('wanderer').

This shared astrological and astronomical tradition concerns not just texts translated from Greek into Arabic into Latin but also material culture. Nowhere is this more evident than in the history of the astrolabe. It is originally a Greek instrument for conducting astronomical measurements. The word literally means 'star catcher' (ἀϲτρολάβοϲ), and in Arabic it is simply known in transliteration (*asṭurlāb*). It normally consists of a fixed sphere and a movable one, together with a pivoted pointer at the back, called 'alidade', a word derived from the Arabic *al-ʿiḍāda* ('support', 'upper arm'). The History of Science Museum at Oxford contains the largest, most diverse, and most significant collection of astrolabes in the world and put together an extremely informative website to explain its history.[47] As the curators of the online exhibition available there put it,

> Astrolabes are the most admired and coveted of scientific instruments, but are also among the least understood. Capturing the movements of sun and stars, they are complex and challenging as well as mysterious, elegant and distant. [. . . The instruments in the Oxford collection] demonstrate that the astrolabe, along with its geometry and astronomy, is a cultural resource shared between Islam and the West.[48]

And indeed, in the Islamic world the astrolabes evolved into complex instruments with many localised varieties and are often works of incredible craftsmanship. Here again, a Greek tradition is transformed and enhanced in the Muslim world; and this tradition, in turn, is at the start of many European innovations that have consequences for both navigation and astronomical discoveries, from the Renaissance onwards. Moreover, the Greek tradition also reached China, thus illustrating how far ideas and instruments travelled.[49]

## The Syriac Connection

Scholars have expended an enormous amount of energy investigating the mechanics of how Greek texts were rendered into Arabic. Here the role of Syriac intermediary translations has recently come into greater focus, although much research still remains to be done. We have a few instances where we can compare the Greek source texts with Syriac and Arabic target texts. In philosophy we have the most fundamental texts of the curriculum:

Aristotle's *Categories* and *On Interpretation* (the first two books of the *Organon*) and Porphyry's *Introduction* (*Eisagōgē*) to the *Categories*, all dealing with the basic principles of logic and argumentation.[50] In medicine we have the Hippocratic *Aphorisms* and *Prognostic*, two fundamental teaching texts in Late Antiquity and the later medieval tradition, as well as Galen's *Simple Drugs*, books six to eight, containing an alphabetical list of medicinal plants, their description and uses.[51] Pilot work comparing the Greek, Syriac, and Arabic versions of *Simple Drugs* suggests that the older Syriac and the older Arabic translations are more paraphrastic, use coordination (parataxis) much more than subordination (hypotaxis), and are generally less sophisticated than their newer counterparts.[52] In the area of terminology, in particular, the older translators felt the need not just to translate the names of plants but also to transliterate their Greek equivalents. In the newer translations the terminology was more established and, as a result, the need to give transliterated Greek names no longer existed.

These texts, for which we still have Syriac intermediate versions, had an enormous influence on the Islamic tradition. For instance, fundamental logic was not important just for philosophy but also for Islamic speculative theology (*kalām*) and jurisprudence (*fiqh*). Likewise, Galen's *Simple Drugs*, together with Dioscorides' *Medicinal Substances* (to be discussed in chapter 4), formed the basis of how pharmacology evolved and provided the theoretical framework for describing new drugs from India and China such as emblic and beleric myrobalan, and cinnamon.[53]

## The Bible and the Church Fathers in Arabic

Generally scholars have paid far greater attention to Arabic versions of Greek secular texts than to Arabic versions of religious works, including the Bible. And yet there are literally more than a thousand Greek Christian works translated into Arabic whose

Arabic versions survive in manuscript: 'an estimated ninety-nine percent of them remain unpublished, and their critical study has barely begun', as one prominent scholar put it.[54] For instance, there are more than 8,000 manuscripts containing Arabic translations of the Old Testament.[55] Moreover, most of the translators of the secular Greek texts were Christians; and we should not forget that the New Testament, originally written in Greek, was also rendered into Arabic numerous times. Although there were oral translations in pre-Islamic and early Islamic times, written translations were produced only towards the end of the seventh and the beginning of the eighth century.[56] It was Christian monks in Palestine, the Levant, and Sinai who composed these translations, as they were bilingual or trilingual – in Greek, Syriac, and Arabic. They often did not render the Greek original but rather existing Syriac versions such as the Peshitta; yet at times they translated directly from the Greek. It was not just the New Testament that appeared in Arabic but also the Old Testament, the Hebrew Bible of the Jews that we have just mentioned. Here again, we have translations directly from the Hebrew, but also from Greek or Syriac intermediary translations. For instance, we have an Arabic manuscript dated to around 755–75 that not only contains parts of the New Testament such as the Acts of the Apostles and the so-called Catholic Letters in Arabic, but also quotations from many Old and New Testament books, including 'Genesis, Deuteronomy, Job, the Psalms, Isaiah, Jeremiah, Daniel, Ezekiel, Micah, Habakkuk, Zechariah, Malachi, and Baruch, along with the Gospels of Matthew, Luke, and John'.[57] These Arabic versions were not read only by Christians: some Muslims took an interest too, and Jews produced their own Arabic versions of the Hebrew Bible.

Nor should we forget the translations of Greek church literature. The motivation for producing these translations was probably different.[58] As Christian texts, they were aimed at a Christian audience and were largely sponsored by Christians, although it is also clear that non-Christians sometimes engaged with this literature. In the early period from the late eighth to the early tenth century, these translations were mainly associated with Palestine, and especially from the monastery of Mār Sābā, located halfway between Bethlehem and the Dead Sea. After this early period, the focus shifted to Antioch (Antakya in modern south-eastern Turkey), whose reconquest by the Byzantines in 969 led to a burgeoning of Graeco-Arabic translations. But other localities such as Cairo and Damascus also produced a significant amount of translation. The range of these Christian Graeco-Arabica is vast; they encompass sermons, hagiography, guides to salvation, theological works, and church history.

## Arabic into Greek: How to Interpret Dreams

This flow of ideas from Greek into Arabic was not a one-way street. Many Arabic works were also rendered into Greek.[59] These were not just works on medicine such as *On Smallpox and Measles* by Abū Bakr Muḥammad Zakarīyā' al-Rāzī (d. 925) and a medical encyclopaedia titled *Sustenance of the Travel and Food for the Sedentary* by Ibn al-Ǧazzār (d. 980), but also works on astronomy and astrology, alchemy, agriculture, geomancy (a form of divination where earth, in Greek *gē*, is thrown on the ground and then interpreted), and magical practices.[60]

An interesting case is the treatise known as *Oneirocriticon of Achmet*, or *Achmet's Book on Dream Interpretation*.[61] It is a complex text that incorporates Greek literature on dream interpretation such as the *Interpretation of Dreams* by the second-century Artemidorus, a treatise subsequently translated into Arabic.[62] The Arabic text of Achmet's book was then rendered into Greek, probably in the ninth or tenth century, and we no longer have the Arabic original.[63] To give an example of how dream interpretation works, we can look at the image of the head.[64] If one dreams of having one's head cut off, this can mean freedom for a slave but ruin for a banker. The image of eating a head indicates that one will acquire high office or riches. These interpretations are found not just in Artemidorus' Greek text and Arabic translation but also in Achmet's book and later Arabic manuals on dream interpretation. This illustrates yet again that translation is not a linear movement: texts and ideas can circulate back and forth, from Greek into Arabic and back into Greek. And on top of this various Latin translations were produced both from the Greek and from the Arabic.

By way of conclusion, therefore, one could say that, by the late tenth century, the transfer of knowledge from Alexandria to Baghdad was largely accomplished and most Greek texts were available in Arabic. Whole disciplines – philosophy (called *falsafa* in Arabic), theology, physics, astronomy, mathematics, alchemy, engineering, medicine, and so on – were based on Greek models and then further refined and developed. But the production of knowledge in Arabic was also in full swing, and Arabic texts that were often based on Greek originals – as we saw with *Achmet's Book on Dream Interpretation* – began to be rendered 'back' into Greek or Latin.

## Islamic Humanism

I have briefly mentioned the renowned philosopher al-Fārābī (c. 870–951), who lived in Baghdad and belonged to a circle (or school) of thinkers known as the Baghdad Aristotelians.[65] Joel L. Kraemer (1933–2018), a prominent scholar of Islamic culture, spoke of 'Humanism in the Renaissance of Islam' to characterise the age of al-Fārābī.[66] He saw in particular parallels with the Italian Renaissance, in that intellectuals engaged critically with the Greek heritage to formulate a new vision of what it means to be human. For instance, the Christian philosopher and pupil of al-Fārābī, Yahyā ibn 'Adī (893–973), and the Muslim polymath Miskawayh (932–1030) both wrote books titled *The Refinement of Morals*, in which they advocate a 'classical' education in the sense of being based on a canon of Greek works that any civilised person ought to master. There is a strong parallel between this curriculum and the one that developed in the Latin Middle Ages, where pupils went through what they called the trivium and the quadrivium. The former consisted of the basic disciples of grammar, logic, and rhetoric, the latter of the more advanced disciplines of arithmetic, geometry, music, and astronomy, and, together, they formed the seven 'liberal arts' (*artes liberales*), a concept that still survives today, especially in US higher education.

The pre-eminent historian and Arabist George A. Makdisi (1920–2002) argued that there is a generic link between the development of educational institutions in the Islamic world and their development in the West. He first formulated this idea in his book *The Rise of the Colleges*, in which he described how colleges (Arabic singular *madrasa*) proliferated in the Islamic world and were pivotal to the development of philosophy, theology, and jurisprudence.[67] As he himself put it,

> The situation in fourteenth-century Paris shows the doctors of the Faculty of Theology relating to bishop and pope in the same way as the doctors of Islamic religious law related to the caliph and those to whom he delegated power. The doctors of Islam gave the juridico-theological reasons, and the sovereign power applied the penalty in matters involving dogma.[68]

He later made the specific point that humanism arose both in the East and in the West, and other leading scholars have accepted his arguments.[69] Even if one does not agree with all of Makdisi's arguments about the ways in which institutions evolved in Christendom and Islam during the medieval period, there can be no doubt that both sides partook in the same enterprise of engaging with Greek thought, and both often wrestled with the same philosophical and theological questions – for example whether the world is created or eternal; how to equate God with the First Cause; how to describe God; and how to accommodate God's providence and human suffering, or reconcile predestination with free will.[70]

While Makdisi saw a parallel between the doctors of theology and the ruling elites in Paris and Baghdad, an English historian of philosophy compared Averroes' *Commentary on Plato's 'Republic'* to lectures given by teachers of philosophy at Oxford, stating:

> Averroes is treating his text [*sc.* Plato's *Republic*] much in the same way as it used to be treated in our oldest University [*sc.* Oxford]. He is using it for the purposes of a course for future civil servants in the science and art of politics. [. . .] we are to think of him as the prototype of the Balliol don of a couple of generations ago expounding the Eternal Truths of Government, and the passing failings of governments, in the guise of lectures to undergraduates on these Greek texts.[71]

Balliol College and the Greats (or literae humaniores) – that is, in ordinary language, the classics course at Oxford – had a track record of producing imperial administrators for many generations. Leon Roth (1896–1963), who made this remark, studied Greats at Exeter college, Oxford and was in a unique position to have insights into the intellectual climate of both modern Oxford and twelfth-century Cordoba.

Whatever one may think about these comparisons between the universities of Paris and Oxford and the colleges of the Islamic world, both sides were very much concerned with the same classical authors and treated them in a similar way. And engagement with all things Greek is not limited to these texts, but encompasses the popular literature, as the next chapter will show.

# 3

# Menander and Alexander Retold

We should not forget that Greek was not just the language of a past Greek culture; it was also spoken by Byzantines. The Arabs distinguished the two, generally referring to the former as *Yūnān* (literally 'Ionians') and the latter as *Rūm* ('Romans'), just as the Byzantines called themselves 'Romans' (Ῥωμαῖοι). We have already explored the Greek culture in evidence at the hunting lodge in Quṣayr ʿAmrā, which belonged to a future caliph; but caliphs also came in contact with Greek speakers in other ways. We know of a number of Greek or, better, Byzantine slave girls who were married to various caliphs, and some even became mothers to an heir apparent – in other words gave birth to future caliphs. A prominent example is Šaġab (d. 933), who bore the Caliph al-Muqtadir (r. 908–32). Such was her influence at court that she was simply known as 'the Lady' (*al-Sayyida*).

Another, less well known example is al-Ḫaršā, one of the slave girls in the harem of Hārūn al-Rašīd (r. 786–809). According to a thirteenth-century source, she adopted her nephew – 'Isaac, son of the Eunuch' (as Hārūn had had his father castrated) – and 'educated him in the culture of the Romans and taught him how to read their books. He learned the Greek language in such a way that he gained complete mastery in it.'[1] Isaac and his friend

Joseph, son of Abraham, who relates the episode, were frequent guests at literary salons held at court. On one occasion, when Isaac had fallen ill, Joseph visited him at home and encountered

> a man with hair that covered him and some of it hid his face from me. He was walking back and forth whilst reciting some poetry in Greek, namely by Homer, the Greeks' chief poet. His inflection resembled that of Ḥunayn, whom I had not seen for more than two years. I said to Isaac, son of the Eunuch, 'This is Ḥunayn', yet he denied it in such a way that it resembled more an affirmation. I called out to him 'Ḥunayn', and he answered me and said: 'The son of the working girl Rassāla, [Yuḥannā ibn Māsawayh], claimed that it was impossible for any member of the 'Ibādī tribe [to which Ḥunayn belonged] to learn medicine. May I renounce the Christian religion if I study medicine before I have achieved a more comprehensive mastery of the Greek language than anyone else in this age!'[2]

Yuḥannā and Ḥunayn were rivals at court, and this anecdote shows that Ḥunayn considered it important to have complete command of Greek, including the Greek of Homer, if you wanted to study medicine. So Ḥunayn recites Homer to his sick friend Isaac, and Isaac, as we have seen, is steeped in Greek learning through the instruction he received from his aunt, a Greek slave girl of Hārūn. To be sure, Homer is not recited in front of the caliph and his courtiers, who did not know Greek.[3] And yet some of those attending the literary salons were well versed in Greek culture, including Homer, and undoubtedly brought their knowledge to bear in conversation.

This episode illustrates that Homer was held in high esteem not just among the Greeks but also among members of the caliph's court. He was never translated into Arabic in the medieval period, and this holds also for the many works of poetry that classical Greece is so famous for: the epic poems of Hesiod, the lyrical poems of Sappho and Pindar, the tragedies of Aeschylus,

Sophocles and Euripides and the comedies of Aristophanes and Menander. The same applies to the works of the great historiographers Herodotus and Thucydides. Some have claimed that this absence reflects the application of a criterion of utility to the works that were translated into Arabic, but nothing could be further from the truth.[4] For, as we shall see in this chapter, there are plenty of works lacking 'usefulness' that were rendered into Arabic.

## Gnomology in Arabic

I said above that Menander was not translated into Arabic. This is not entirely true. Of course, we do not have any whole play such as the *Cantankerous Curmudgeon* (also known as *Dyskolos* – a transliteration of the Greek title, Δύϲκολοϲ) in medieval Arabic translations, but there is a collection that circulated under the title *Menander Sentences*, witty one-liners in iambic trimeters presumably taken from his plays.[5] Examples include the following:

Δέϲποινα γὰρ γαμοῦντι νυμφίῳ γυνή.
(1) The wife is mistress over the bridegroom who marries her.
Θεὸν προτίμα, δεύτερον δὲ τοὺϲ γονεῖϲ.
(2) Honour God above all, and then your parents.
Ἰατρὸϲ ἀδόλεϲχοϲ ἐπὶ τῇ νόϲῳ νόϲοϲ.
(3) A chatty doctor is a disease in addition to the disease [that he treats].
Ξένουϲ ξένιζε, καὶ ϲὺ γὰρ ξένοϲ γ' ἔϲῃ.
(4) Treat strangers hospitably, as you, too, will be a stranger.
Χεὶρ χεῖρα νίπτει, δάκτυλοι δὲ δακτύλουϲ.
(5) One hand washes the other, and fingers wash other fingers.[6]

On the whole, these verses give advice, prescribe certain behaviours, and poke fun at institutions such as marriage or the doctor–patient relationship.

Such one-liners attributed to Menander in the Greek sources appear for instance in the *Witty Saying about Greek Maxims* by Abū l-Farağ ibn Hindū (d. 1019). In their Arabic form, these maxims no longer follow metric conventions but rather appear without any attempt at rhyme or assonance. The examples quoted above are translated as follows:

١) إنّ المرأة مولاة من يتزوج بها.

(1) The wife is mistress over him who marries her.

٢) قدّم كرامة الله أوّلا ثم كرامة الوالدين ثانيا.

(2) Honour God first, then your parents second.

٣) كثرة كلام الطبيب مرض آخر للعليل.

(3) The physician talking too much is another disease for the patient.

٤) أنصف الغرباء لعلك تكون غريبا يوما ما.

(4) Treat strangers justly, for you will perhaps be a stranger one day.

٥) إنّ اليد تغسل اليد والإصبع الإصبع.

(5) One hand washes the other, and one finger the other.[7]

We can perceive some subtle differences, as for instance in sentence (4), where the Greek asserts bluntly 'you will be a stranger', whereas the Arabic is more circumspect: 'perhaps you will be a stranger'; or in sentence (5), where the Greek plural 'fingers' turns in Arabic to the singular 'finger'. But largely these maxims are faithfully rendered into Arabic.

The *Witty Saying about Greek Maxims* by ibn Hindū belongs to a genre called gnomological literature: collections of memorable utterances by famous people from the past. This genre goes back to Greek models, and we still have many Greek gnomological collections.[8] Again, in Arabic the genre is transformed: it now includes a short sketch of a famous author's life, followed by the *bons mots* attributed to him. The most popular such collection, entitled *Choicest Maxims and Best Sayings*, was written by Mubaššir ibn Fātik roughly around the year 1048.

Mubaššir begins with some mythical characters such as 'the prophet Seth', Hermes, and Asclepius, the god of healing; then he focuses on famous Greek personalities: Homer, Solon, Zeno, Hippocrates, Pythagoras (see previous chapter), Diogenes, Socrates, Plato, Aristotle, and Ptolemy; and he concludes with Basil, Gregory, and Galen. At the very end he provides some anonymous sayings. Let us look at the entry for Homer:

> He was the oldest Greek poet, and the Greeks held him in the highest regard. He lived roughly five hundred and fifty years after Moses (peace be upon him). He produced many maxims and beautiful and glorious poems. All Greek poets who came after him imitated him: they took and learnt from him. He was their model.
>
> He was captured, and the slave monger took him away to sell him. One of the people wanting to buy him asked him: 'Where are you from?' He replied: 'I am from my father and mother.' The person then said: 'Do you think that I should buy you?' He answered: 'You have not bought me yet. Have you made me your financial advisor?' The person bought him.
>
> Someone else wanting to buy him asked: 'What are you good for?' He retorted: 'Freedom.' The buyer felt compassion for a while, and then Homer was freed. He lived a long life.
>
> He was of moderate stature, beautiful appearance and brown complexion; he had a large head, but the area between his shoulders was narrow. He walked quickly, and often looked around. On his face there were scars from smallpox. He joked a lot, was fond of insulting those who preceded him, and was funny. He frequented chieftains. He died at the age of one hundred and eight years.
>
> His utterances include the following.
>
> He said: 'The intelligent man [*al-'āqil*] is he who restrains [*'aqala*] his tongue from blame.'[9]

This description shows how accurate information about Homer in the first paragraph (his being a famous Greek poet and a model for others) is mixed with anecdotal material that has no basis in the historical record. We know nothing about Homer's life, but it is unlikely that he was a slave. But the exchanges with potential buyers appear here to illustrate Homer's wit and have parallels in other popular Greek literature, for instance the *Aesop Romance*.[10] Finally, there are thirty-six maxims attributed to Homer and I have quoted here only the first. It could hardly have been Greek in origin, as the pun is entirely based on a play of words in Arabic: *ʿāqil* means 'intelligent person' but is the active participle of a verb *ʿaqala*, which also means 'holding back' – the sense employed here.

Mubaššir's work was extremely popular not just in the Islamic world, but also in Europe.[11] It was first translated into Spanish in the thirteenth century, under the title *Bocados de oro* (literally 'bites of gold', also perhaps 'golden utterances'), and this Spanish translation was then rendered into Latin by the end of the century. The Latin version spawned a number of vernacular renderings in French, Provençal, and English. In fact there are several English versions, including one in verse by George Ashby (d. 1475). The prose translation by Earl Rivers (d. 1483) was the first book printed in England: it was printed in 1477 by William Caxton (c. 1422–91), a merchant who first introduced printing into England. These versions no longer carry the name of Mubaššir ibn Fātik, but still enjoyed an enduring popularity well into the nineteenth century; the 'dictes or sayengis of the philosophres' (to quote the title given by Caxton) seem to have spoken to very diverse audiences across time. Here again, we find a genre that began in Greece transformed into something new and highly influential. And some of these utterances even reached China.[12] Obviously, this whole literature aimed at enlightening and entertaining, not at achieving some abstract usefulness.

## Alexander the Great

Mubaššir also has a long entry on Alexander the Great's life and utterances.[13] This points to the importance and popularity of Alexander, who became something of a mythical figure in the Islamic tradition. The main Greek source for much information about Alexander is what we know as the *Alexander Romance*, one of the most popular Greek texts of antiquity. It tells the story of Alexander, yet also contains numerous supernatural elements. For instance, Alexander is the child of Olympias, the wife of King Philip of Macedon, and an Egyptian priest. He kills his Egyptian father, gets educated by Aristotle, and competes successfully in the Olympic Games. After his alleged father Philip dies, he becomes king and embarks on a campaign of conquest that leads him to Egypt, Persia, India and China. Alexander prays to God that two mountains, 'the Breasts of the North' (οἱ Μαζοὶ τοῦ Βορρᾶ), draw closer to each other and create a narrow pass; this then allows him to erect a gate that keeps out the hostile people of Gog and Magog. The further east Alexander travels, the more marvellous the things he encounters are. He travels to the land of the giants, meets other magical creatures, corresponds with the Amazons and is invited to visit them, and so on. Now there are quite a few versions of the Greek *Alexander Romance*, including one in Byzantine verse, and not all episodes and stories are contained in all of them. Then there are numerous translations, most famously into Syriac and Armenian, the Syriac version playing a particularly important role in the transmission of this material into Arabic. Already in the Greek *Romance*, Alexander is transformed into a god-like creature; but, as the stories are retold, he can become a philosopher king, an envoy sent by God to spread and uphold religion, including the belief in the one true God, or a ruthless and cunning warrior, well versed in the techniques of military deception.

In Arabic, Alexander first appears, famously, in the Qur'ān, in the *Sura of the Cave* (*Sūrat al-kahf*) (18:83–100), which tells of the

Two-Horned – 'the man with two horns' – who erects a dam or a wall to keep out Gog and Magog (called Yāǧūǧ and Māǧūǧ in Arabic). I quote and translate here just four verses (18:92–5):

ثُمَّ أَتْبَعَ سَبَبًا \ حَتّى إِذَا بَلَغَ بَيْنَ السَّدَّيْنِ وَجَدَ مِنْ دُوْنِهِمَا قَوْمًا لا يَكَادُونَ يَفْقَهُونَ
قَولًا \ قَالُوا يا ذَا القَرْنَيْنِ إنَّ يَاجوجَ وَمَاجوجَ مُفْسِدُونَ في الأَرْضِ فَهَلْ نَجْعَلُ لَكَ
خَرْجًا عَلى أن تَجْعَلَ بَيْنَنَا وَبَيْنَهُمْ سَدًّا \ قَالَ مَا مَكَّنّي فِيهِ رَبّي خَيْرٌ فَأَعِينُوني بِقُوَّةٍ
أَجْعَلْ بَيْنَكُم وَبَيْنَهُم رَدْمًا

> Then he followed a path so that, when he reached [the place] between two dams [i.e. mountains; sg. *sadd*], he found beyond them people who hardly understood what was said. They said: 'O you possessing the two horns. Gog and Magog sow corruption in the land. Can we offer you money for you to build a dam [*sadd*] between us and them?' He replied: 'Whatever my Lord has enabled me to do is good. So help me with all your strength, and I shall build a dam [*radm*] between you and them.'

Alexander is sometimes described as 'possessing two horns' already in Greek and Syriac sources, and later exegesis of these verses generally takes it for granted that the passage is about Alexander the Great. And we also have the story of Gog and Magog in the *Alexander Romance*.

The Qur'ān is by no means the only Arabic text talking about Alexander the Great. There are numerous medieval adaptations of the Greek *Alexander Romance*.[14] We can usefully divide the Arabic literature that features Alexander into three general categories: first, gnomological works such as Mubaššir's *Choicest Maxims and Best Sayings*, which we have already discussed; second, historical works and generalist accounts; and, third, specific works on Alexander. To illustrate the second category, famous historians such as al-Ṭabarī (d. 923) in his *History of Prophets and Kings* and al-Mas'ūdī (d. c. 956) in his *Meadows of Gold* have long sections on Alexander the Great, whom they identify with the Two-Horned. Likewise, in a general encyclopaedia called *Utmost*

*Skill in the Literary Arts*, its Egyptian author al-Nuwayrī (d. 1333) devotes a chapter to Greek kings in which he narrates various stories from Alexander's life.[15] For instance, when Alexander is in China, the Chinese king comes to him disguised as a mere ambassador. Later, when Alexander meets the king again, he realises what the latter has done and is mightily impressed. This version of the story also recurs in a later work of historiography. But it is, in a way, an inversion of what we find in the Greek and Syriac *Alexander Romance*, where it is Alexander who disguises himself as an ambassador and visits the king, and only later reveals himself to be Alexander the Great.

Alexander is also an excellent letter writer. Already in the *Alexander Romance*, there are long exchanges of letters, for instance between Alexander and his mother Olympias; some scholars have even talked about epistolary novellas nested within the *Romance*. In the Arabic tradition we find an exchange of letters between Alexander and Aristotle, his former teacher. Al-Nuwayrī has one version of it, in which Alexander writes to Aristotle enquiring whether he should kill certain soldiers of whom he is suspicious without having definite proof. The Greek philosopher advises him to give them the benefit of the doubt and to provide them with comely women who can assuage their desires.

We even have an anonymous epistolary 'novel'.[16] It begins with letters sent by Alexander's father to Aristotle, asking him to educate Alexander, then continues with Aristotle's 'testament' to Alexander when his father dies and with various letters that congratulate Alexander on his various conquests. A long letter follows in which Aristotle explains to Alexander how to organise political life in Persia once he conquers it.[17] This advice contains a good deal of popular philosophy and can at times sound like a recital of platitudes – for example 'magnanimity and generosity are both praiseworthy' (الكَرَم والسَّخاء مَمْدوحان).[18] The correspondents go on to talk about how one should behave as a king and treat ministers, and end on more philosophical topics such as the makeup of the world. This epistolary novel is just one of many texts that are entirely devoted to Alexander the Great in the Arabic tradition. Another such text bears the title *Life of Alexander* and survives in various versions.[19]

So far we have looked at the Arabic prose versions of the *Alexander Romance*. But it was through poetry, namely in Persian verse, that Alexander reached perhaps his greatest fame.[20] The celebrated Persian poet Firdawsī (d. 1020) already included Alexander in the *Book of Kings* (*Šāh-nāma*). This work enjoyed enormous popularity among Persian speakers and is generally seen as a national epic par excellence. In it, Firdawsī makes Alexander the descendant of the Persian King Darius II through a Greek mother and depicts him as a philosophical sage who, tempered by Aristotle's education, rejects the world and abstains from its tawdry pleasures. In this account, Alexander has the Avestan books translated into Greek and thus draws on Persian wisdom. He embarks on a journey of conquest and defeats the Persian King Darius III, but also mourns his death and shows high regard for his family. His conquests, even that of Persia, are depicted as heavenly sanctioned events, in which kings and realms succeed one another of necessity. He emerges as both Persian hero and philosopher king.

While Alexander is just one king among many in the *Book of Kings*, Niẓāmī (d. 1209) devotes a whole epic to him, namely the *Book of Alexander*. He also portrays Alexander differently, even though he draws on sources similar to those of Firdawsī (most prominently the *Alexander Romance*). Niẓāmī places much more emphasis on Alexander as a divine character and as a philosopher and thinker and pays much less attention to his military exploits. The *Book of Alexander* is divided into two parts: the first, called *Book of Honour*, largely retells the events narrated in the *Alexander Romance* and therefore focuses on Alexander's campaigns and military achievements; the second, the *Book of Good Fortune*, contains philosophical reflections and theological discussions. In particular, Niẓāmī sees Alexander as the Two-Horned mentioned in the Qur'ān: a king guided by God to protect his people, a just ruler who will bring peace and prosperity. He also includes the episode of Gog and Magog.

Yet Alexander as portrayed by Firdawsī and Niẓāmī also embraces new things, not found in the Greek sources. Two examples can briefly illustrate this. In the *Book of Kings*, Alexander visits Mecca to pray at the Kaʿba. This shows him as a proto-Muslim, fully aware of the importance that the Kaʿba should play later on, during the Muslim pilgrimage. And Alexander is depicted as a bit of a lady's man. He practises polygamy and has his own harem, which grows as his campaigns take him to ever farther places. Niẓāmī, for instance, details at some length his erotic encounters with a Chinese girl. Aristotle at times criticises Alexander for his sexual overindulgence, but he does so not for moral reasons but because of potentially detrimental effects on Alexander's health. And when his soldiers encounter beautiful women, Alexander says:

> When Alexander saw fairy-bodied [creatures] resembling pure silver
> [And that] all the soldiers were thirsty whereas they [the girls] are like water,
> He contemplated the army's needs,
> For a woman is a woman without any doubt and a man a man.[21]

The poem abounds in such similes and Niẓāmī repeatedly addresses a cupbearer, asking him to pour wine so that Niẓāmī may forget the wretchedness of the human condition. This fairly free attitude to sexual encounters reflects the much more relaxed attitude that existed in the Islamic tradition by comparison with Christian Europe, for instance.

Alexander's fame spread through the entire Islamic world and reached far-flung places such as the steppes of central Asia, Malaysia, and Indonesia. In Bulghar versions, for instance, we find Alexander accompanied by Socrates as the two are visiting the region along the Kama river – including the city of Yelabuga

– in what is now the Republic of Tatarstan in the Russian Federation.[22] Likewise, there are no fewer than three different accounts about Alexander in Malai: the *Story of Two-Horned Alexander*; the *Story of King Alexander*; and the *Story of Gog and Magog*.[23] In this way the *Alexander Romance* reached all the corners of the Islamic world and was transformed and retold hundreds of times. One constant element in many of these retellings is local colour: Alexander is of Persian origin in a Persian epic, but visits the local city of Yelabuga in a Bulghar version.

Alexander also appears in works that offer political advice to rulers – a genre that has been dubbed 'mirrors for princes'. The most famous example in the Islamic tradition is the *Book of Government*, written in Persian by Niẓām al-Mulk (1018–92), a vizier who spent much of his life advising the Ghaznavid and Seljuk rulers. He fell victim to the famous Assassins, an Ismaili religious order involved in the assassination of numerous high-profile figures. They are nicknamed *ḥaššāšīyīn* ('hashish users') by their detractors, and this term gave us the word 'assassin'. They assassinated Niẓām al-Mulk on 14 October 1092, while he was travelling from Isfahan to Baghdad. Niẓām al-Mulk mentions Alexander as one of the kings who 'possess divine grace, sovereignty, and knowledge', who 'were wise', and whose 'names . . . will be blessed until the resurrection'.[24]

This chapter has thus shown that Muslims did not limit themselves to translating what is useful but took an enormous interest in Greek popular culture, as reflected in gnomologics and the many versions of Alexander's life and sayings. While Firdawsī composed his *Book of Kings* and Niẓāmī his *Book of Alexander*, interest in the learned Greek tradition continued as well; it did not simply stop at the end of the tenth century, as we shall see next.

# 4

# From Aphorisms to Alchemy

> Among the Greeks before the advent of Christianity there were men who distinguished themselves through their great zeal for research and their efforts to advance things to the highest degree and to bring them to perfection. If Dioscorides had lived in our region and had directed his efforts at knowing the things in our hills and valleys, the plants would have all become remedies, and their fruits would have been turned through his expertise into medicaments.[1]
>
> Al-Bīrūnī (d. c. 1051)

This is how the great polymath al-Bīrūnī (d. c. 1051) praised Dioscorides in his own work on pharmacology. Dioscorides had written a treatise *On Medicinal Substances*, which was translated probably in the ninth century by a Stephen, son of Basil (Iṣṭifān ibn Bāsil), and Ḥunayn slightly revised it.[2] *On Medicinal Substances* is a work in five books, on simple drugs, mostly plants; in each case Dioscorides first describes the plant in question and then lists the medicinal effects of its roots, leaves and so on. When Galen wrote his own treatise *On Simple Drugs*, he incorporated a lot of the information contained in Dioscorides' work. And yet the latter remained extremely popular, not just in the original Greek but also in Arabic translation, as can be seen from al-Bīrūnī's opening quotation.

The translation efforts did not cease in the tenth century. For towards the end of that century a certain al-Nātilī further revised Stephen's translation. And two more translators in the twelfth century produced Arabic versions based on the Syriac rendering by Ḥunayn ibn Isḥāq. This is just one of the many instances where interest in a Greek text continued well beyond the heyday of Graeco-Arabic translations.

## The Hippocratic Aphorisms

Another text that remained extremely popular is the *Aphorisms* attributed to Hippocrates.[3] These are pithy sayings on a variety of medical topics, ranging from the mundane to the profound. The beginning of the first aphorism is most famous: 'Life is short, the art long' – a sentence often quoted in its Latin form, *Vita brevis, ars longa*, although it reached great fame in Arabic too (العُمْرُ قَصيرٌ والصِّناعةُ طَويلة). Other aphorisms state that 'peak fitness in sport is dangerous' (1.3) or that 'if fear and despondency last for a long time, this is something melancholic' (6.23).[4] Galen wrote a commentary on this work, which was itself translated into Arabic; and there it spawned a rich commentary tradition.[5]

Two of these commentaries, namely those by Abū Bakr Muḥammad ibn Zakarīyā' al-Rāzī (d. 925) and Avempace (Ibn Bağğa, fl. twelfth century), survive only in short quotations.[6] Another commentary, falsely attributed to Palladius, has come down to us in incomplete form, in a single, privately owned manuscript, and belongs to the earlier stage of Arabic translations, as we have already seen.[7] Two eleventh-century authors, Abū Sahl Sa'īd ibn 'Abd al-'Azīz al-Nīlī (d. 1029) and 'Alī ibn Riḍwān (d. 1068), penned short commentaries in the tradition of medical teaching in Late Antique Alexandria. Then we come across Ibn Abī Ṣādiq (d. after 1068), known as a 'second Hippocrates': his commentary was by far the most popular and influential. It is preserved in over forty extant manuscripts and more than one version: there is the 'normal' arrangement in seven books already found in the Greek tradition, and then a thematic one, where the aphorisms are grouped into twenty subject categories. These two arrangements are also found in the twelfth-century author al-Singārī.

Maimonides (Mūsā ibn 'Ubayd Allāh; d. 1204), the most famous Jewish intellectual of the medieval period, was originally from Cordoba, lived most of his life in Cairo, and then served as personal physician to the Ayyubid rulers. Towards the end of the century Maimonides wrote a short commentary on the *Aphorisms* where he explains his motivation in the preface:

> Since I realised that the *Book of Aphorisms* by Hippocrates is of the utmost usefulness, I decided to write a commentary on them. For all physicians need to commit them to memory. I have even seen people who are not doctors make their children learn them by heart in school. Thus people who are not physicians know many aphorisms by heart, because they had learnt them as young children in school.[8]

This clearly shows the popularity of the *Aphorisms* in twelfth-century Cairo, and it continued into the thirteenth century as well.

'Abd al-Laṭīf al-Baġdādī (d. 1231), Naǧm al-Dīn Aḥmad ibn al-Minfāḫ (d. c. 1258), Ibn al-Quff (d. 1286), and Ibn al-Nafīs (d. 1288) all produced commentaries on the *Aphorisms*. Ibn al-Quff's is by far the longest, amounting to nearly 300,000 words of Arabic text. Without going into details, in these thirteenth-century commentaries one really feels the influence of the *Canon of Medicine* by Avicenna (Ibn Sīnā; 980–1037) and the abridgements, commentaries and super-commentaries written on it (a topic to which I shall return later).[9]

In the fourteenth century we meet four very diverse commentators on the *Aphorisms*: al-Kīšī (fl. c. 1300), ʿAbdallāh ibn ʿAbd al-ʿAzīz ibn Mūsā al-Sīwāsī (early fourteenth century), Ibn Qāsim al-Kīlānī (fl. 1340–56), and ʿAbd al-Raḥīm, the physician (d. between 1383 and 1387). Like Maimonides, al-Kīšī makes a startling observation in the preface to his work:

> I saw that a favourite group of my medical students who often came to me put in a lot of effort to learn Hippocrates' *Aphorisms* by heart. Yet I also noticed that this book not only contains beautiful extracts and superb sayings, but that it is also boring for students, because it has such long-winded expressions and phrases, even if the instances of meaning in it still amazed them. Therefore I decided to abridge its text gently, so as to reduce it to half its size or less.[10]

So al-Kīšī abridged the text and then, later, ʿAbd al-Raḥīm wrote a commentary on this summary. Al-Kīlānī wrote a commentary on the whole Hippocratic text and, in it, he betrays his debts to Avicenna and later commentators in the *Canon* tradition. The text is badly transmitted, but al-Kīlānī was quite an innovative thinker.[11] The last commentator was Al-Manāwī (d. 1488), who breaks each passage up and explains it word by word, having recourse to previous exegetical authorities such as Ibn abī Ṣādiq; his method resembles the approach we find in some Qurʾān commentaries.[12] The earlier al-Sīwāsī also drew heavily on Ibn Abī Ṣādiq; but he is interesting for another reason. Kâtip Çelebi (Ḥāǧǧī Ḫalīfa, 1609–57), the most prominent Ottoman intellectual of the seventeenth century, quotes from al-Sīwāsī's introduction in a massive bibliographical survey of his own, titled the *Discovery of Opinions about the Names of Books and Arts*. This shows the interest that Çelebi clearly took in al-Sīwāsī's commentary on the *Aphorisms*.

This brief survey demonstrates how profound and creative the engagement with the Hippocratic *Aphorisms* was in the Arabic commentary tradition. It reveals that even school children learnt some of the aphorisms by heart, as did medical students. Also, because many of the aphorisms were concise and somewhat obscure in places, they could be interpreted in ever-changing ways. Besides, the *Aphorisms* is not the only Hippocratic text commented upon by Galen that had its own afterlife in the Islamic world; others are the *Epidemics* (already discussed in chapter 2) and *Airs, Waters, Places*, a text that investigates the influence of the environment on population health and offers a first medical anthropology.[13] But it is not just in commentaries on a seminal Hippocratic text that we can witness the dynamism of the Arabic engagement with Greek ideas. We also find it in the work of Avicenna, and especially in his philosophical and medical output.

## Avicenna

Avicenna marks a true watershed in both medicine and philosophy. His influence was enormous not just in the Arabic tradition but also in the Latin West, including among the Jews under Christian rule; and it was of course seminal in Avicenna's native Persian culture.[14] Avicenna was aware of his own genius and created a highly original system. Adamson has rightly summarised Avicenna's contribution to philosophy in the following terms: 'he had an unparalleled impact on Muslim philosophers and theologians – who mostly ceased responding to Aristotle in order to engage instead with Avicenna'.[15] We have seen something similar happen with the commentaries on the *Aphorisms*: in the commentaries on this Hippocratic text, Avicenna replaces Galen as the main reference point.

Whereas there is a good body of work on Avicenna's philosophy, his contributions to medicine have hardly been studied in any comprehensive way. Take his *Canon of Medicine* as an example: it is *the* most influential medical text of the medieval period and possibly of all times, and yet we still do not have either a critical edition of the Arabic text or a scholarly translation into English (or any other modern language, for that matter). It is therefore too early to make detailed statements about Avicenna's impact, but my personal working hypothesis is that he replaced Galen as a main reference point in medicine just as he replaced Aristotle in philosophy. This does not, of course, mean that he had little regard for Aristotle and Galen; on the contrary. But his genius was in part to turn into the main reference point himself. In Avicenna, we can study how Greek philosophical and medical systems are modified, refined, and enlarged and how the resulting new systems continue to exert enormous sway. In other words, the transformed Greek tradition continues to be highly relevant even today, as we shall briefly show through the example of Avicennian philosophy and medicine.

Avicenna's main philosophical work is the *Book of Healing*, also called the *Cure*, which is sometimes mistaken for a medical encyclopaedia because of its title. It is divided into four main parts: logic, physics, mathematics, and metaphysics.[16] Each part is further subdivided into topics taken from the Aristotelian curriculum. For instance, in the part on physics, Avicenna discusses astronomical phenomena, meteorology, minerals, plants and animals, and psychology (understood as the study of the soul); hence 'physics' here has a much broader semantic field than it does in current English usage. These topics are closely mapped onto works by Aristotle such as *On the Heavens*, *History of Animals*, and *On the Soul*, to name just a few. By writing this encyclopaedia – or *summa*, the sum total of what one needs to know about philosophy – he created his own system. This system was so persuasive that, as we have seen, it replaced that of his main source, Aristotle.

Now, in a book like the present one it is simply impossible to do justice to the output of a genius like Avicenna's. Consequently I have decided to illustrate how Avicenna transforms Greek thought with the help of three concrete examples.[17] A major problem in philosophy is the body–mind problem: where is the intersection that allows biological processes to turn into thoughts and, ultimately, into a notion of self? To put it in modern terms: can a person's thinking, her mind, be reduced to synapses firing in the brain, and where exactly do the physical processes become thought? The position that thought consists only of physiological occurrences is called materialism, as opposed to the 'dualism' to which, very roughly speaking, both Aristotle and Avicenna adhered (as did most of the medieval philosophers).[18] Aristotle discusses this at length in his *On the Soul*; and Avicenna discusses it in the part of the *Book of Healing* dedicated to psychology.

Avicenna adhered to a notion of inner senses supposed to correspond to the five 'outer senses' (touch, taste, smell, hearing, and sight). On this view, each of these inner senses is located in a specific part of the brain: common sense and receptive imagination in the anterior part of the brain; active imagination, estimation, and thinking in the middle part of the brain; and active and passive memory in the posterior part of the brain. Common sense functions as an interface between the five external senses and the soul, allowing us to perceive an object through different senses simultaneously. Imagination is divided into two faculties, one that receives the images and another that combines them. Estimation allows both animals and humans to make instinctive judgements. Memory is twofold as well, allowing us to store and recall images. In the *Book of Healing*, Avicenna explains his concept of common sense – a notion already present in Aristotle's *On the Soul* 3.1, where it is called 'common sense' (κοινὴ αἴϲθηϲιϲ) too:

> the faculty called 'common sense' [حِس مُشْتَرَك] [. . .] is the centre of the senses. The shoots branch out from it, and the senses lead to it. It is really the [faculty] which senses.[19]

Common sense is further aided by imagination to comprehend things, and it interfaces with thought. But Avicenna's real invention is estimation, a notion he is the first to introduce. In his conception estimation is one of the five internal or inner senses:

> Estimation is the greatest judgement in animals. It judges by way of an imaginary impression, without its being affirmed as true. An example of this is the fact that one regards honey as abhorrent, because it resembles bile. Estimation judges that it [honey] is according to this judgement, and the soul follows this [judgement], even if the intellect declares this to be false.[20]

Therefore the mere resemblance between bile and honey leads to the instinctive judgement that one should recoil from both; yet by using the intellect one can rectify this judgement. Another example of estimation in animals is the sheep's perception of a wolf as hostile; this is what we might call instinct. Avicenna has thus transformed Greek notions of the body–mind interaction and created something new, which was to be instrumental for later discussions on the subject, both in the East and in the West.

Another important topic is medical epistemology: how can we know that treatments work? how can we test drugs? Galen had introduced the idea of 'qualified experience': experience on its own is dangerous and rather needs to adhere to a number of conditions.[21] The entire book 2 of the *Canon of Medicine* deals with simple drugs. At the beginning of this book, Avicenna discusses the conditions under which drugs need to be tested and lists the following:

1: the experience 'should be free from any acquired quality';
2: 'the experience should be conducted on a simple illness';
3: it should be tested on a drug as well as on its opposite;
4: the strength of the drug should correspond to the strength of the illness;
5: the time the drug needs to take effect should not be too long;
6: the effect should be constant and occur in most cases;
7: the human body should be used for testing, and not the body of animals.[22]

Avicenna explains each of these seven conditions in some detail. Here is for instance what he says about the last one:

> The seventh [condition] is that experiments should be carried out on the human body. If the experiment is carried out on the bodies of [other animals] [. . .] it might fail for two reasons. First, the medicine might be warm in relation to the human body, yet cold in relation to the body of a lion or a horse, if the drug is hotter than the human being and colder than the lion and the horse. I believe that it is possible for rhubarb to be extremely cold in relation to a horse, but warm in relation to a human being. Second, it is possible that the drug has a specific quality in relation to one body, but not the other. For instance, aconite has a specifically poisonous quality in relation to the human body, which it does not have in relation to the body of starlings.[23]

In this passage we see humoral pathology in action: health consists of the balance between blood, phlegm, yellow bile, and black bile. Each of the humours has two of the four cardinal or primary qualities, which come in pairs of opposites, warm and cold, dry and moist. Drugs themselves have warming, cooling, drying, or moistening 'powers' or 'faculties' and thereby help to regulate the balance between these primary qualities in the living body. Now things can be harmful if they have one or two of these qualities in excess. But whether they have a cooling or a warming effect on a given animal depends on its 'temperament' – that is, the 'mixture' of humours that is specific to that animal. When stipulating his seven conditions, Avicenna draws on the Greek notion of qualified experience; however, he significantly expands it in order to improve the epistemological foundations of drug testing.

My final example comes from the *Four Discourses* by the Persian author Niẓāmī ʿArūḍī Samarqandī (d. after 1152), who relates how Avicenna treated lovesickness.[24] As Avicenna arrives in Gurgān, he begins treating the populace. His success is so great that King Qābūs ibn Wušmagīr hears about this skilled healer. When one of the king's relations falls seriously ill and none of the usual physicians can diagnose the disease, the king calls for Avicenna. The latter feels the patient's pulse and has someone call out districts to begin with, then streets, then houses, and then inhabitants; for at a certain point the patient's pulse would flutter. By this method, Avicenna deduces that there is a certain girl with whom the patient was ardently in love. Eventually the patient marries the girl and is thus saved from his lovesickness.

Now, this story is a commonplace: we already find similar episodes in many classical texts, and Galen himself relates how he diagnosed lovesickness in a female patient by taking her pulse.[25] But the common stories found in literature reflect what happens in real life. For instance, two lovers taking leave of each other in a railway station or an airport are a common occurrence, both in life and in literature. Importantly, Avicenna mentions in the *Canon*, in a chapter 'on lovesickness' (*ʿišq*): 'I have tried this [*sc.* taking the pulse and mentioning the names of potential lovers] a number of times.' He also details the method of mentioning various locations, streets, and neighbourhoods, and then says:

> We have tested this and derived benefit from what we have thus established. Then if the only treatment that you can find is to bring the two lovers together in a way that religion and law allow, do it. For we have seen [patients] to whom health and strength returned.[26]

Avicenna also advocates distracting the lovesick patients and trying to make them fall in love with someone else, 'with whom the law permits'. Avicenna thus takes elements of the Greek tradition and adapts them to his own situation, for instance by insisting on the legality of the resulting relationships.

The *Canon* spawned not only direct commentaries and commentaries of commentaries (so-called super-commentaries), but also abridgements and commentaries of abridgements in which physicians and philosophers debated various topics critically. If one looks only at direct commentaries and super-commentaries, there are twenty-three distinct works preserved in more than two hundred manuscripts. These commentaries run from the twelfth to the eighteenth century and cover much of the Islamic world. This just shows how the engagement with Greek concepts continues for centuries to come, and on a massive scale.

The commentaries offer new insights and discoveries, too. A famous case can illustrate this. In his *Commentary on the Anatomy of the 'Canon'*, Ibn al-Nafīs challenged Galen's idea that there is a hole in the septum – the membrane that separates the left from the right ventricle of the heart. He states bluntly that 'this hole does not exist' and argues that blood must pass via the lungs.[27] We now know that blood is oxygenated in the lungs and circulates through the body. But Ibn al-Nafīs did not yet have a notion of either oxygenation or circulation. Blood circulation was discovered only in 1628, by William Harvey, and oxygen more than a century and a half later.

We saw that Avicenna replaced Aristotle as the main reference point in philosophy. Although this is generally right, we need to be mindful of Averroes (Ibn Rušd, 1126–98), whom we encountered in chapter 2 as a commentator on Plato's *Republic*. But, apart from his work as a physician and judge, he was primarily a staunch Aristotelian and wrote a large number of commentaries on and paraphrases and abridgements of various works by Aristotle.[28] Many were later rendered into Latin and Hebrew and had an important effect on the development of scholastic theology. Averroes was eagerly read throughout the Arab world as well, from his native Muslim Spain to the Levant and Transoxania, and resonated deeply in Persian circles.[29] So, when we look at commentaries, be they on the Hippocratic *Aphorisms*, on works of Aristotle, or on Avicenna, the later tradition is both innovative and vibrant. We therefore have to abandon the idea of a decline and fall that dominates so much of the intellectual history of the late medieval and early modern Islamic world.

## The Ottomans

This chapter serves to demonstrate that the engagement with the classical tradition goes well beyond the tenth century. Our next vignette, on the heyday of the Ottoman Empire, will also show this. For the Ottoman rulers had a profound interest in all things Greek, as illustrated by Sultan Mehmet II (1432–81), who is best known for sacking the city of Constantinople and thus putting an end to the Byzantine Empire in 1453. He was therefore called 'the Conqueror' (Al-Fātiḥ) and greatly admired, and even feared, by friend and foe alike. His interest in Greek literature and thought can be gleaned from the fact that he continued to run the Greek scriptorium in the city he conquered.[30] In fact he amassed an enormous library of Greek works in his palace, and one manuscript is a copy of Homer's *Iliad*.[31] We also hear of recitals of Homer at his court; and these events moved him to such an extent that he decided to visit the site of ancient Troy, where the battle between Greeks and Trojans described in the *Iliad* took place. A Greek-speaking Christian chronicler gives this account:

> He [*sc.* Mehmet II] himself with his army crossed the Hellespont . . . and reached Ilium. He observed its ruins and the traces of the ancient city of Troy, its size and position and all the advantages of the country, and its favourable location as to land and sea. He also inquired about the tombs of the heroes – Achilles and Ajax and the rest. And he praised and congratulated them, their memory and their deeds, and on having a person like the poet Homer to extol them. He reportedly shook his head a little and said, 'for a long period of years, God has kept in store an avenger of this city and its inhabitants, and it is I. For I have subdued their enemies and have plundered their cities.'[32]

In this way Mehmet II identifies with the Trojans and sees himself as fulfilling the task of avenging the city after all this time. In chapter 6 we will see that the famous Palestinian poet Maḥmūd

Darwīš also identifies with the Trojans, but obviously in a different way. The interest in Homer and Troy is not the only instance of such preoccupations at the court of Mehmet II. Nor are they confined to works from a far-flung past, like the *Iliad*.

Mehmet II was also involved in theological and philosophical controversies that raged among rival groups of Christian scholars, who often appealed to him for help. George Gemistus Pletho (c. 1360–1452), a Neoplatonic philosopher who attended the Council of Ferrara and Florence during its 1438–9 phase, took part in many such controversies. He was instrumental in reintroducing Platonic ideas to Italy and the Latin West, where philosophy and theology were dominated by scholastic Aristotelianism. He attacked western thinkers for their adherence to Aristotle, which he blamed in part on the influence of figures such as Averroes, author of many commentaries on Aristotle. Yet Pletho had his own detractors in Byzantium.

The exact extent of Pletho's paganism is disputed, but he became embroiled with two prominent figures in the Greek Orthodox Church: Gennadius Scholarius (c. 1400–72), a staunch advocate for increasing the use of Aristotle in the church; and George of Trebizond (c. 1395–1486), who attacked Pletho viciously and repeatedly. When Scholarius became patriarch in 1454 after the Fall of Constantinople, he had Pletho's *Laws* (Νόμοι) outlawed and burnt.

Yet at Mehmet II's court some of Pletho's works were translated from Greek into Arabic, and one of them was the *Laws*. This translation survives in a unique manuscript in the Topkapı Palace Library that also contains a version of his *Summary of the Zoroastrian and Platonic Doctrines*.[33] In the *Summary*, Pletho explains how various gods of the Greek pantheon such as Zeus, Hera, Poseidon, Helius and so on are related to one another and how our world owes them its continued existence. The parts of the *Laws* translated into Arabic include hymns to Gods such as Apollo and Artemis. Given that one of the most fundamental tenets of Islam is the affirmation that God is one (*tawḥīd*), it is surprising that Mehmet and his entourage were interested in this text. In a preface, the translator even distances himself from Pletho's pagan ideas and states that 'the entire book was thrown to the fire and burnt out of fear that the ordinary people will be led astray by the propagation of his doctrine'.[34] This is a clear allusion to the famous burning of Pletho's *Laws* ordered by Scholarius. Whatever the reason for Mehmet's interest, it is clear that he was dragged directly into these controversies, as both George of Trebezond and Scholarius dedicated to him their polemical works against Pletho.

We already encountered the foremost intellectual of the next century, Kâtip Çelebi (Ḥağğı Ḫalıfa, 1609–57), who took an interest in *Aphorisms* commentaries. But he was concerned not just with the past but also with the present. For instance, with the help of a French convert, Çelebi also rendered Latin texts into Turkish and Arabic – for example recent publications by Gerardus Mercator (1512–94), the famous Flemish geographer, cosmographer, and cartographer. He translated the *Small Atlas* (*Atlas minor*) by Mercator and Jodocus Hondius (1563–1612) from Latin into Turkish and annotated it heavily. His version bears the poetic title *Rays of Light Shining into the Darkness of the 'Atlas minor'*. A shorter compilation, also taken from the *Atlas*, is entitled *A Guide for the Confused about the History of the Greeks, Romans, and Christians*. These are just some examples of scientific exchange between Europe and the Ottoman Empire, and we find many others.[35]

## Alchemy and Medicine

In the field of medicine many Latin texts, for instance by followers of Paracelsus (1493–1541), were also rendered into Arabic and Turkish under the Ottoman Empire during the sixteenth and seventeenth centuries.[36] Paracelsus broke with the Galenism taught in the universities of Europe and introduced a new medical philosophy, based on alchemical principles. This approach drew on the alchemical tradition of the medieval period, which in its turn went back to Greek models. The chief physician Ibn Sallūm (d. 1669) commissioned the translation of works by two of Paracelsus' followers and called the resulting Arabic translation *The New Alchemical Medicine of Paracelsus*.

Alchemy also shows perfectly the cultural cross-pollination that we see at work again and again. For it began in Egypt, with the Greek writings of Zosimus of Panopolis in the early fourth century; and these were eagerly translated and used in the Arabic tradition.[37] Alchemy then thrived as its own discipline in Arabic, where it had many further developments; and here the figure of Ǧābir ibn Ḥayyan (c. 721–815) loomed large. Writings attributed to him enjoyed great popularity in both the Arabic and the Latin traditions; in the latter he was known as Geber. Not just Paracelsus but also luminaries such as Isaac Newton (1643–1727) read and used extensively works attributed to Geber and other Latin translations of Arabic alchemical texts.[38]

When Ibn Sallūm had the works by Paracelsus' followers translated from Latin into Arabic and Ottoman Turkish, he integrated them back into the framework of humoural pathology, the very doctrine against which Paracelsus had inveighed so vehemently. This does not mean that medicine in the Islamic world stagnated, but merely that it followed a paradigm that still dominated medicine at universities in Europe as well. All this illustrates yet again that the exchange between classical and Islamic cultures was not one-sided. Nor did it end in the medieval period; it rather continued at pace in Ottoman times – and the same can be said about the modern period, as we shall see next.

# 5

# Colonial Struggle and Intellectual Manumission

The nineteenth and twentieth centuries in the Islamic world are dominated by colonialism and the fight to throw off the yoke of foreign oppressors. The British and French effectively ruled large swathes of Asia and North Africa, and frequently competed for power and influence in these regions. In parts of the Ottoman Empire, the colonial powers replaced Ottoman rule with their own, as the examples of Algeria, Lebanon, Syria, Palestine, and Jordan show. In what follows we shall focus on Egypt; I therefore start by offering a brief sketch of its history in the nineteenth and twentieth centuries that should serve as background for the ensuing discussion.

The traditional narrative of Egypt's modern history generally begins with Napoleon's occupation of Egypt (1798–1801).[1] After defeating the French, Muḥammad ʿAlī (r. 1805–48), the charismatic figure, took the reins of power and embarked on a massive process of modernisation. In 1826 he sent a delegation of students to Paris. One of them was Rifāʿa Bey al-Ṭahṭāwī (1801–73), who learnt French and immersed himself in Parisian culture. Al-Ṭahṭāwī became the first director of the School of Languages in Cairo, founded in 1836, and exerted a profound influence as a translator.

Muḥammad ʿAlī's successors – ʿAbbās I (1848–54), Saʿīd (1854–63), Ismāʿīl (1863–79), and Tawfīq (1879–92) – continued this policy of modernisation and achieved some stunning successes, especially in the area of infrastructure and public works; these are best exemplified by the Suez Canal and the construction of railroads. Their reigns, however, were marred by foreign debts that spiralled out of control. Britain formalised its influence by occupying Egypt in 1882 and ruling the country indirectly. At the beginning of the First World War, Britain formally declared Egypt a protectorate and installed a puppet regime. But under the leadership of Saʿd Zaġlūl (1857–1927) the Egyptians formed a party called the Wafd ('Delegation') and demanded independence.

The British occupation partly met the Wafd's demands and granted Egypt formal independence in 1922 by way of creating a parliamentary monarchy, but Britain remained largely in charge. Both King Fuʾād (r. 1922–36) and King Fārūq (r. 1936–52) often clashed with parliament and with the Wafd in particular, while also trying to accommodate their British overlords. The Second World War brought greater direct involvement of the colonial countries, as the axis powers vied for influence in the region.[2] The Free Officers, a group of high-ranking military personnel with an anti-royalist and anti-colonial agenda, swept away the old regime in a revolution that took place in 1952 and instituted a republic. Through the ensuing reforms, upper echelons of society lost significant amounts of their property. By 1954, Ǧamāl ʿAbd al-Nāṣir was firmly in power, supported by a loyal group of army officers; as president of the republic, he pushed through many policies inspired by socialism and moved Egypt closer to the Soviet Union, especially after the Suez Crisis in 1956. He died in 1970 and was succeeded first by Anwar al-Sadāt (1918–1981), then by Ḥusnī Mubārak (1928–2020).

## Ṭāhā Ḥusayn: The Struggle for Classical Scholarship in Egypt

The most influential Arab intellectual in the first half of the twentieth century was undoubtedly Ṭāhā Ḥusayn (1889–1973). Hailing from Upper Egypt, he first attended a Qur'ān school and later al-Azhar, the most famous university in the Muslim world. But when the secular University of Cairo opened in 1908, he moved there, and in 1914 obtained a doctorate with a thesis on the celebrated poet Abū 'Alā' al-Ma'arrī (973–1058). He later republished it under the title *Together with Abū 'Alā' in His Gaol*, as al-Ma'arrī and Ḥusayn were both blind. This thesis also won him a scholarship to Paris, where he studied at the Nouvelle Sorbonne from 1915 until 1919. On his return, he first served as professor of ancient history at the then private University of Cairo and was appointed to a chair of Arabic when it became public in 1925. Over the next three decades he played a crucial role in the development of higher education, and was even appointed minister for education from 1952 to 1954.

In the fight for independence, cultural and religious identity became a battleground in which classics had a major role to play. For instance, Ḥusayn rejected the idea that Arabic and Muslim culture is fundamentally different from European culture, and he did so by emphasising the close ties between the Graeco-Roman and the Egyptian civilisations. In his influential book *The Future of Education in Egypt*, published in 1938, he states:

> Therefore the ancient Egyptian intellect is not eastern, if one understands by 'the East' China, Japan, India, and other adjacent regions. The origin of the Egyptian intellect is in Egypt, yet [this intellect] is influenced by the natural and human conditions that surrounded it and contributed to its shaping, so that it grew and developed, influencing other neighbouring peoples and being influenced by them. The first people who were most influenced by the Egyptian intellect and then influenced it most were the Greeks.

> If we have to search for a family where we can situate the Egyptian intellect, then it is the family of the peoples who lived around the Mediterranean. The Egyptian intellect was the oldest among those born in this part of the earth – and the most influential.[3]

Ḥusayn makes two important points here: first, that Egypt had a significant influence on Greek culture and occupied a privileged position among the Mediterranean civilisations; and, second, that Egypt was in turn heavily influenced by Greece. Ḥusayn thus echoes what I have emphasised more than once in this book: that there was a constant give and take, a play of mutual influence, between the Muslim civilisation and the Greek, just as there had been between the ancient Egyptians and the Greeks in the earlier period.

Many intellectuals from colonial powers such as Voltaire, the orientalist Ernest Renan, and various European professors at the University of Cairo denied these close ties between modern Egyptians and the Greeks and claimed that the former were incapable of writing their own history, as they could not read the relevant primary sources, which were predominantly Greek and Latin.[4] Consequently Ḥusayn strongly advocated the teaching of Greek and Latin in state secondary schools and university departments, as this dispassionate argument from *Future of Education* shows:

> The practical conclusions to be drawn from my remarks are as follows: (1) the Faculty of Arts [at the University of Cairo] must have a strong Department of Greek and Latin Studies offering the BA, MA, and PhD degrees, staffed with competent teachers. Students must be prepared for this in general schools; (2) Latin, and in some cases Greek, should be prerequisite for would-be majors in the humanities; again, students must be prepared for this in the general schools; (3) our national pride and interest demands that we train Egyptians to take over certain of our basic institutions that have been directed by non-Egyptians since the

> beginning of our modern renaissance [*nahḍa*], e.g. the Egyptian Service of Antiquities, which will doubtless have to remain under their present management until there are Egyptians who know Latin and Greek very well before starting to specialise in the field. [. . .] Egyptian history, except for the modern phase, has been largely written by foreigners without any fruitful participation by Egyptians. We are still beginners in our ancient, Graeco-Roman, and Islamic periods. Those who call for Egyptian historical studies, if they are serious, should at the same time advocate the use of such logical and indispensable tools as Latin and Greek. It is shameful to have to repeat over and over again the elementary facts that the relation between Egypt and Greece is very old, that the Greeks fashioned this relation through their writings and other creative works, that Egypt was subject to Graeco-Roman authority and institutions for ten centuries, an indelible part of our national history (the source material for which is in Greek and Latin), and that Egypt was linked during the Islamic period both to Byzantium and Western Europe (the source material for which is also in Latin and Greek). The objectors to Latin and Greek should re-examine their position; for they are virtually condemning us to ignorance of our history except for what we can learn from foreigners. I cannot conceive of any proponent of Egyptian nationalism being happy about this patently disgraceful situation.[5]

These are strong words. And Ḥusayn succeeded, at least in part: classics as an academic subject is thriving in Egypt, where hundreds of freshers embark on degrees in Greek and Latin each year. Even such strongholds of Islamic orthodoxy as al-Azhar now teach classical studies, and the same is true for most of the large Egyptian universities. By contrast, foreign universities such as the American, German, and French ones in Cairo do not offer any instruction in Greek and Latin. When I attended the annual classics conference held at Cairo University and organised by the Egyptian Association for Graeco-Roman Studies, hundreds of delegates listened to dozens of papers on subjects that ranged from Homeric themes in Sappho to Late Antique Greek medical texts.[6]

Yet one has also to admit that Ḥusayn failed at some level. He encountered tremendous resistance from many quarters. As suggested above, many European professors thought that the Egyptians were not 'ready' to study Latin and Greek; and some of their Egyptian colleagues questioned the usefulness of learning these two languages. Some conservative intellectuals also doubted the close relationship between Egypt and Greece. Moreover, Greek and Latin were never introduced as subjects in state schools. To my knowledge, the only schools teaching classical Greek in Egypt today are the Greek schools in Alexandria and Cairo; and Latin is mainly available at the French school – and a vanishing proposition even there. Thus colonial hegemony over Greek and Latin education is still manifest. On the other hand, what was then called the Egyptian Antiquities Service (currently the Ministry of Tourism and Antiquities), as well as the museums, are now staffed with Egyptians competent in areas such as Egyptology and papyrology, including Greek papyrology.

Ḥusayn argued that Egypt's 'intellect' belonged not to the East but to the common culture shared around the Mediterranean, especially that of Greece. Here the field of papyrology is particularly important, for most Greek papyri that survived until today come from Egypt. Therefore Egyptians can claim a special bond with the Greek texts produced and preserved on their soil. While Europeans excavated and studied these sources, Egyptians were largely excluded from access to this heritage – a fact that Ḥusayn greatly lamented, as we shall see very soon. Moreover, the topic of ownership of historical artefacts, which are often transferred to the homelands of colonial powers, has come into much sharper focus recently and many classicists now question previous practices.

A good example of such practices is Sir Ernest A. W. Budge (1857–1934), an English orientalist in the service of the British

Museum. In November 1896 he was in Cairo and bought what came to be known as the (now famous) Bacchylides papyrus.[7] Budge bought it under dubious legal circumstances and removed it from Egypt, in full knowledge that this was illegal at the time. Undaunted, he broke the papyrus up, hid it in orange crates, and smuggled it out through the Suez, as we know from his own account of this episode.[8] The *Times* welcomed and commended Budge's initiative: 'The British Museum has once again the satisfaction of announcing the recovery of one of the lost classics . . . In the present instance it is one of the great lyric poets of the earlier days . . . who is thus, in part at least, *restored to us*.'[9] Clearly, for the journalists at the *Times*, Bacchylides belonged to England much more than to Egypt; therefore the removal of the papyrus from its native soil and its display in the British Museum meant that the lyrical poet has come home.

Access to the classical heritage taken from Egypt's soil remains a highly controversial topic. When I came to Oxford as a Rhodes Scholar in 1997, I was keen to avail myself of the opportunity to work on Egyptian papyri directly and was able to do so under the supervision of Dirk Obbink, who shortly afterwards, in 2001, received a MacArthur 'genius' award for his papyrological work. He allowed my fellow students and me to be co-authors in the prestigious Oxyrhynchus Papyri series.[10] Even today, I would have relatively easy access to the collection, whereas my Egyptian colleagues might struggle to get a visa and to finance a research trip to Oxford. I mention this personal experience for a specific reason: Obbink rose through the ranks and was placed in charge of the Oxford papyri collection for many years, but today he stands accused of selling papyri that did not belong to him and has left the university with his reputation in tatters. In 2024, my former colleague Roberta Mazza authored a fascinating account called *Stolen Fragments: Black Markets, Bad Faith, and the Illicit Trade in Ancient Artefacts*.[11] Behaviour such as Obbink's further complicates the debate about the ownership of cultural artefacts, and also poses a clear question: to whom do the Greek papyri from Egypt belong?[12]

A hundred years ago, Ṭāhā Ḥusayn was appalled by the fact that Greek papyri from Egypt were edited, translated, and studied by European scholars without much reference to any of his contemporary Egyptians. In 1919, as professor of ancient history, Ḥusayn translated Aristotle's *Athenian Constitution*, which had been discovered some thirty years earlier among Egyptian papyri. It was not just of historical but also of political interest, as it favoured democracy as a political model. For Aristotle focuses on the democratic system reintroduced after 'the rule of the thirty tyrants' (as we call it). The tyrants' oligarchic coup of 404–3 BC was supported by a foreign power, Sparta. In the heated days of Egypt's early 1920s, when a constitutional monarchy had just been imposed by the British, Aristotle's view of Athens offered a poignant alternative.

Yet in the preface to his translation, which he titled *Regime of the Athenians*, Ḥusayn complained about the fact that his fellow Egyptians had paid no heed to it:

> I learnt about this book, which I present today to the readers of Arabic, by accident in Paris: one of our professors at the Sorbonne assigned it to us. When I returned [to Egypt], I found out that it had been discovered in Egypt in the year 1891. Then it was transferred to the British Museum in London. Then a facsimile of it was published. Then it was printed in London, Paris, Berlin, and other European cities. Then it was translated into English, French, German, Italian, and other modern languages. Then it was the object of criticism and commentary in all these languages. Then it was studied in the universities of Europe. Then European historians benefitted from it. Then they corrected the errors in the history of Athens and filled in the gaps. Then thirty years passed without the Egyptians knowing anything about it.
>
> When I was teaching Greek history at the University [of Cairo], I had taken it upon myself to explain to the students from time to time certain primary sources in ancient history, so that

> they could get used to reading historical works critically, and benefit from them. In this year, I decided on this book. Yet I could not begin with this course without being overcome by shame: I would explain a book found in Egypt, but read its French or English translation, since reading the Greek source is neither easy nor beneficial, as none of the students had taken the trouble [to learn] this language. So why should I not explain it in Arabic translation, given that the misfortune has befallen us not to care for the ancient languages, and not to pay close attention to their study? After all, I owe Egypt this translation, since I did not study just to benefit myself by what I had learnt.[13]

Ḥusayn does not really critique Europeans for taking the papyri and studying them, but rather inveighs against his own countrymen. For in his opinion they do not make enough of an effort to give Egyptians the skills to write their own history and decipher, edit and translate these Greek papyri. For him, this is a matter of pride and a source of embarrassment. Only when Egyptians have the same level of competence in the classical languages as Europeans can they write their own history. And he fights on two fronts: against those Egyptians who think that knowledge of Greek and Latin is useless; and against those Europeans who think that Egyptians are incapable of reaching such a level.

The classicist, playwright, and intellectual Aḥmad ʿEtmān (1945–2013) dealt with Ḥusayn's struggle to establish the discipline of papyrology in a play entitled *The Goats of Oxyrhynchus*.[14] It is a clever engagement with both Sophocles' satyr play *The Trackers* (*Ichneutai*) and Tony Harrison's play *The Trackers of Oxyrhynchus*. The Oxford papyrologists Grenfell and Hunt discovered important fragments of the former in the sands of Egypt. Harrison used this historical event to construct his play, thus drawing both on Sophocles' satyr play and on the historical circumstances surrounding its discovery. ʿEtmān, for his part, linked Ṭāhā Ḥusayn's struggle to establish a department of Greek and Latin at Cairo University with Grenfell and Hunt's discovery of the Sophocles papyri. For 'Etmān's play opens with a scene in which Ṭāhā Ḥusayn and his European colleagues Enno Littmann (1875–1958) and Alfonso Nallino (1872–1938) discuss the usefulness, desirability, and feasibility of teaching Latin and Greek at their university. Both Nallino and Littmann make the point that Cairo University is not ready for Latin and Greek, as the Egyptians hardly know anything about their classical past.[15] In the next scene, the same three professors discuss excavations at Oxyrhynchus, where the action now shifts. From now on, Grenfell's and Hunt's search for papyri occurs in parallel with the search for some goats that had been stolen. It is in these parts that Tony Harrison's influence is most strongly felt, although 'Etmān's play obviously approaches the subject quite differently from his English predecessor. Suffice it to say that the Egyptian 'Etmān portrays the English papyrologists somewhat more sympathetically than did the English Harrison, although in both plays Grenfell and Hunt take an interest in the 'natives' mostly as a source for ancient ritual.

Ḥusayn argued for introducing classics at the university, whereas the European professors maintained that Egyptians were not yet ready. There was, however, also a third front, manned by those who thought that the claims of cultural kinship with the Greeks were wrongheaded and who insisted on religious, cultural, and linguistic purity. To put it differently, they denied that Greek or Latin were needed for the writing of Islamic history; they often treated the pre-Islamic period with contempt, as one of idolatry, not worth studying in detail; and they saw the Qur'ān as written in pure, unadulterated Arabic. This attitude is best reflected in the opposition to a series of lectures delivered by Ṭāhā Ḥusayn as the newly appointed professor of Arabic, in the academic year 1925–6.

According to the traditional narrative, early Arabic poetry developed when the desert-dwelling tribes of the Arabian Peninsula produced a number of outstanding poets, who celebrated glory and exploits, sorrow and grief, and, most importantly, love and longing.[16] Reciters then continued to perform these odes, thereby transmitting them from generation to generation. Pre-Islamic poetry found its first stable home, so to speak, in the poetry collections produced during the second half of the eighth century; and these were then quoted in later works, such as the majestic *Book of Songs* by Abū l-Farağ al-Iṣbahānī (d. 967). One finds many linguistic affinities between the language of the Qurʾān, revealed approximately between 610 and 632, and these pre-Islamic poems. For this reason, from the earliest times onwards, Qurʾān commentators relied on pre-Islamic poetry to explain the Holy Writ.[17]

Ṭāhā Ḥusayn basically applied the tools of historical criticism, and notably radical doubt, to this standard narrative and argued that it could not have been correct. In a methodological chapter of his *On Pre-Islamic Poetry*, he invokes the philosophical method of René Descartes (1596–1650), saying that, like him, he will embrace radical doubt: everything needs to be examined critically.[18] Ḥusayn argued that the poetry generally known as 'pre-Islamic' did not in effect originate in the pre-Islamic era, but was wrongfully ascribed to it in later times. In his view, one would not expect the great thematic and linguistic consistency found across pre-Islamic poetry, since the poets belonged to various periods and to tribes that spoke different dialects.

When discussing the reasons for the wrongful ascription of poetry, Ṭāhā Ḥusayn begins by stating that those who reached the wrong conclusions about Arabic literature and history did so because they neglected to compare the Arabic past with that of other ancient nations. His discussion is focused on only two such nations, the Greeks and the Romans, because in antiquity they had a historical and political development similar to that of the Arabs during the Middle Ages. These three glorious nations – the Greeks, the Romans, and the Arabs – also shared a feature related to their literary history: they all ascribed poetry wrongfully to certain ancient authors. But historical criticism has shaken many beliefs about the Greek and Roman past, and will continue to do so. Ṭāhā Ḥusayn addresses the reader directly, with these words:

> If you consider this, you will agree with me that this movement of [historical] criticism arose when literary and historical scholars were influenced by this method which we advocated at the beginning of this book, that is to say, the philosophical method of Descartes.
>
> Whether we want to or not, we cannot help but be influenced by this method in our scholarly and literary research, as Westerners before us were influenced by it.[19]

Ḥusayn continues by praising the arrival of western methods in Egypt, and then returns to the subject of classics:

> I would like you to familiarise yourself a little with any [. . .] of the many books nowadays published in Europe on the history of Greek and Latin literature. Ask yourself afterwards if the beliefs about the literary history of these two nations to which the ancients adhered remain intact. Is it true what the ancients thought about the *Iliad* and *Odyssey*? Is it true what they related, and even believed, about Homer, Hesiod, and other epic poets? Are the stories of the Greeks and the Romans true which they took as the foundation for their political order, science, literature and all [aspects of their] life? It would be delicious to read what Herodotus wrote about Greek, and Livy about Roman history, and what modern authors now write about these two nations. Yet you barely find any difference between the account of Ibn Isḥāq [a major source for the Life of the Prophet, d. c. 761] and the stories of al-Ṭabarī [the major early Muslim historian and Qurʾān commentator, d. 923] regarding Arabic history and literature, and the writings of modern historians and literary critics about the Arabs.[20]

Thus Ṭāhā Ḥusayn sought to modernise the history of the Arabic language and literature by deliberately taking European classical scholarship as a model. He had first come into contact with these critical approaches when he studied at Cairo University with Carlo Alfonso Nallino (1872–1938) and David Santillana

(1855–1931), two Italian orientalists, and with Louis Massignon (1883–1962), the French doyen of Islamic studies, who devoted most of his life to the Muslim mystic Manṣūr al-Ḥallāǧ (d. 922).[21] During Ḥusayn's time in Paris, German historicism made a great impression on him; he notably read all eleven volumes of Theodor Mommsen's monumental works on Roman constitutional and penal law in French translation.

## Ṭāhā Ḥusayn Rejected

Ḥusayn first gave the lectures in 1925–6, then published them in 1926 under the title *On Pre-Islamic Poetry* and the next year issued a revised version titled *On Pre-Islamic Literature*. The first reaction to his ideas was a veritable barrage of vicious criticism in the daily press, notably in the most important Egyptian paper, *The Pyramids* (*al-Ahrām*). The second onslaught came in the form of two commissions set up by al-Azhar University in which clerics led by Sheikh Muṣṭafā al-Qayyātī petitioned the university authorities and the government to censure Ṭāhā Ḥusayn. He was even accused of apostasy and dragged before the courts, although he was ultimately acquitted.[22]

A prominent critic of Ṭāhā Ḥusayn was Muṣṭafā Ṣādiq al-Rāfiʿī, a conservative literary scholar (1880–1937). He was one of those who attacked Ṭāhā Ḥusayn – first in the press, then in an influential book titled *Under the Banner of the Qur'ān: The Struggle between the Old and the New*, published in the same year in which Ḥusayn's *On Pre-Islamic Poetry* appeared. The book bears the telling subtitle *Articles on Arabic Literature in the Egyptian University, the Refutation of the Book* On Pre-Islamic Poetry *by Ṭāhā Ḥusayn, and the Elimination of the New Heresy of Those Calling for a Renewal of Religion, Language, the Sun, the Moon . . .*[23]

The title and subtitle already indicate the tone of al-Rāfiʿī's criticism. He claims to defend the Qur'ān while fighting under its banner and accuses Ḥusayn of *bidʿa*, which originally meant 'innovation, novelty', but came to designate religious innovation in the sense of dangerous heresy. The end of the title indicates, of course, a polemic attack, suggesting that Ḥusayn and his followers wanted to reinvent even the 'sun and the moon'. In his preface, al-Rāfiʿī sets the tone for the onslaught to follow:

> Their [*sc.* the modernisers'] most vicious, wicked, and stupid [representative] was this Dr Ṭāhā Ḥusayn, professor of Arabic literature at the Egyptian University. His first studies *On Pre-Islamic Poetry* were blasphemy against God and mockery against the people, for he lied about religions and declared [previous] historical accounts as silly, while multiplying errors and misconceptions. No other force in nature could have helped him bear all this and carry it out, except his arrogant obstinacy.[24]

Al-Rāfiʿī continues on this vexatious tone, mocking Ṭāhā Ḥusayn and declaring him to be both impious and incompetent. His main argument can be outlined as follows. If renewal and reform imply that one should abandon the marvellous language of the Qurʾān and the ancients, then surely this novelty is wrong; this does not, however, imply that new words cannot be found for new concepts. But Ṭāhā Ḥusayn and his followers want only to belittle Arabic and Islamic culture, out of an exaggerated esteem for all things European. To take just one more example, al-Rāfiʿī vilified Ḥusayn's idea of free and unfettered intellectual inquiry, saying:

> It should not escape our friend [i.e. Ṭāhā Ḥusayn] that the many opinions in this age, the many thinking intellects and the complete independence of thought without limits and bounds, then the wish that each intellect have an influence on society, and each influence have an indication, and each indication have followers – all this will result in a sickness of society that can only be cured through godly limits, which are called 'religions'. But we see in Europe and America that neglect is a 'confession', stupidity

> is a 'confession', the base fulfilment of desires is a 'confession', madness is a 'confession', each deviation is a 'confession', and not having a 'confession' is a 'confession' as well.[25]

The point is not exactly subtly argued. It is brought home rather through rhetoric: too many opinions lead to complete relativism, which ought to be cured through recourse to religious authority. Europe and America offer examples of diseased societies in which everything is acceptable.

Apart from religious themes, al-Rāfiʿī also argues extremely strongly against the idea of abandoning 'the pure Arabic language' or denigrating the literary legacy written in it. Another intellectual who was no less offended by Ṭāhā Ḥusayn's ideas on pre-Islamic poetry was Maḥmūd Muḥammad Šākir (1909–97). He apparently stormed out of one of Ṭāhā Ḥusayn's lectures when he heard them as a young student at Cairo University, in the mid-1920s. We shall meet Šākir again, when discussing a student of Ḥusayn's: Louis ʿAwaḍ, who proved just as controversial a figure as his teacher.

## Louis ʿAwaḍ: Continuing Ḥusayn's Legacy

Louis ʿAwaḍ (1915–90) hailed from a Coptic middle-class family in Minyā province in Upper Egypt. His father insisted that he study law, and he enrolled in 1931 at Cairo University, but soon lost any interest in jurisprudence and attended lectures in the Arts Faculty.[26] When his father learnt of this change of subject, he cut off his son's funding, but ʿAwaḍ managed to live by his pen and so excelled in his studies that he was offered a scholarship to read English at King's College, Cambridge (1937–41). In 1942 he obtained an MLitt there, with a thesis titled 'The Theory and Practice of Poetic Diction in English, with Reference to the Same in French and Arabic'. On returning to Egypt, he joined the English Department in the Faculty of Arts at Cairo University.

He later obtained a doctorate from Princeton University (1953) with a thesis on the myth of Prometheus in English and French literature.[27] Because of his Marxist and critical tendencies, he was forced to resign from his post at Cairo University and lived the rest of his life as an author, editor, and public intellectual. He recounted his time in Cambridge and Princeton in his *Memoirs of a Scholarship Student*, published in 1965, but written much earlier, in 1942, in the Egyptian dialect.[28]

As can be seen from his choice of a dissertation topic, ʿAwaḍ was greatly interested in literary theory, comparative literature, and in particular the reception of Greek and Latin works, ideas, and myths. This love for the classics is evident in an early publication: his edition and Arabic translation of Horace's *Art of Poetry*. ʿAwaḍ worked on it mostly during his time in Cambridge, but it only appeared in 1947, and then saw two further editions in Egypt, in 1969 and 1988, and other reprints elsewhere.[29] He dedicated this book to his teacher Ṭāhā Ḥusayn, calling him 'the foremost revolutionary and leader', 'the protector of Arabic literature and the Arabic language in the university', and 'a true enemy of ignorance and bigotry'.

Horace's *Art of Poetry* is probably the most influential Latin text on poetics and had an enormous impact on European literature, especially during the Renaissance and the early modern period. It is in fact the last of Horace's *Letters*, consisting of 476 hexametric lines. ʿAwaḍ produced a typical critical edition with a facing translation and an apparatus of variant manuscript readings. His substantial introduction deals with 'the Greeks and Romans' in general; 'the role (or function) of poetry'; 'drama'; and the topic of 'art and inspiration'. The introduction is followed by the text and translation and, finally, by notes to the text. ʿAwaḍ makes it clear that his main aim is not to offer a critical discussion of Horace's ideas but rather to make them accessible to his (Arab) readers.

Ancient literary criticism was to remain one of ʿAwaḍ's abiding interests, and in 1965 he brought out a substantial compendium of source texts in Arabic translation entitled *Greek Texts on Literary Criticism*.[30] While working on this volume in 1964, ʿAwaḍ also translated Aristophanes' *Frogs*, because the play deals with aspects of literary criticism: the merits of the old tragedy (Aeschylus), compared with those of the new (Euripides). ʿAwaḍ was particularly interested in the fact that the play is constructed around a *katábasis* – a 'descent' into the underworld. The protagonists journey there and attend the contest between Aeschylus and Euripides. The descent into the underworld is a familiar theme in Arabic literature. In Abū ʿAlāʾ al-Maʿarrī's *Epistle of Forgiveness*, the protagonist – Ibn al-Qāriḥ, a recently departed pious Muslim scholar – travels to the Hereafter.[31] There he witnesses, to his great astonishment, how many poets whom he considered heretics have found forgiveness – hence the title of Maʿarrī's work.

In a number of articles published between 16 October and 11 December 1964 in the *Supplement* to *The Pyramids* (*al-Ahrām*), Louis ʿAwaḍ investigated the parallels between al-Maʿarrī's *Epistle*, Greek antecedents (notably Homer and Aristophanes), and Dante's *Divine Comedy*. In these studies ʿAwaḍ availed himself of the tools of comparative literature. He paraphrases a number of *katabáseis* in various Greek works, then hypothesises how al-Maʿarrī could have known about them. His historical case rests mainly on two points: during the ʿAbbāsid age Arab culture became increasingly Hellenised; and in the latter half of the tenth century Byzantine troops occupied parts of Syria, hence al-Maʿarrī is likely to have come into direct contact with Greek speakers. ʿAwaḍ then explores parallels between the Greek sources and al-Maʿarrī, and concludes with a chapter on how Dante was influenced by al-Maʿarrī in his *Divine Comedy* – which, after all, is also a *katábasis*.

To illustrate ʿAwaḍ's methodology, it is useful to look at an example.[32] One of the things that the recently deceased Ibn al-Qāriḥ observes in paradise is that everybody is restored to splendid beauty and eternal youth. He encounters two alluring nymphs ('houris', *ḥūr*). They tell him that they were extremely ugly in their previous life. The second nymph confesses that she used to be a black slave girl who fetched books 'in the House of Learning in Baghdad'.[33] This leads Ibn al-Qāriḥ to exclaim: 'There is no god but God! You were black and now you are more dazzlingly white than camphor.'[34] After relating this scene, 'Awaḍ makes the following observation about the feature he found in paradise whereby the formerly ugly becomes fair:

> The fact that in paradise mankind returns to a state of eternal youth and is clothed in radiant beauty despite its original ugliness does not have any support in Ibn 'Abbās or in the [other] Islamic sources on which the story of [Muḥammad's] journey to heaven relies.[35] What corresponds to this is what happens to Odysseus and his men in the agreeable company of the nymph Circe when they are all returned to eternal youth and lofty manliness by drinking a surplus of the magical plant potion 'moly'. Something similar also occurs in Hesiod's *Works and Days* when this poem turns to the description of the next world. Aristophanes also describes something similar in *Frogs*, where we find a chorus of initiates imploring Iacchus, the lord of vegetation and renewal, to restore them to youth. Perhaps al-Maʿarrī's description of the renewal of youth and beauty in paradise was a literary imagination of the noble Hadith, influenced by the descriptions of the ancients.[36]

The 'journey to heaven' (*miʿrāǧ*) to which 'Awaḍ refers here is a complex concept. The word *miʿrāǧ* originally means 'ladder', then comes to designate the prophet Muḥammad's nightly journey to heaven (*isrāʾ*) and 'the furthest place of worship' (*al-masǧid al-aqsā*), later identified as Jerusalem. By al-Maʿarrī's time, the *miʿrāǧ* symbolised the soul's ascent to heaven, where it is judged.

'Awaḍ therefore maintains that, since the idea of eternal youth in Paradise is not found in Islamic sources, al-Maʿarrī is 'perhaps' influenced by similar accounts in Homer, Hesiod, or Aristophanes. This example clearly illustrates 'Awaḍ's enthusiasm for drawing parallels between Greek and Arabic literature. Yet one might offer an objection: the dream of eternal youth is almost universal; al-Maʿarrī would not have needed Greek sources to develop it. Moreover, it is doubtful whether al-Maʿarrī could have had access to the *Odyssey* and the *Frogs* in Arabic.[37]

The *Epistle of Forgiveness* belongs to the high or elite register of Arabic literature. But Louis ʿAwaḍ was also interested in popular literature, and in particular in a popular medieval romance, known as *al-Zīr Sālim*. The origin of the story goes back to the fifth century, when two tribes were fighting against each other in Yemen; but the story itself has undergone myriad transformations in its various versions.[38] ʿAwaḍ saw parallels between this popular romance and the story told in Aeschylus' trilogy *Oresteia – Agamemnon*, *Libation Bearers*, and *Eumenides*. Between 1966 and 1969 ʿAwaḍ translated these plays into Arabic free verse;[39] then in 1968 he published a study titled *The Myth of Orestes and Arabic Epic Poetry*, in which he draws numerous parallels between the Greek myth and the popular romance constructed around the figure of al-Zīr Sālim.[40]

In this work ʿAwaḍ retells the story of al-Zīr, often giving more than one version, and then compares the episode he has just recounted with its treatment in other sources, mostly Greek, but sometimes also ancient Egyptian.[41] Here I am just going to give a very general outline of the Oresteia and of the story of al-Zīr (according to ʿAwaḍ), in order to explore some of the parallels.

Agamemnon and his army gather at Aulis to set sail for Troy. Because he killed a deer in a grove sacred to Artemis, the goddess changes the winds so that the fleet cannot sail. To appease the goddess, he sacrifices his eldest daughter, Iphigenia. Ten years later, after the Greeks have sacked Troy, he returns home with his concubine Cassandra. Clytemnestra, Iphigenia's mother and Agamemnon's wife, still bears him an enormous grudge and plots to kill him with the help of her lover, Aegisthus. Cassandra, a prophetess, then predicts Agamemnon's murder and that of his lover. Clytemnestra kills both. Later on Orestes, Agamemnon's son, arrives to avenge his father's death. Joined by his sister Electra, he kills both his mother and her lover.

Some elements of this intergenerational blood feud among family members are also visible in the story of al-Zīr Sālim: Ḥassān, the king of Yemen, conquered Syria and wants to marry the beautiful Ǧalīla, the daughter of one of the local chieftains. Yet Ǧalīla had previously been betrothed to her cousin Kulayb, who kills Ḥassān during the wedding celebrations and marries her in his stead. Ḥassān's sister, the sorceress Suʿād, vows to avenge her brother's death. Through false prophecies, she gets Ǧalīla's brother, Ǧassās, to kill Kulayb. But at the time of his death Ǧalīla is pregnant with Kulayb's firstborn son, Hiǧris. Ǧalīla's daughter Yamāma hates her mother for the role she played in Kulayb's death and drives her out of his household. Ǧalīla goes to live with her brother Ǧassās. Now the plot thickens: Kulayb has a brother too, al-Zīr Sālim, and Yamāma appeals to him to avenge her father's death. After some further twists and turns, al-Zīr confronts Ǧassās and his men, including Hiǧris. But al-Zīr realises that Hiǧris is Kulayb's son, and tells this to Yamāma. She, in turn, persuades Hiǧris to change sides and fight against Ǧassās, whom he eventually kills. Then al-Zīr cuts off his head, and the two take it to al-Yamāma. Hiǧris becomes king.

Now, one can already detect a few general parallels between the two stories: there is internecine strife within an extended family, and a son – Orestes, Hiǧris – eventually avenges his father's death. There are also two prophetesses of sorts, Cassandra and Suʿād, whose predictions play an important role in the plot. Yamāma urges her paternal uncle, al-Zīr Sālim, to take revenge on her maternal uncle, Ǧassās, just as Electra incites her brother Orestes to avenge himself on Aegisthus, their mother's lover and their father's killer. ʿAwaḍ also draws more detailed parallels between episodes that involve apples as a means of recognition, or etymological links, for instance around the name of one character, Sulṭān, which

> has elements of Seth. Perhaps the two overlap in the name Soter [Cωτήρ, 'Saviour'], which is one of Zeus' attributes in Greek. It is thought that it is derived from the ancient Egyptian term 'Soneter', meaning 'great god' (compare also 'Sothis' [Cῶθιc], the [name of the] star Sirius [Cείριοc] in Greek, which is thought to have an etymological link to Šayṭān, Satan [Cατᾶν], Sathan.[42]

Two points are important to make here. First, 'Awaḍ draws etymological and other parallels between the Greek and the Arabic material, although many of these are tenuous at best. Experts in etymology would find 'Awaḍ's list of cognate terms naive. And yet his eagerness still illustrates a desire to relate the Greek and Arabic literary traditions and to see them as mutually influential, just as his teacher Ṭāhā Ḥusayn did. Although they may be historically incorrect or untrue, they still show to what extent Greek literature was important to 'Awaḍ and others in their understanding of their own Arabic traditions.

Finally, let us briefly look at one of Louis 'Awaḍ's own poems. It comes from a thin volume of poetry entitled *Plutoland and Other Poems*, published in 1947. In what he calls 'Sonnet 1', he first quotes two lines of Horace's Ode 3.30 in Latin, then continues in Arabic free verse written in the Egyptian dialect:

> 'I built a monument longer lasting than bronze, / higher than the royal site of the Pyramids.'
>
> Not the marble of the Romans, nor their forts, / Nor the mastabas in Memphis' burning heat, / Nor the temples carved by the ancients, / Nor the obelisk of Ramses' column / Will endure forever like my poetry / And will fill each soul with humility. / I am the one who received the revelation, I am the artist.
>
> I translated the enigma of creation with tears. / One tear for Nini, one tear about my friends, and my tear, make three tears. / I squeeze the rest of my heartblood onto the ground / And lament

with it the mortals before death. / I say again: all this is clear: I am/ the owner of the building, am built, and the builder.

Cambridge, 31 May 1940[43]

'Awaḍ begins with a quotation from the last poem in his original volume of Horace's *Odes*, which only comprised three books (he later added a fourth). Horace picks up an old trope, that literature will endure whereas other things perish – as 'Awaḍ explains in a 'comment' to the poem: 'The idea conveyed in this poem is one known in the literature of the East and the West. Al-Mutanabbī (915–61), for instance, says: "If you compose a poem, eternity will recite it" [إذا قُلْتَ شِعْرا، أَصْبَحَ الدَهْرُ مُنْشِدا].'

'Awaḍ goes on to quote other examples from Renaissance literature such as William Shakespeare ('Not marble, nor the gilded monuments / of princes shall outlive this powerful rhyme', *Sonnet* 55) and Pierre de Ronsard (d. 1585), the celebrated French 'prince of poets and poet of princes'.

In the first part of this poem 'Awaḍ elaborates on this theme, although there is also a certain irony to his treatment, as he writes in the colloquial dialect, a register not normally associated in Arabic with high-brow literature that can endure for centuries. In the second part he contrasts human mortality with the eternal life of the poem. This piece shows yet again that 'Awaḍ is keen to situate Arabic literature as a whole, as well as his own lyrical output, in the tradition of classical literature as it continued in both Europe and the Arab world.

## Plato and the Iranian Republic

But perhaps the clearest example of the influence of Greek thought on the modern Middle East comes not from the Arab world but from Iran, where the new Islamic Republic was partially modelled on Plato's *Republic*. Our story begins in Ḫuzistān, the south-western region of Persia that we encountered when talking about translations from Greek into Syriac, in chapter 2. In 1908 British geologists found there significant amounts of oil and founded the Anglo-Persian Oil Company (APOC) to extract it. APOC and its successor, British Petroleum, played a significant part in how history unfolded over the next seventy years, as they propped up various regimes and vied for influence with other colonial powers such as tsarist Russia. In 1925 the Pahlavi dynasty ousted the Qajars and established its power base with Britain's help. Although APOC nominally shared its profits equally with the Iranian state, it refused to have its books audited. When Prime Minister Mohammad Mosaddegh (Muḥammad Muṣaddiq, 1882–1967) nationalised the oil industry, the American and British secret services, CIA and MI6, overthrew him and his government and increased the power of Mohammad Reza Pahlavi (Muḥammad Rižā Pahlavī), the shah of Iran. The latter pursued a policy of westernisation and reduced the influence of the Muslim clergy. The shah's secret police – the notorious Bureau for Intelligence and Security of the State, known by its acronym SAVAK – was particularly brutal. The shah's regime was finally overthrown by the Iranian Revolution of 1979 led by Ayatollah Khomeini (Rūḥullāh Ḫumaynī, 1900–1989).

Khomeini, as the name indicates, hailed from a small town called Khomein (Ḫumayn) in central Iran. He had a traditional religious education, inculcated in him from an early age. He studied in Arak (Arāk) and Qom (Qumm), where he took a particular interest in Islamic jurisprudence and mysticism, as well as in philosophy more generally. He eagerly read authors such as al-Fārābī (d. 951 or 952), Avicenna (980–1037), the Sunni mystic Ibn ʿArabī (1165–1240), Šīhāb al-Dīn Suhrawardī (1154–91), the Persian founder of the illuminist (*išrāqī*) school, and Mullā Ṣadrā (c. 1570–1640), its most prominent adherent.[44] The latter belonged to the school of Isfahan, which developed illuminism still further and re-engaged much more deeply than before with Neoplatonic ideas, including mysticism – following in the footsteps of Shiite thinkers, as we saw in chapter 2. All this had a profound influence on philosophy in nineteenth- and early twentieth-century Iran.[45] To put it another way, philosophical enquiry was part and parcel of the curriculum in Iran's religious colleges during the twentieth century. Ever since the time of the legal scholar, theologian, and philosopher Faḫr al-Dīn al-Rāzī (1150–1210) (not to be confused with the clinician Abū Bakr al-Rāzī), this instruction came under the heading of 'wisdom' (*ḥikma*) and 'speculative theology' (*kalām*) rather than *falsafa*, the Arabic loanword derived from Greek *philosophía*.[46]

It therefore comes as no surprise that Khomeini took a strong interest in Plato and Neoplatonic thought already during his formative years in Arak and Qom. He then spent most of his career as a teacher in various seminaries and rose through the ranks of the Shiite hierarchy, becoming a qualified jurist (*muǧtahid*) in the 1940s, a 'sign of God' (*Āyatullāh*) in the 1960s, and 'source of emulation' (*marǧa'-i taqlīd*) and 'great sign of God' (or 'grant Ayatollah', *Āyatullāh al-'uẓmā*) in the 1970s. In parallel with this meteoric rise as a Shiite cleric, he also distinguished himself through his opposition to the shah's regime, most notably to his policy of westernisation. This policy culminated in the White Revolution of 1963, when a number of measures were promulgated by the shah, including a land reform that greatly diminished the wealth of the clergy. Khomeini made a number of speeches against the shah and his regime and ended up in exile, first in Bursa (Turkey) in 1964, but then in Najaf (Iraq), which is home to an important pilgrimage shrine for Shiites. In early 1970 he gave there a series of lectures in Arabic, which expounded his theory of the guardianship of the jurist and were later printed in Beirut.[47] This theory served as a blueprint for the later Islamic Republic.

One scholar, Vanessa Martin, argued that Khomeini's ideas about how a state should be organised, including the concept of guardianship of the jurist, have close parallels in Averroes' *Commentary on Plato's 'Republic'*, which we discussed in chapter 2.[48] Averroes also transformed Plato's philosopher-king into a jurist-king: the order of the state derives from the religious laws interpreted by the jurist (*faqīh*). This jurist is an accomplished philosopher, who masters both theoretical and practical sciences and is of unimpeachable moral character. When Averroes and Khomeini wrote their works, they very much endeavoured to improve the society around them, and both advocated the restoration of Islamic law as a key to this process: Averroes criticised the Almohad rulers and Khomeini inveighed against the shah's regime, which he regarded as godless. Both wanted to restore the political system by imposing religious laws. Martin finds many more parallels between the two, but the overall picture is clear as she concludes: 'Both writers demonstrate the continuing role of the thought of the Greeks in the politics of Islam and the quest for answers in that thought to the eternal tensions between the real and the ideal.'[49]

Did Khomeini use Averroes' *Commentary* as a source of inspiration for his ideas about the guardianship of the jurist? I personally find this unlikely, as this text is transmitted in Hebrew translation and was published and translated into English no earlier than in 1956. It is far more likely that the many parallels between the two go back to the fact that a lot of Averroes' thought is based on Plato, but also on philosophers such as al-Fārābī, who had also read Plato and with whom Khomeini was intimately familiar, as the theological discourse on which he was brought up included Platonism, as we have just seen.

Moreover, we have the personal testimony of a close collaborator who tells us that Khomeini felt inspired to formulate his concept of the guardianship of the jurist after reading Plato's *Republic* itself.[50] Therefore the parallels discussed above should give us no surprise. We can find similarities even in the nomenclature of the institutions. Whereas Plato envisaged Guardians who protected the ideal city, Khomeini set up a Guardian Council to safeguard the Islamic Republic.

After the revolution in 1979, Khomeini became supreme leader and guardian jurist, and organised the new Islamic Republic according to his ideas. In that, he betrayed his left-wing allies, who had hoped for a democratic system after the collapse of the shah's regime. Be that as it may, the Iranian Republic is a monument to the influence of Plato on the modern world. But poetry, which is outlawed in Plato's *Republic*, was keenly adapted and adopted by Arab and Muslim authors, as we shall see next.

# 6

# Lysistrata and Oedipus in Baghdad and Cairo

On a warm summer's eve in mid-June 1904, the entrance of Cairo's Shepheard's Hotel, the leading house in Egypt and one of the most luxurious establishments in the world, was illuminated by colourful electric lights for a very special occasion.[1] When the guests entered and made their way through the splendid foyer into the inner courtyard, they were engulfed in a festival of lights, as chandeliers hung from the trees and torches adorned the garden. Exquisitely crafted crockery and cutlery graced the tables, and menus in French and Arabic not just listed the finest food but also displayed a fitting image: the pyramids and the sphinx next to Mount Lebanon and its cedars – 'symbols of Egypt and [Greater] Syria', as one guest put it – and above them the sun of knowledge, whose rays shone on everything equally.

What was this 'spectacle that had not been seen before'? Some hundred personalities, representing the 'literary and intellectual elite', came to celebrate the publication of the first Arabic translation of the *Iliad*. Only those who had subscribed to it had been invited; even so, the list of subscribers had to be closed, as there was simply too much demand. After dinner, a long list of luminaries addressed the guests in Arabic, English, French, and modern Greek, all extolling the virtues of this new venture. Some of those who could not attend sent telegrams that were read out at the gathering, and one of them was from Grand Mufti Muḥammad ʿAbduh (1849–1905) – the Egyptian Islamic scholar, judge, and reformer.

This translation was the result of decades-long efforts by a high-ranking statesman of Lebanese origin who served as a minister and senator in the Ottoman government: Sulaymān al-Bustānī (1856–1921).[2] It bore an elaborate title: 'Homer's *Iliad*, translated into Arabic verse, with a historical and literary commentary; prefaced with an introduction on Homer and his poetry, as well as the literature of the Greeks and the Arabs; and appended to it are a general lexicon and indices'.[3]

As al-Bustānī himself explains in his preface, he decided to render the *Iliad* into Arabic verse, but was of course faced with a number of difficulties.[4] The greatest one was the difference between Greek and Arabic metre. Like its Greek counterpart, Arabic metre is quantitative: a fixed sequence of short and long syllables constitutes each verse. However, it also requires all verses in a poem (and sometimes also the end of each hemistich in the first verse) to rhyme among themselves (something known as monorhyme). Having been influenced by the fads and fashions of his age, al-Bustānī opted for a neoclassical style in which he changed the metre and the rhyme regularly after a certain number of verses. Often his vocabulary was both recondite and recherché, so that he had to explain many of his expressions in the copious notes that accompany the translation.

A Princeton Arabist analysed the quality of al-Bustānī's translation with special reference to the sixth book. He came to the conclusion that al-Bustānī often failed to render all the subtleties and poetic expressions of the Greek original into Arabic. For instance, stock phrases such as 'he uttered winged words' (ἔπεα πτερόεντα προσηύδα) are simply rendered as 'he said' (*qāla*). Likewise, al-Bustānī employed Arabic clichés, which do not convey the exact meaning of the original. This criticism is to a certain extent justified and, according to the German Arabist Jörg

Krämer (1917–61), '[t]he profound impact on the movement to renew Arabic literature for which he [*sc.* al-Bustānī] had hoped as a recompense for decades of painstaking work failed to materialise'. In other words, the complicated language and copious notes limited the impact that this translation had.[5]

And yet al-Bustānī had a profound influence through his preface, which could be regarded as a monograph on the topic of comparative poetics. It shows that he was acutely aware of the European scholarly debates of the time. He devoted, for instance, a section to the Homeric question: who is the author of the extant epic poetry attributed to Homer? He expounded in particular the 'Wolfian view', by which he meant a thesis developed by the German classical scholar and philologist Friedrich August Wolf (1759–1824): the *Iliad* and the *Odyssey* were not written by a historical Homer but were rather the result of a conscious sixth-century BC 'recension', under the tyrant Peisistratus of Athens, of a multitude of oral epic poems (basically performed songs, *carmina*) created and circulated throughout the centuries by itinerant bards who called themselves Homerids. And al-Bustānī sides with Wolf against the more traditional opinions.[6]

In general, al-Bustānī compared the social and religious structures of pre-Islamic Arabia and archaic Greece, as well as the poetic and metrical conventions of their traditions. He saw certain parallels in their political organisation, and even studied some issues that were talking points in his day, such as the situation of women, contrasting the women in the *Iliad* with those in pre-Islamic Arabia. We can thus appreciate how al-Bustānī paved the way for Ṭāhā Ḥusayn's later discussions of pre-Islamic poetry that we encountered in chapter 5: just as Homer as a poet did not really exist, and just as the Homeric poems were the result of later composition and recension, so too the pre-Islamic poetry really originated at a much later time than was generally believed.

Homer's epic poems continued to fascinate Arab authors, and this is reflected in two ways. On the one hand, we find extensive studies of al-Bustānī's translation, and especially his preface by later critics: in 1956 Joseph al-Hāšim, for instance, published a monograph entitled *Sulaymān al-Bustānī and the Iliad* in which he explored al-Bustānī's life and work, with special reference to his translation of the *Iliad*; and Miḫā'īl Ṣawāyā devoted a book to the same subject.[7] On the other hand, a number of authors produced further Arabic adaptations of the *Iliad* from the 1950s until today.[8] Some are retellings of the events of the Trojan War in paraphrastic prose of various lengths; they relay the stories of the Trojan War, sometimes from the beginning to the end, proceeding roughly in chronological order. They start with Zeus catching a glimpse of Thetis and falling in love with her, then follows her marriage to Peleus, and the sack of Troy comes at the end. Certain scenes were particularly famous and recounted in detail; one of these was Hector's encounter with his wife Andromache and infant son Astyanax in book six, as he leaves for battle, never to return.

But we also have complete translations. The famous Syrian writer Mamdūḥ 'Adwān rendered each verse, although he, too, like all previous translators, worked largely from English translations of the Greek original – which means that all these renderings are in reality translations of translations. The late and lamented classicist Aḥmad 'Etmān broke the mould and produced an Arabic translation directly from the Greek. It was published by the Supreme Council of Culture in 2004, as number 750 of the National Translation Project, to mark the centenary of al-Bustānī's translation – which was reissued as number 712 in the same series.[9] 'Etmān's new translation was launched at a conference held from 29 May to 1 June 2004 on 'the *Iliad* throughout the Ages', in which both Egyptian and international scholars partook.[10] The Egyptian delegates gave papers on subjects ranging from the myth of Agamemnon in epic poetry and tragedy, or Egypt and the Egyptians in Homer, to pronouns that indicate relative clauses in the *Iliad*, the reception of the *Iliad* in English and French literatures, and how Homeric scholarship influenced the study of popular Arabic epic traditions. This range illustrates scholarly engagement with the *Iliad* in all its aspects; in other words, contemporary Egyptian classicists resemble very much their American and European counterparts in that, when they study something like the *Iliad*, they do it from the vantage points of linguistics, literary criticism, history, and reception studies.

Today there is a large number of classical scholars who work in Egyptian universities, and some of them are extremely productive. ʿEtmān is one such scholar: he also translated numerous Greek plays directly from the original into Arabic. To give just two further examples, the Hellenist Munīra Karawān, one of the scholars who collaborated to produce the Arabic version of the *Iliad*, also translated Aeschylus' *Oresteia*, six plays by Sophocles, ten plays by Euripides, and Aristophanes' *Lysistrata*.[11] Likewise, under the general editorship of ʿAbd al-Muʿṭī Šaʿrāwī, a team of Egyptian Latinists rendered Virgil's *Aeneid* into Arabic; and this is just one of the many Latin texts that were translated into Arabic directly from the original over the past half century or so.[12] All these achievements indicate the vibrancy of classical studies in Egypt, but also the availability, to the Arabic reading public, of high-quality translations of Greek texts produced directly from the original. In many cases there is even choice between several scholarly translations of the same text.

## Oedipus in Arabic

But translation is only the first step. Many classical themes were tackled more than once, and a prime example is the story of Oedipus, which spawned numerous versions already in antiquity and continues to fascinate playwrights today. Sophocles' play *Oedipus King* in particular generated a number of Arabic adaptations. It was performed in 1912 at the Cairo Opera House, with the acclaimed actor George Abyaḍ (1880–1959) in the lead role. This adaptation was produced by the prominent Christian intellectual Faraḥ Anṭūn (1874–1922).[13] When Abyaḍ took his troupe on a tour in 1926 and put *Oedipus King* on stage in the two Iraqi cities of Basra and Baghdad, one of the actors, Ḥaqqī al-Šiblī, was so overwhelmed by the experience that he founded the first Iraqi theatrical company. He himself later became a famous actor and theatre coach, and set up a drama department within the Iraqi Academy of Arts in 1939.[14] You can still listen to a wonderful radio play of *Oedipus King* with George Abyaḍ in the main role, lavishly produced by the Egyptian Radio and Television Union.[15]

No fewer than five Arab playwrights have written their own *Oedipus* adaptations.[16] Tawfīq al-Ḥakīm and ʿAlī Aḥmad Bākaṯīr wrote their *Oedipus* plays in the aftermath of what became known as the Catastrophe (*Nakba*): the expulsion of the Palestinians in 1948 and the subsequent declaration of the state of Israel. They both endeavoured to create plays that reconcile the Greek myth with the religious sensitivities of their coreligionists. Let us look at al-Ḥakīm's adaptation more closely. It is the most interesting one, as it contains a preface in which al-Ḥakīm reflects in more general terms on the problems of introducing drama in general and tragedy in particular into the Arabic tradition:

> If only a literary figure had risen among us during the last century or two to cry out questioningly: 'O Arabic literature, from ancient times there have been between you and Greek thought close ties and bonds. You have, however, turned your face away from the poetry it has. How far will this rupture go? When will a reconciliation be achieved between you and Greek poetry? Consider it a bit. Allow it to be translated and researched. Perhaps you will find in it something to reinforce your heritage and to augment your legacy to future generations.' This voice was not raised during the past centuries. [. . .]
>
> [T]he reconciliation between the two ancient literatures is incumbent upon us. [. . .] Here we approach the great question: how can this reconciliation be achieved? Is it sufficient to be, with care and concern, devoted to Greek dramatic literature, rendering all of it into our Arabic language? This is obviously necessary,

> and most of that has been accomplished. Indeed, *Oedipus King* by Sophocles was performed for all to see on the Arab stage more than a third of a century ago.
>
> But merely rendering Greek dramatic literature into the Arabic language does not achieve for us the establishment of a dramatic literature in Arabic. Similarly, merely rendering Greek philosophy [into Arabic] did not create an Arabic or Islamic philosophy. Translation is only a tool which must carry us to a further goal. This goal is to draw water from the spring, then to swallow it, digest it, and assimilate it, so that we can bring it forth to the people once again dyed with the colour of our thought and imprinted with the stamp of our beliefs. This was the way the Arab philosophers proceeded when they took on the works of Plato and Aristotle. We must proceed in that same way with Greek tragedy. We must dedicate ourselves to its study with patience and endurance and then look at it afterwards with Arab eyes. [. . .]
>
> That is the way to the reconciliation, indeed the marriage, between the two spirits and the two literatures. There must occur a marriage between Greek literature and Arabic literature with respect to tragedy comparable to the marriages that took place between Greek philosophy and Arab thought and between French literature and Greek literature.[17]

Al-Ḥakīm clearly states that he considers a return to Greek sources necessary if Arabic literature is to have new life breathed into it and be allowed to gain equality with French literature. Such aspirations should, of course, be seen in the context of Egypt's intense political debate and struggle to gain independence, which succeeded in 1952. According to al-Ḥakīm, this literary manumission cannot be achieved merely by translating Greek texts; one also needs to engage with them critically and creatively, in order to incorporate them into the Arabic tradition. In the case of *Oedipus King*, he does this extremely successfully.

In keeping with his own beliefs, al-Ḥakīm drew on the Greek sources of the legend, notably Sophocles' play, but transformed the plot so as to make it more relevant to his audience and to bring it in harmony with his own philosophy. One of the main ideas in Sophocles' play is the immutability of fate: Oedipus is condemned to kill his father and subsequently marry his mother. Despite all efforts to avoid this outcome – for instance by his parents, when they abandon the newborn Oedipus – fate inextricably takes its course, indifferent to the intentions of the human actors in the play. In al-Ḥakīm's plot, however, Tiresias, who is more of an ambitious politician than a clairvoyant seer, is the origin of the tragedy: he sets the wheels in motion by persuading Laius that his son would kill him and by showing Oedipus how to solve the riddle, which leads to his becoming king of Thebes and marrying his mother Jocasta. Thus human action, and not an oracle foretelling the inevitable future, triggers the events that will lead to the tragic outcome. As one critic put it,

> Al-Ḥakīm would not have the gods work against man, and has to put the blame for the downfall of Oedipus on Tiresias, in the first place, and on Oedipus' insistent search for the truth. As an Oriental, he [*sc.* al-Ḥakīm] says, he cannot see man as the only power in the universe, as his own god. The gods are just: they give us what we deserve.[18]

Al-Ḥakīm also dispensed with some of the more pagan aspects of the myth – for instance he replaced the sphinx with a fierce lion – since, as he himself says, 'I had to strip the story of some of the superstitious beliefs that the Arab or Islamic mentality would scorn'.[19]

Like al-Ḥakīm's play, Bākaṯīr's *Tragedy of Oedipus* is also based on Sophocles. In fact Bākaṯīr often draws inspiration from al-Ḥakīm and follows his lead. This is not the case in the other three plays. In his *Return of the Absent* (1968), Fawzī Fahmī favours a different version of the ancient narrative. His Oedipus repents of his incestuous transgression, marries a young girl, and begets offspring with her. ʿAlī Sālim's *Comedy of Oedipus, or You're the One Who Killed the Beast* (1970) departs significantly from Greek antecedents. He situates the action in the Egyptian rather than the Greek Thebes, and mixes modern politics and concerns much more prominently with the action than did his predecessors. His Oedipus is modelled on the (failed) Egyptian president Čamāl ʿAbd al-Nāṣir. The population of Thebes reveres Oedipus because he was able to 'kill the beast' and thus save them, so in a new crisis they turn again to a hero. Sālim's message is, undoubtedly, that the populace should not rely on a hero (such as ʿAbd al-Nāṣir), but should rather confront the enemy (the monster, the sphinx) themselves, and thus gain protection. Finally, in his *Oedipus: A Modern Tragedy* (1981), the famous Syrian playwright and dramatist Walīd al-Iḫlāṣī also changed Sophocles' version significantly. Here the action takes place in a university computer lab, and the oracle is represented by a computer. The protagonist, called Sufyān, is foretold by the computer that he will kill his son and love his daughter. He becomes infatuated with the young and beautiful Sulāf who, he later discovers, is his daughter; then, on the brink of suicide, he puts a lethal dose of pills into a glass of water, which he decides not to drink, and this leads to his son's accidentally consuming the deadly cocktail. Thus the computer's prophecy is fulfilled.

## Greek Comedy on the Arab Stage

It was not just Greek tragedy but also Greek comedy that was adopted and adapted for the Arab stage. This can again be illustrated by an example, namely Aristophanes' *Assemblywomen*, which served as an important source of inspiration for Arab playwrights. Tawfīk al-Ḥakīm wrote a play called *Praxa*, which is based on Aristophanes' comedy.[20] He published it in two parts. *Praxa* I appeared in 1939, at the end of a politically tumultuous decade, and bears the following dedication:

To Aristophanes! . . .
Master of Greek comedy! . . .
I present my misdeed! . . .
And I ask for:
Forgiveness! . . .[21]

In the brief statement preceding the play itself, al-Ḥakīm explains the relationship between his *Praxa* and Aristophanes' *Assemblywomen*:

> I wrote the play on the basis of an ancient comedy by Aristophanes, *The Assembly of Women*, which was produced in 392 BC. Those who have gathered crumbs from Aristophanes' table in order to make a new dish are many [. . .] I would like it that any meticulous reader or scrupulous critic refer to Aristophanes' original before perusing this book; doing so will show them many stylistic particularities. For just sharing one play with Aristophanes has revealed to me what the experience of fifteen theatrical plays that I wrote has not; has taught me secrets of this difficult art that I did not know; and has disclosed to me features and faults that were not easy to grasp.[22]

The play is set in classical Athens, in which any reader or spectator immediately recognises contemporary Cairo. In act I, which follows the Greek model much more closely than the rest, Praxagora leads a group of women, who disguise themselves as men and take part in the assembly. They want to end the men's political folly by hook or by crook, and manage to get Praxagora elected as leader of the government. The session itself of the assembly is not staged, but rather foreshadowed in a preparatory meeting of the women and reported by one of the male citizens, Chremes, to his neighbour, Blepyrus, who is in fact Praxagora's husband.

Already in the first scene of this act, al-Ḥakīm's criticism is only thinly veiled. Praxagora, for instance, says in her speech:

> My heart bleeds, because I see that corruption has crept into the body of the state like a slow death. I see that the state has put its affairs into the hands of presidents who only care for themselves, not the state. [. . .] No man has yet appeared who would make the state a single circle at the centre of which is the public benefit, and who would then remove himself only to watch over it from far, like a God.[23]

In the second act, the protagonist is no longer called Praxagora but rather Praxa, indicating that the plot now moves beyond Aristophanes' play. She is installed in the palace, as the ruler. Different factions of the people make demands on her, and she does not have the courage to disappoint them, promising them contrary things. She is also under the spell of the beautiful general Hieronymus, who urges her to spend more money on the military and to go to war with Sparta. She even retires with him to her boudoir and neglects the affairs of the state. Praxa also puts her friends and family in high-ranking and lucrative positions. At the end of act II, a disgruntled crowd appears, requesting regime change. At the beginning of the next act, which is set in a gaol cell, we learn that Hieronymus has seized power. Hippocrates, the philosopher who had previously advised Praxa, is imprisoned. Praxa comes to see him first, and they are later joined by Hieronymus. All three discuss the merits of different types of government. For Hieronymus, Praxa represented anarchy; for Praxa, Hieronymus symbolises barbarism. The general praises the merits of his type of government in no uncertain terms:

> HIERONYMUS: I am order! Since I have seized the reins of power, have you heard a single faction proffer a request? or has anyone praised an opinion? or has any mouth opened to cry? or has anybody raised his voice to shout a slogan? All that is past. The age of the parties has come to an end. The differences, struggles, and competitions have been wiped out. I have brought together the whole nation, and united the country's

voice. Everything is now as if one. The people are like one individual.

THE PHILOSOPHER [HIPPOCRATES]: It is you!

HIERONYMUS: Yes! It is I. There is nothing else but I; no wish but mine. And I will give the people with this hand the most eternal glory.

PRAXA: And what is this glory?

HIERONYMUS: Triumph and victory![24]

Hippocrates argues that the best type of government would be to have all three, Hieronymus, Praxa, and himself, rule together as equals. But Hieronymus dismisses this idea, and has Praxa join Hieronymus in gaol at the end of the act.

This was the end of the play as it was published in 1939. In his preface to the 1960 edition of the play, Tawfīq al-Ḥakīm laconically states:

> *Praxa or the Problem of Government* first appeared in 1939 in three acts only. At that time, it would not have been easy to publish more than that. After it had been translated [into French] to be published in Paris in 1954, it appeared complete for the first time.[25]

A short summary of the second part, consisting of acts IV to VI, will show why publication was difficult at that time.

In act IV, Hieronymus has lost the war against Sparta and fears the wrath of the people. He recalls Praxa and Hippocrates in prison, in the hope that they might help. During their deliberations, Praxa's husband Blepyrus arrives. Then Praxa, Hippocrates, and Hieronymus decide that it would be best to make him king: the three hope that they can easily control the gullible husband, who is under his wife's spell. He ascends to the throne and is acclaimed by the people. In act V, however, we see the three together in prison. For other people gained Blepyrus' confidence and persuaded him to have the former rulers thrown in gaol. Finally, in act VI Chremes, Blepyrus' former neighbour and current advisor, conducts a show trial against the three in front of the people. They are not accused of betraying the country, as they first think, but of adultery. But the trial turns sour for Chremes when Hieronymus tries to persuade the people that Blepyrus is weak and his regime corrupt:

> HIERONYMUS (shouting): I say that these people alone are duped today. O Athenians! Search a little in your heads, and you will find the answer. Think a moment and it will become clear that they betray you and rob you. It is they who keep you occupied with a small and paltry matter which does not concern you, so that you do not become aware of greater matters which touch your rights and your interests directly. It is high time that you pay attention. It is high time to observe the hands which fiddle with your pockets in darkness.[26]

Chremes attempts to calm the populace and severely inveighs against Hieronymus:

> CHREMES (through his teeth): So be it. Since you wanted it so, then listen, Hieronymus. You were an absolute ruler over Athens. And what have you done for its people? You deprived them of their freedoms, their possessions, their food, and their sons. You threw all this away for a war through which you supported your rule and built, as you believed, your glory.[27]

Finally, Hippocrates urges the people to govern themselves. Since all failed – Praxa, who tried only to please everybody, Hieronymus, the military dictator, and Blepyrus, the feeble and gullible king – the people themselves should seize power. He addresses them directly:

> O people, can you not walk one path or another yourselves? Then, where are you? What do you do? Do you always sit like this? You

> observe, and listen, and shout? You may be excused for this, if you have in front of you one of the shrewd snake charmers [. . .] But only swindlers and pickpockets are left. Then what is the wisdom in sitting around? What are you waiting for?[28]

In the end, the people, together with Hippocrates, storm the palace.

At the end of act III we see Hieronymus embodying the absolute dictator, who equates himself with the state and abolishes democratic debate and political parties. Yet at the end of act VI he is deposed and defeated; the various rulers emerge as snake charmers who dupe the people. At the end of the 1930s, Egypt was still a monarchy and its colonial overlord, Britain, was calling the shots for the most part. The second half of *Praxa* was a much more direct criticism of the political system of that time, and this prevented its publication. With the revolution and overthrow of government on 23 July 1952, the situation changed.

But the story of Praxagora in Arabic does not end in the 1950s, or even on al-Ḥakīm's death in 1987. For – to give just one example – shortly afterwards Aḥmad ʿEtmān, whom we encountered earlier as the translator of the *Iliad*, wrote a new version of *Praxa*. He had written a comparative study titled *The Classical Sources in Tawfīq al-Ḥakīm's Theatre*.[29] ʿEtmān's play is called *Al-Ḥakīm Does Not Follow the Common Crowd*.[30] In it, al-Ḥakīm encounters Aristophanes on his deathbed, in a dream, and discusses his play with him. The two then attend the rehearsal of a different version of *Praxa*, where Praxa is married to Pedro. Through the clever use of self-reference and allusion, ʿEtmān thus constructs an updated criticism of Egyptian society. The play was originally published in 1988. It was originally produced in Luxor, in July 1990, and then twice in 1991 – first in somewhat difficult conditions, at the Sāmir theatre in Cairo, and then at the sumptuous Cairo Opera house.[31]

A new musical *Praxa* by Nādir Ṣalāḥ al-Dīn (Nader Salah Eddin) was also performed at the Cairo Opera House (on the main stage) at the end of July 2009. It featured 'a cast of 62 actors and dancers, in addition to the six main characters, including the star singer, film star Boshra'.[32] One theatre critic reviewed this show in quite scathing terms, but that does not detract from the fact that it marked a major cultural event in Cairo at the time.[33] Again, this shows that classical themes can reach a larger audience; the classical play, first adopted and adapted by al-Ḥakīm, thus went through further iterations.

The *Assemblywomen* is often confused with Aristophanes' *Lysistrata*, as women become involved in politics in both. To illustrate the continuing relevance of Greek comedy to political theatre in Egypt, let us briefly look at an adaptation of *Lysistrata* that grew out of a protest movement against the US invasion of Iraq in 2003. In the build-up to this invasion in February and March, various protest movements sprung up in many cities across the world. On one day alone, as many as 10 million protestors descended onto the streets to voice their opposition to the American aggression: that day was 15 February 2003.[34] I was in Paris at the time and I still remember demonstrating every day against this war.

Two New York-based actors, Kathryn Blume and Sharron Bower, organised a different kind of protest: the Lysistrata Project, 'a global act of theatrical dissent'. Through grassroots activism, they got more than 200,000 supporters to organise public readings of Aristophanes' play so as to voice through it their objection to the war.[35] One of the people who picked up the call for action was Marina Kotzamani from the University of the Peloponnese, who went beyond the readings: she set up a project where she invited Arab theatre professionals to sketch how they would stage *Lysistrata*, then published these sketches in an article. But one playwright went even further.[36] The prominent Egyptian author and director Lenin al-Ramlī (1945–2020) wrote an adaptation of Lysistrata and produced it – again, at the Cairo Opera House – on 14–24 December 2004. It is called *Peace of Women* and set in pre-war Baghdad.[37]

The protagonist, Labība (Labeeba), organises an anti-war coalition of Iraqi and Western women who have come to Iraq to demonstrate against the imminent US invasion and to serve as human shields. They swear to abstain from sex in order to prevent the war. They occupy the Oil Ministry, to gain power over the vital resource at the heart of the conflict. At some stage, the husband of one of the women is allowed to enter the occupied building. He has been enjoined to break the sex strike, and to this end he begs his wife to have sex with him, claiming that otherwise Ṣaddām would punish him. But, although she agrees, he cannot perform because of the psychological pressure. As the women's movement gathers force and gains support, cracks appear in the united front: western women chide their Arab sisters for wearing the veil, while the latter rebuke them for their loose morals and consumption of alcohol. One Arab woman turns into a suicide bomber, and the Americans begin to bomb Baghdad. Some drunken people confuse the bombardment with fireworks, and at the end Labība is seen roaming among the ruins and rubble, in search for her son.

In the prologue, al-Ramlī implicitly comments on the intentions of his play and its relationship to the Aristophanic model:

> You have come to attend our show, although we are still just
> amateurs, and no stars are among us.
> This is a singular and wondrous thing! It will not be remembered
> by the history of our theatre.
> At the beginning . . . this is a play,
> only just a play,
> a theatrical play that has no political goals.
> It shows how people behave, and how humanity thinks.
> In it we imitate this humour invented by Aristophanes,
> the most skilful of those who wrote comedy in the land of the
> Greeks.
> We take from it the shape and structure,
> we mix it with some of its spectacle and its happy end.

For just as war has enemies, so peace has enemies, who are
stronger,
and this is the human nature, everywhere –
from times of old, until now, until now.[38]

Thus al-Ramlī warns the spectators that they should not reduce the play to a political or sociological message. He lets the coalition of Arab and western women descend into conflict and chaos. In this, of course, he departs from his Greek source, as he himself acknowledged.[39] The prologue also highlights another issue: that of style and language register. In all his previous plays and productions, al-Ramlī had used colloquial Arabic, as the Egyptian dialect brings much more immediacy and accessibility. But in the present play he chose standard Arabic, a language in which many Arabs are not fluent, to create a distance between the spectator and the play.[40]

This process helped al-Ramlī to address yet another concern, and one with which Tawfīq al-Ḥakīm struggled too: the explicitly sexual references and the crude display of private parts (such as phalluses) in the Greek original. Al-Ramlī used Amīn Salāma's translation, in which the more explicit passages had already been bowdlerised. But the staging itself posed problems in this respect. Al-Ramlī obtained funding from the Greek Cultural Centre in Cairo to put on an amateur production, but the actresses had no inclination to expose themselves in an Aristophanic way. So al-Ramlī cast many men as women, thereby both achieving a comic effect and resolving a staging problem.

## Arabic, Persian, and Turkish Lyrical Poetry and Greek Myth

Let us now turn from drama to lyrical poetry and look at two of the greatest modern poets of the Arabic-speaking world: the Iraqi Badr Šākir al-Sayyāb (1926–64); and Maḥmūd Darwīš

(1941–2008), Palestine's national poet and arguably the most famous poet in the Arab world today. In her *Classical Mythology: A Very Short Introduction*, Helen Morales noted that the period after the Second World War saw a number of Arab poets use the new form of free verse and adapt various classical myths.[41] She mentioned specifically a group of new poets that included Badr Šākir al-Sayyāb (1926–64).

A collection of poems by al-Sayyāb entitled *Rain Hymn* explores the theme of rebirth through rain in various guises.[42] Three poems in particular are important here: 'Sinbad's City', 'Rain Hymn', and 'Cerberus in Babylon'. The first and the third contain direct allusions to the classical myth of Adonis, the beautiful and eternally young man who is loved by both Persephone and Aphrodite: during the winter he resides with one in the netherworld, then ascends to be with the other in the summer. Adonis is also equated to Tammūz, a figure from ancient Mesopotamian mythology whose descent into the underworld marks the beginning of autumn and the withering of vegetation. Incidentally, there is a famous Syrian contemporary poet whose pen name is Adonis (b. 1930; his birth name is 'Alī Aḥmad Sa'īd Isbir). The first poem in *Rain Hymn* makes references to the story of Sinbad, the traveller from Baghdad celebrated in the *Arabian Nights*, whereas the third employs the figure of Cerberus, the savage dog who guards the gates of the underworld. The metaphor of rain as an agent of rebirth is strong in all three poems, as well as in the collection as a whole. On 'Rain Hymn', which contains no direct reference to Adonis and Tammūz, the influential literary critic Iḥsān 'Abbās remarks: 'seen in its context, the poem is merely a translation of the myth [of Tammūz or Adonis] that does not make the fertility symbolism explicit'.[43]

Thus al-Sayyāb wove classical mythology into his poetry; but the political context of Iraq in the 1950s is also very important for understanding the imagery. For instance, we repeatedly find the idea that in Iraq rain does not lead to rebirth and growth, but falls on sterile ground and causes hunger and misery. Moreover, the image of Cerberus is undoubtedly a thinly veiled reference to the dictator ʿAbd al-Karīm Qāsim (1914–63), who seized the reins of power in a coup in 1958. The misery of many Iraqis is in stark contrast to their country's wealth, so unequally distributed by the dictator as well as by his predecessors – rulers from the Hashemite dynasty.

In al-Sayyāb's poetry the classical allusions are explicit, but we find refractions of classical influences in later compositions by others. We have already seen that the US invasion of Iraq led Lenin al-Ramlī to write a play based on Aristophanes' *Lysistrata*. But it also prompted Maḥmūd Darwīš to engage with al-Sayyāb's 'A Stranger in the Gulf' and 'Rain Hymn', and therefore indirectly with classical themes. Darwīš's poem first appeared in the daily paper *Arabic Jerusalem* (*al-Quds al-ʿArabī*), after the first American bombs had fallen on Baghdad. I vividly remember reading it at the time in Paris and despairing at our collective inability to prevent this war through peaceful protest. It bears the title 'There Is Only Iraq'.[44]

In this poem, Darwīš uses a number of direct allusions: to ancient Near Eastern literature (Gilgamesh, hero of the eponymous epic; Hammurabi, king of the Old Babylonian Empire, known for promulgating the first law code); to the historic events that led to the sack of Baghdad in 1258, by the Mongol ruler Hülegü; and, most importantly, to al-Sayyāb himself. Darwīš entertains the notion that poetry originated in ancient Mesopotamia: 'poetry is born in Iraq; therefore be an Iraqi in order to become a poet, my friend (إنَّ الشِعْرَ يُولَدُ في العِراق، فَكُنْ عِراقيًا لتُصْبِحَ شاعِرا يا صاحِبي)'. Incidentally, Darwīš was not the first to suggest that poetry was born in that part of the world. In fact, according to Lucian of Samosata, a second-century Syrian satirist who wrote in Greek, Homer 'said that he came, of course, from Babylon' (εἶναι μέντοι γε ἔλεγεν Βαβυλώνιος).[45] Classicists have seen this as a clear attempt by Greek intellectuals who hailed from the Levant to claim Homer for the Fertile Crescent rather than leaving him in the Greek heartland.[46] This underlines yet again the fluid identity of being 'Greek' and makes Darwīš's reassertion of the priority of Iraqi over western culture even more poignant.

Maḥmūd Darwīš's engagement with Homer has recently come under scholarly scrutiny.[47] In 2002 Darwīš published a relatively long poem, 'Under Siege', in which he enmeshed numerous allusions to various narrative traditions, including the book of Genesis in the Hebrew Bible (the story of Adam). Moreover, he stated there twice that 'there is no Homeric echo' (لا صَدى هوميريّ لِلشَيء). Jean-Luc Godard's 2004 film *Notre musique* contains a scene in which the protagonist, played by the French-Israeli actress Sarah Adler, talks to Maḥmūd Darwīš ('himself' in the credit line), asking him about this poem. She addresses him in Hebrew, saying this:

> Maḥmūd Darwīš, you have written that 'he who writes his own history inherits the land of words'.[48] Do you not belittle the connection of the Israelis with this land? And you add that there is no place for the Homeric poet, and that you are trying to be the poet of Troy, and that you love the defeated. Be careful; you begin to sound like a Jew.

To this he replies, in Arabic: 'I hope so, for this is something beautiful.' He then goes on to explain that he endeavours to speak for the Trojans, to give voice to those whose history has not been told. He obviously, at least at one level, establishes a parallel between Palestinians and Trojans, both defeated and voiceless. This parallel also appears in an earlier poem by Darwīš called 'Other Barbarians Will Come':

> The emperor's wife will be abducted. The drums will be beaten. / The drums are beaten, so that the horses will trample over the corpses of people from the Aegean Sea to the Dardanelles. / But what about us? What about our wives in the horse race? The emperor's wife will be abducted. The drums will be beaten and other barbarians will come. / Barbarians fill the void of the cities,

> somewhat higher than the sea, stronger than the sword when madness strikes. / But what about us? What are our children to do with the dynasty of this madman? / The drums will be beaten, other barbarians will come, and the emperor's wife will be abducted from his verse–home [*bayt*].[49] / From his verse–home is born the military attack to bring back the 'groom of the bride' onto his throne. / But what about us? What about the fifty thousand killed in this hastily [arranged] marriage? / Is Homer born after us whereas the myths open their doors for all [of us]?[50]

The poem has a first and fairly obvious meaning, at least to my mind: barbarians (the Greeks) came to Troy and sacked it; other barbarians (the Ottomans) came and sacked it again. This was the fall of Constantinople, when the Byzantine emperor's wife was abducted (just as Helen was before, one might add). The lyrical 'us' are the Palestinians, who face other barbarians (the Israelis). Fifty thousand Palestinians have already been killed; will another Homer tell their (our) story?

This is how Darwīš comes to see himself as giving voice to the voiceless, as fulfilling Homer's function to a certain extent. It is also interesting that, in the interview, Darwīš insists on the ambivalent relationship between the Palestinians and the Israelis. He himself, for instance, encountered Homer first in Hebrew translation, as he grew up in Haifa and learnt Hebrew from an early age. He argues that, in part, Palestinians owe their fame – and the fame of their cause – to the fact that people around the globe are interested in Jews. It is for this reason that the conversation between him and the Jewish journalist is so startling: Darwīš obviously understands Hebrew, but Adler's character is unlikely to master Arabic.

We shall return to Darwīš at the end of the chapter, but now let us look at the reception of Greek poetry in the Persian and Turkish traditions.[51] Suhayl Afnān (1904–90) was 'a great scholar' who was 'translating the Greek classics into modern Persian'.[52] Born in Haifa, Palestine, he received his education largely from western institutions such as a catholic school, the American University in Beirut, and later the Sorbonne and Oxford. He came from a prominent Baha'i family, but had a difficult relation with his coreligionists. When the German geographer Carl Rathjens (1887–1966) met Afnān in 1950 and 'spent a day' with him 'in Frankfurt after the Marburg conference', he was incredibly impressed with him and praised him in various letters, saying that he was 'an extremely learned Persian, probably the most intelligent Oriental, even by European standards'.[53] For Afnān had rendered Aristotle's *Poetics* into Persian in 1948 and had published a Persian translation of Aeschylus' tragedy *Persians* in 1952.[54]

One can see why *Persians* would be an interesting play for modern-day Iranians: it explores the hostility between Greece and Persia, focusing on the battle of Salamis, which ended in calamity for the Persians. In the introduction, Afnān discusses Aeschylus' life and works, *Persians*, the more general history and structure of Greek tragedy, and finally its influence. To illustrate Afnān's approach, let us look at one scene of high drama in the play. The Persian king Xerxes has just returned from Salamis and announced his defeat. The Chorus now pities the Persians' fate, addressing the king directly:

> ὀτοτοῖ, βασιλεῦ, cτρατιᾶc ἀγαθῆc / καὶ περcονόμου τιμῆc μεγάλης, / κόcμου τ' ἀνδρῶν, /οὓc νῦν δαίμων ἐπέκειρεν. [. . .] αἰαῖ αἰαῖ κεδνᾶc ἀλκᾶc. / Ἀcία δὲ χθών, βαcιλεῦ γαίαc, /αἰνῶc αἰνῶc / ἐπὶ γόνυ κέκλιται.

> Alas, my King, for that fine army, / and for the great honour of Persian empire, / and the men who adorned it, / whom now the god/daemon has scythed away! [. . .] Alas, alas, for our brave defenders! King of our country, the land of Asia is terribly, terribly down on her knees![55]

When Afnān translates these verses, he makes subtle changes.[56] For instance, he renders the Greek word δαίμων ('divine being', 'semi-god') as فال ('fate'), and expands on the laconic ἐπέκειρεν ('cut down'), making it 'بِدرَويده' ('has mowed down'), with the added comparison چُو کِشتزار ('like [growing] corn'). Otherwise his translation follows the Greek closely, and effectively uses assonance and rhyme to bring out the tone of the original.

Although it is difficult to think of two states more different from each other, the secular Turkish Republic and the theocratic Iranian Republic have one thing in common: classical studies flourished under their rule.[57] We have examples of translations not just from prose authors or dramatists, but also from lyrical poets such as Pindar and Sappho into Turkish. For instance, the opening lines of Pindar's remarkable sixth Nemean ode – Ἓν ἀνδρῶν, ἓν θεῶν γένος· ἐκ μιᾶς δὲ πνέομεν ματρὸς ἀμφότεροι· ('There is one race of gods and one race of humans, but we both breathe from the same mother') – is beautifully rendered thus: *Biri insanların, biri tanrıların soyu; aynı anadan doğageldik ikimiz* ('Humans have one race, gods have one; from the same mother we have been born, both of us'). The translator is the Turkish poet Can Yücel (1926–99).[58] Yücel had studied Latin and Greek at Ankara and Cambridge and was a popular poet in Turkey, where his critical stance towards the regime earned him some time in gaol as a political prisoner.

A recent three-year research project at Clermont-Ferrand and Paris demonstrates the vitality and continuing resonance of classical theatre on the Arab, Persian, and Turkish stages.[59] The authors state, for instance:

> From the Islamic Revolution of 1979 in Iran, we see a great interest in the staging of Greek plays with a political connotation. [. . .] Since the 1990s, there have been each year in Iran more than a dozen performances of ancient texts: *Oedipus*, *Medea* and *Antigone* are at the top of the list.[60]

As characters, Medea and Antigone are female protagonists who allow the theatre practitioners and their audience to explore subjects such as social justice, the unequal distribution of power and agency, and disobedience in the face of a totalitarian regime. They also give them the license to tackle subjects that would otherwise be difficult to address.[61] Turkey boasts many of the amphitheatres of the ancient world where Greek drama was performed during the Roman Empire. Modern Turkish playwrights and performers are conscious of this heritage when they stage dramas that are inspired by Greek models; and, like Iran, Turkey presents a very active scene.[62]

## The Latin Connection

Throughout this chapter we have focused on Greek material, whether epic, dramatic, or lyrical poetry. But we should not forget the Roman heritage, even if Greek texts had a far greater impact on Muslim culture at large. To illustrate the importance of the Latin element, we shall end by discussing another play by Tawfīq al-Ḥakīm and looking at the figure of Nero, a Roman emperor who inspired Arabic verse. In 1942, al-Ḥakīm published his *Pygmalion*, a play that draws on two myths narrated in Ovid's *Metamorphoses*: that of Pygmalion and that of Narcissus.[63] The plot of al-Ḥakīm's play is as follows.[64] In Pygmalion's house, his friend Narcissus contemplates the statue of Galatea, Pygmalion's most beautiful and perfect creation. It is the festival of Venus, and Pygmalion has gone to the temple to bring offerings to the goddess. There is a chorus of nine young women, visible through a window, who dance and tease Narcissus. Ismene, a young woman in love with Narcissus, arrives and tries to persuade him to come with her to the temple. After some resistance, Narcissus is persuaded and leaves with Ismene. Enter Apollo and Venus, two rival gods who do not cease to mock and tease each other throughout the play. Pygmalion approaches, yearning for his statue to come to life, and Venus grants him his wish, after some discussion with Apollo. He is extremely joyful, but Galatea does not yet know that she is his creation.

At the beginning of act II, we see Pygmalion sitting in sadness, because Galatea has eloped with Narcissus. Ismene comes and tries to stir Pygmalion into action, and the situation is eventually resolved when Apollo gives Galatea greater insight into who she is, all the while inspiring in her a profound love for Pygmalion. She returns, but after a time Pygmalion finds her too ordinary: he does not want her to be mortal, to age, to defile herself by doing housework. It is again the gods who fix the situation, by granting Pygmalion his wish that Galatea be a statue again. Upon reflection, however, Pygmalion realises that he misses the living Galatea. Consumed by sorrow and frustrated with his fate, he destroys the statue and shortly afterwards dies.

The myth of Pygmalion and Galatea is perhaps best known in the English world through the adaptations of William S. Gilbert (1836–1911) (of Gilbert and Sullivan) and George Bernard Shaw (1856–1950). Shaw's play *Pygmalion* (1913) has the phonetician Henry Higgins fall in love with his 'creation', Eliza Doolittle, a cockney-speaking flower girl who learns to master received pronunciation through his instruction. This myth is about a creator, the sculptor Pygmalion (aka Higgins), becoming smitten with his creation, the statue Galatea (aka Eliza). The myth of Narcissus, by contrast, is about swooning, not for one's creation, but for oneself. Towards the end of the play, al-Ḥakīm shows how he intends to bring the two myths together. When Narcissus wants to protect and comfort his friend Pygmalion, who is already physically ill from his sorrows, the latter shouts at him:

> O you scoundrel, you scoundrel! How can I get rid of you? It is always you I see appearing before my face. When I bend over the stagnant pool in the caverns of my soul in order to see an image of myself, I only see your image. Yes, I see you, in your futile beauty, pride, stupidity, and blindness. You are the beautiful, yet sterile

> part of my soul. You are the sin the burden of which each artist, as is preordained, has to carry: to be infatuated with oneself, with one's identity.[65]

In Ovid's *Metamorphoses*, both Narcissus and Pygmalion are uninterested in real-life members of the opposite sex. The former is consumed by self-love, the latter by the love for his creation. The point that al-Ḥakīm makes here is that love for one's creation is basically and fundamentally just love for oneself, if in a slightly different form.

Let us now turn to Nero. The poet Ḫalīl Muṭrān (1872–1949) was born in Lebanon but spent most of his life in Egypt; he was one of the attendees at the banquet that launched Bustānī's *Iliad*. Among his many accomplishments, he wrote a long Arabic poem with a single metre and rhyme. Finding 327 different words ending in *-rā* for the same number of verses was no mean feat: Muṭrān had to scour the Arabic dictionaries and selected many words that would have been unknown to his readers. And yet it was to great acclaim that, on 17 May 1924, at the meeting of the Association for the Invigoration of the Arabic Language at the American University of Beirut, Muṭrān recited his poem in the main auditorium, which was filled to the rafters. The last four lines of the poem can illustrate both the difficulties and the tenor of this work. They run as follows:

> Whoever blames Nero? I myself blame
> a nation that could have scolded him and pushed back against him, for then he would have withdrawn,
> A nation that, had it risen up against him for a time,
> would soon have finished with him, as he retreats in fear.
> He won against her [*sc.* the nation] at first, and unlike her
> has another excuse in history.
> All peoples create their own Nero,
> whether he be called Caesar or Chosroes.[66]

For the first two verses of this extract, Muṭrān, like al-Bustānī before him, had to explain in a footnote the meaning of the last word of the line – the word that forms the rhyme. He gave a speech to introduce the poem and, in it, he showed awareness of his plight: he had to choose recondite words to fit the rhyme:

> Now, gentlemen, I shall recite the longest poem with the same rhyme and on the same subject that the Arabic language has known. It is the longest in terms of number of verses, and the greatest in terms of the aim that this number imposes on it. But I do not know what value it has beside its number. I made every effort to adhere to the objective [*al-ġāya*], but did not produce a marvel [*al-āya*].[67]

The aim and objective was to compose a long ode with a single rhyme, and this constraint has hindered the immediacy with which the reader or listener experiences this poem. Yet it must be said that some verses from this ode are still recited and quoted in the Arab world, and quite often; so Muṭrān is perhaps a bit too modest in his assessment of what he achieved.

When Maḥmūd Darwīš wrote the poem 'On Man' early in his career, he referred to Nero too:

> The night will end.
> The interrogation chamber will not remain,
> nor the links of the chains.
> Nero died, but Rome did not die . . .
> She fights with every fibre of her being![68]

The poem had previously talked about the suffering of a human being: a Palestinian interrogated, imprisoned, separated from his beloved, falsely accused, and driven from his homeland. And yet there was hope: Nero the tyrant could not conquer Rome. Rome prevailed. When Darwīš referred to the Roman emperor in this context, he undoubtedly had Muṭrān's long ode in mind, although he offered a different perspective: whereas Muṭrān upbraids the people for failing to rise against their tyrants, Darwīš celebrates the fact that they do, or at least will in the future. His is a message of hope.

# 7

# From Homer to al-Qāʿida

In the preceding six chapters we have largely explored how Arab and Muslim authors engaged, directly and indirectly, with classical literature and thought. They translated texts, adopted and adapted myths and storylines, and modelled whole disciplines such as philosophy and medicine on Greek antecedents. This process had already begun in pre-Islamic Arabia and continues today. As a result, Muslim culture and religion were touched in nearly all their aspects: Islam as it exists today, in its manifold manifestations, would not have been the same without the classical heritage. The evidence for what classics did for Islam is overwhelming.

In this final chapter I am going to develop a more subtle argument: that the way in which classicists thought about Greek and Latin texts had an impact on how both modernists and traditionalists in the Islamic world conceived of the Qurʾān and its history during the past century. As a first step, we will explore traditional accounts of the Qurʾān, its textual history and exegesis. Then we will compare these accounts with the views of two diametrically opposed figures, the Saudi traditionalist and Salafist cleric Ibn ʿUṯaymīn (1929–2001) and the reformer and modernist Ṭāhā Ḥusayn, whom we have already encountered in chapter 5.

How can we read works from the distant past, such as Plato's *Republic*, the New Testament, or the Qur'ān? Generally speaking, you are likely to read a modern English translation based on a modern edition in the original language. This edition is in turn based on medieval manuscripts that are still extant and transmit a text that was copied, century after century, from manuscripts that are now lost. For the New Testament and the Qur'ān, we have some early witnesses that are close in time to the original date of composition, but are still separated by a few generations; the early witnesses are also very short and fragmentary. It is for this reason that whole disciplines developed that are dedicated to tracing this textual history and reconstructing the original text. We shall explore later how classical studies established a methodology to tackle these tasks; for now, let us focus on the Qur'ān.

## The Richness of the Qur'ān: Its Ambiguity

During the medieval period, a number of 'sciences of the Qur'ān' (عُلوم القُرآن) emerged that studied the text in its historical context ('the circumstances of revelation' [أَسْباب النُّزول]) or discussed the different readings ('the science of [variant] readings [عِلْم القِراءات]').[1] The general medieval account of how the text of the Qur'ān was established runs as follows. The Qur'ān was successively revealed over the last twenty years or so of the prophet's life, that is, during the period 610–32. The revelation was oral: the archangel Gabriel recited different suras at different times, some in Mecca and some in Medina. While the Prophet was still among them, his companions learnt these suras by heart, and thus preserved them for posterity. Even during Muḥammad's lifetime, various readers recited the full Qur'ān more than once. They transmitted their versions largely orally to their pupils, so that chains of transmissions from Muḥammad's time exist. The Qur'ān was also written down, first under the auspices of the first rightly guided caliph, Abū Bakr (r. 632–4), and then under the third one, 'Uṯmān

(r. 644–55). These early versions contained only the 'skeleton text' (*rasm*), which did not have diacritical marks or vowel signs. This absence made the text extremely ambiguous. For instance, without diacritical marks and vowel signs, the word ىوم could be read as بُوم (*būm*, 'owl'), ثُوم (*ṯūm* 'garlic'), نَوم (*nawm* 'sleep'), or يَوم (*yawm* 'day'); and these are just some of the possibilities. The skeletal condition of these early manuscripts illustrates that the oral text still had priority over the written one, as the ambiguities do not exist once the text is recited. Moreover, the adoption of a skeleton text was a deliberate choice on the part of the scribes, since diacritical marks had been invented long before, as we know from inscriptions. They could have employed them but deliberately favoured the ambiguity of the skeleton text.

As a result, we have numerous reports about variant readings of the Qur'ān from medieval sources, and scholars both in the Muslim world and in the West have endeavoured to document them. Muslim scholars published a monumental *Lexicon of* [*Variant*] *Qur'ānic Readings* and the Berlin-Brandenburg Academy recently completed the *Corpus Coranicum* project.[2] Today some regard as authoritative the 'first Cairo' edition, printed in 1924 by the Survey and Land Registration Office in Gizeh, others the 'second Cairo' edition, printed in 1952 and adopted by the King Fahd Complex for the Printing of the Holy Qur'ān in Medina. Yet there are many other versions, printed in various countries. One cannot therefore speak of one authoritative text, agreed upon by all or most Muslims.[3]

There is an utterance (*ḥadīṯ*) attributed to the Prophet in which he says: 'This Qur'ān was sent down in seven *aḥruf*. Therefore recite of it whatever is easy [إِنَّ هٰذَا الْقُرْآنَ أُنْزِلَ عَلَى سَبْعَةِ أَحْرُفٍ، فَاقْرَؤُوا مَا تَيَسَّرَ مِنْهُ].' The meaning of the word *aḥruf* in this context is unclear and has been variously interpreted.[4] Arabic *aḥruf*, singular *ḥarf*, signifies 'letter', which does not provide a very satisfying meaning. Scholars therefore proposed other senses, such as 'reading', 'version', or even 'dialect'. This has led to the notion that there are seven authoritative (or 'canonical') readings of the Qur'ān; but many medieval scholars rejected the idea that the number is limited to seven. The celebrated Qur'ān scholar Ibn al-Ǧazarī (1350–1429), for instance, wrote an influential manual on the topic, and its title, *Publication about the Ten Readings*, already indicates that there are in his view more than seven readings. In this book, Ibn al-Ǧazarī actually explains that one cannot simply reduce the large number of readings to seven or ten, although some readings are obviously more plausible than others.

According to the German Arabist Thomas Bauer, the figure of Ibn al-Ǧazarī exemplifies what he calls a 'culture of ambiguity'.[5] Bauer persuasively argued that premodern Muslim culture embraced this ambiguity and saw it as something positive. To put it simply: that the Qur'ān can be read and interpreted in many different ways is part of its richness. It also future-proofs the Sacred Text: each generation can discover new aspects and meanings in it, and this way it never becomes stale or ossified. Ibn al-Ǧazarī put it eloquently himself:

> From the first beginnings to the end of time, the scholars of this nation have always and will always produce evidence, arguments, proofs, knowledge and so on from it [*sc.* the al-Qur'ān] that earlier ones had not discovered and later ones will not be restricted to. Rather, it is a vast, unfathomable, and boundless sea, the limits of which one shall never reach.[6]

So the many possible readings of the Qur'ān are something positive that is to be celebrated. Such different readings can best be illustrated with a famous example. The fourth verse of the first sura, 'The Opening' (*al-Fātiḥa*), has the following skeleton text: ملک بوم الدىں (*mlk ywm 'l-dyn*). This is generally dotted and vocalised as مٰلِكِ يوْمِ الدِّينِ (*māliki yawmi l-dīni*, 'the possessor of judgement day'), but other readings such as مَلِكِ يَوْمِ الدِّينِ (*maliki yawmi l-dīni*, 'the king of judgement day'), مَلَكِ يَوْمِ الدِّينِ (*malaki yawmi l-dīni*, 'the angel of judgement day'), and so on are also transmitted.

On the other hand, it is also possible for the same text with the same readings to have numerous different and contradictory interpretations that can all be true. For instance, sura 79 opens with a number of oaths ('by the . . . by the . . . by the . . .' etc.) that have baffled interpreters. Verse four reads *fa-l-sābiqāti sabqan* [فالسَّابِقَاتِ سَبْقًا], where *fa-* is a particle with the genitive introducing the oath ('by'), *l-* is the article ('the'), *sābiqāti* is the feminine plural of the active participle of the verb *sabaqa* ('get ahead of', 'precede', 'overtake'), and *sabqan* is a verbal noun used as an inner accusative, to reinforce the verb ('a lot', 'greatly'). So a literal translation could be: 'By those who greatly precede'; but that does not mean much. Three questions immediately come to mind. Who are these entities in the feminine plural who 'precede'? What do they get ahead of, or what do they do earlier? And whom do they precede or overtake? The context offers no help here, because the three preceding oaths (verses 1–3) are just as enigmatic. One prominent commentator of the Qur'ān, al-Māwardī (974–1058), offers six solutions: (1) angels overtake satans in delivering God's revelation; (2) stars overtake one another; (3) death overtakes the souls; (4) souls overtake one another at death; (5) horses overtake others in battle; and (6) souls overtake bodies in reaching Paradise at death.[7] Importantly, al-Māwardī does not say that any one interpretation is right or wrong; they can all simply coexist. Today, however, most interpreters of the Qur'ān would reject the idea that more than one interpretation is correct or that the many readings of the Qur'ān are a blessing, as the example of Ibn ʿUṯaymīn can illustrate.

## Salafists, a Product of Modernity

Ibn ʿUṯaymīn was an extremely prominent and influential Wahhabī (and, by implication, Salafī) cleric. He adhered to the strict teachings of Muḥammad ibn ʿAbd al-Wahhāb (1703–92), who founded the Wahhabī movement. One of the core aims of this movement is to strive to imitate the pious ancestors (called *salaf* in Arabic), who knew and supported the prophet Muḥammad. Ibn ʿUṯaymīn's general attitude towards Greek thought was unambiguous: he condemned *falsafa* (Greek philosophy) as 'wrong' or 'reprehensible' (*munkar*) and distinguished it from 'wisdom' (*ḥikma*), which is permitted and necessary. This distinction began in the late twelfth century.[8]

But let us look at Ibn ʿUṯaymīn's account of 'the writing and compilation of the Qur'ān' in his work *On the Foundations of [Qur'ānic] Exegesis*.[9] He distinguishes three stages in the composition of the Qur'ān: first, during the prophet's lifetime, the Qur'ān was memorised and written on palm leaves and other materials; second, the caliph Abū Bakr produced a first edition of the Qur'ān; and, third, the caliph ʿUṯmān produced an authorised text in the language of the Qurayš, as the Qur'ān was originally revealed in this dialect. Then Ibn ʿUṯaymīn explains the rationale behind the two different 'editions' produced at stage 2 and stage 3:

> The difference between his [i.e. ʿUṯmān's] and Abū Bakr's [. . .] compilation is the following. The compilation in the age of Abū Bakr [. . .] aimed at writing down the whole Qur'ān as a collection in an exemplar, so that nothing of it would be lost, but without bringing the people to agree on *one* exemplar. For no trace of difference in their readings had become evident that would have called for bringing them to agree on *one* exemplar. The compilation in the age of ʿUṯmān [. . .], however, aimed at writing down the whole Qur'ān as a collection in *one* exemplar that brings the people to agree on it, because the *frightening sign of difference in readings had appeared*.[10]

This account is diametrically opposed to the one given in traditional works of Qur'ānic scholarship such as that by Ibn al-Ǧazarī. For the latter, there is no doubt that various versions and ways of reading the Qur'ān existed during the Prophet's lifetime.

Moreover, whereas Ibn ʿUṯaymīn appears to attach importance only to the written transmission, al-Ǧazarī prioritises the oral one. After all, the Qurʾān copies of both Abū Bakr and ʿUṯmān contained only the *rasm*, the skeleton text, so they could hardly be read without knowledge of the oral tradition – a fact conveniently omitted by Ibn ʿUṯaymīn.

But the greatest difference between traditional scholarship and Ibn ʿUṯaymīn is in the view of what it means for the Qurʾān to have variants. Ibn al-Ǧazarī celebrates this as something positive, whereas Ibn ʿUṯaymīn talks about the 'frightening sign of difference in readings'. Being different is bad, having just one reading is good; ambiguity is utterly rejected. Ibn ʿUṯaymīn also abhors the idea that there can be different meanings of the Revelation that can be correct and exist side by side. Al-Māwardī offered no fewer than six interpretations of verse 79:4, *fa-l-sābiqāti sabqan* [فَالسَّابِقَاتِ سَبْقًا], yet Ibn ʿUṯaymīn chooses only one: '*Fa-l-sābiqāti sabqan* refers to the angels; they carry out earlier the commandment of God, the Mighty and Exalted, [by doing] what he orders them to do.'[11]

Ibn ʿUṯaymīn justifies his choice by quoting a number of parallels in the Qurʾān where angels are mentioned; but he does not employ any of the more traditional techniques of the science of variant readings. Also, his solution is new: it does not belong to the six listed by al-Māwardī, for instance. The latter does speak of angels' overtaking satans in delivering God's revelation, but that is obviously different from angels' carrying out God's order more readily than others.

Although Ibn ʿUṯaymīn was a Salafist and therefore looked back to the past, his approach is entirely modern. He rejects traditional Qurʾān scholarship and its views regarding the text, and replaces them with his own views. There is a substantial body of literature arguing that fundamentalist movements such as that of the Salafists are the result of modernity; it is therefore not surprising that Ibn ʿUṯaymīn fits squarely into the mould of modern fundamentalism.[12] More surprising is the fact that his view on the univocity of the Qur'ān is shared with the modernist reformer Ṭāhā Ḥusayn.

## Ṭāhā Ḥusayn Rejects Qur'ānic Ambiguity

Ḥusayn discussed the textual character of the Qur'ān and its variant readings in his famous work *On Pre-Islamic Poetry* and its revised version, *On Pre-Islamic Literature*, already mentioned in chapter 5. What he says there presents clear parallels with some of Ibn 'Uṯaymīn's ideas:

> The Qur'ān was recited in one language and one dialect, namely the language and dialect of the Qurayš. No sooner had the reciters from different tribes received it than the [different] readings multiplied, and the dialects used for it diversified and fluctuated greatly. Later reciters and scholars made an effort to edit it with precision and established a science, or specific sciences, to this end. [. . .]
>
> Some clerics understood the seven readings to be continuously transmitted from the Prophet, to whose heart [the archangel] Gabriel had revealed them. Therefore, if one were to deny them, one would without the shadow of a doubt be an infidel. The only proof that they advanced this opinion was to say that among the canonical [utterances of the prophet] one finds the following: 'The Qur'ān was sent down in seven *aḥruf*.'
>
> But the truth is this: these seven readings do not belong to the revelation either in their detail or in their general outline. Nor is one an infidel, a sinner, or a detractor of religion simply for denying them. They are just readings originating in differences of dialect. People may argue about them, and deny some of them and accept others. In fact people did argue about them and disputed them, and some accused others of error. Yet I do not know of any Muslim who accused anyone of unbelief because of this.[13]

Ḥusayn goes on to explain that the seven *aḥruf* are not the 'readings' (*qirāʾāt*) but the 'languages' (*luġāt*) – that is, the dialects that put different vowels and quantities. Yet the prophet constantly forbade dialects to create different meanings in this manner. After his death, people continued to recite in these different versions, 'so that disagreements and arguments became more severe, to the point that sedition [*fitna*] threatened to break out among the people'.[14] ʿUṯmān was worried about this situation and feared that the text of the Qurʾān would present discrepancies similar to those of the gospels. He therefore produced one authoritative copy, thus eliminating six of the seven *aḥruf*: only one remained, that of the Qurayš, the tribe of the prophet. Ḥusayn succinctly formulates his belief in the univocity of the Qurʾān through a rhetorical question: 'How is it possible for there to be disagreement among the people, when there is one teacher and one body of knowledge without different aspects?'[15]

For Ḥusayn, God's message is univocal just as God is one. The variants across the Qurʾānic texts are due to human failure and frailty, not divine economy, as Ibn al-Ǧazarī still thought. We have seen above that Ḥusayn wanted to apply the method of René Descartes: radical doubt. Descartes himself was a firm believer in univocity, and Ḥusayn follows him in this regard as well.

## European Positivism

The Cartesian care for clarity continues in the nineteenth and twentieth centuries. Bruno Latour argued that so-called modernity was characterised by the wish to distinguish between knowledge of people and knowledge of things, as illustrated in the works of Thomas Hobbes (1588–1679) and Robert Boyle (1627–91), and that this distinction, and therefore the notion of modernity itself, is profoundly flawed.[16] Following on from Cartesian philosophy and the scientism of the Enlightenment, positivism came to dominate much of nineteenth-century academic discourse.

Scholars became increasingly confident that they would be able to define the world around them by describing it in great detail. Classical and biblical scholars in particular developed the tools of textual criticism to reconstruct sources, and I shall now briefly outline the main developments from the late eighteenth to the early twentieth centuries.

Our story begins in Göttingen, where the German classical scholar and archaeologist Christian G. Heyne (1729–1812) trained two students, Johann G. Eichhorn (1752–1827) and Friedrich A. Wolf (1759–1824). Both were interested in textual criticism; Eichhorn worked on the Hebrew Bible, Wolf on Homer.[17] Their two objects of study shared a number of problematic features that they tried to overcome. First, the transmitted text relies on medieval manuscripts, mostly from the eleventh century onwards, which include a scholarly apparatus. In the case of the Hebrew Bible, this is the Masorah: remarks by Jewish scholars who tried to establish the right reading. The Masorah goes back roughly to the period between the sixth and the eighth centuries. The manuscripts of Homer contain scholia, short annotations explaining the text, which possibly go back to Hellenistic Alexandria in the third and second centuries BC. Yet, although the Masoretes and the scholiasts had access to older manuscripts, they often made poor textual choices and corrupted the text of the manuscripts that survive today. Moreover, between them and the respective redactions of the Homeric epics and Hebrew Bible lie many centuries. Wolf argued that the former are the product of revisions by many anonymous rhapsodes who recited Homer at courts; as for the latter, it includes diverse books written at different times. Wolf developed methods to tackle this problem and to reconstruct the archetype – that is, the oldest manuscript, lost to us, that can be reconstructed from the available textual evidence. Importantly, both Wolf and Eichhorn adhered to a positivist outlook: both were of the view that, evidence permitting, one can see clearly which is the right and which the wrong reading.

Wolf's *Prolegomena* exerted a huge influence on subsequent generations of classical philologists. One of these was Karl K. F. W. Lachmann (1793–1851), who refined the method of reconstructing an archetype through textual criticism.[18] The central idea is this: manuscripts are copied over time, one from another; hence they resemble an extended family. Newer members descend from older ancestors, which branch out; and the result is a sort of tree or genealogy called 'stemma'. At the top of the stemma is the archetype, and from it descend the extant manuscripts. The relationships between them are determined by what we call 'conjunctive' mistakes – that is, mistakes shared in a branch of the transmission that bind its members together; for such mistakes emanate from a common ancestor and must have been copied from one manuscript to the next. As one recent scholar put it, '[t]he genealogical method – also called [. . .] "Lachmann's method" [. . .] – played a pivotal role in developing a *scientific* approach to textual criticism, and it still remains an essential research tool.'[19]

The belief in textual criticism as a scientific discipline that deals in certainties is strong even today among many classicists. Lachmann's ideas were further refined and enhanced throughout the nineteenth century, but what characterised this discipline was the fundamental and unshakable confidence that a true archetype can be reconstructed. The general idea remained the same: the author produced an unambiguous text which could be reconstructed through recourse to the methods of philology and textual criticism. In this way, the new tools would lead to a new text, which is identical with the archetype.

Another aspect of this philological approach is the search for lost sources. Just as an archetype (now lost) can be reconstructed, so can the original text – namely from the extant evidence. Homer is a prominent case, and generations of classicists have endeavoured to find the original material in the *Iliad* and *Odyssey*. Similarly, German theologians such as Heinrich Ewald (1803–75) discerned redactional layers in the biblical books; Ewald stated that '[t]he investigation of the origin and source of *Genesis* is, like the investigation of the formation and sources of the gospels, one of the most difficult and most important that biblical criticism ought to consider within its purview'.[20]

He then distinguished two different authors in Genesis: the 'Elohist' and the 'Jahwist'. One used the Hebrew word for 'god' (*ʾĕlōhīm* אֱלֹהִים), the other used God's four-letter Hebrew name, the tetragrammaton (*Yahweh* יהוה). As Ewald said, for the gospels, New Testament scholars also tried to identify lost sources, the most famous being 'Q'. Q was called *Logionquelle* in German, because it contains Jesus' utterances (*lógia* in Greek; and *Quelle* means 'source' in German). These efforts started in the early nineteenth century and continue today, even if some scholars question the existence of Q.[21] In other words, faced with complicated textual traditions, the nineteenth-century biblical and classical scholars searched for the original source, the *Urquelle*, which their sophisticated methodology promised to reveal.

In chapter 5 we have seen that Ṭāhā Ḥusayn was directly inspired by the methods of historical criticism formulated by ancient historians like Theodor Mommsen. Al-Bustānī had espoused the 'Wolfian' view, and Ḥusayn argued that many of the poems thought to come from pre-Islamic Arabia were actually products of later times. Ḥusayn's confidence is high and he argues his case vigorously. We can now detect parallels here with what happened in the subfield of textual criticism and source analysis.

While Ḥusayn himself trained in classics and served as professor of ancient history, Ibn ʿUṯaymīn had no such instruction. And yet his outlook, too, is deeply influenced by the positivism that pervaded nineteenth-century classical scholarship. Its methods and ideas became so ubiquitous that Ibn ʿUṯaymīn adopted them. Although he and Ḥusayn are in many ways diametrically opposed, they agree in their views on the textual history of the Qurʾān. Both place particular importance on the notion that there is a continuous transmission of the text, from the Prophet Muḥammad via Abū Bakr and ʿUṯmān to the present day.[22] Both insist that the right readings, those of the Qurayš, were chosen and now appear in the text. Again, we find a parallel here with classical philology, as it, too, strives to restore the correct readings in the text and has developed tools to exclude incorrect ones.

## Under the Banner of the Qurʾān

I also briefly mentioned that pre-Islamic poetry constituted a battleground between conservative and religious thinkers and modernisers. Both Ṭāhā Ḥusayn and Louis ʿAwaḍ found themselves at the receiving end of a great amount of criticism. One could say that Ṭāhā Ḥusayn was vilified for his use of the historical and textual criticism that he had studied in Paris. Because ʿAwaḍ employed the methods of comparative literature that he had learnt in Cambridge and Princeton, he attracted a great deal of opprobrium.

Immediately after ʿAwaḍ published a series of articles on al-Maʿarrī in late 1964, his critics attacked him in the Egyptian and Arab press; at times, their censure took vitriolic forms. Left-wing intellectuals accused him of being right-wing, right-wing authors accused him of being a left-leaning Marxist; some said that he was 'the last consul of the Christian world in Egypt since the Crusades', thus attacking his Coptic family background, and yet others claimed that he promoted Egyptian 'Pharaonic' nationalism over Arab nationalism.[23]

Maḥmūd Muḥammad Šākir, who had stormed out of Ḥusayn's lectures as a young student in 1926, also pilloried ʿAwaḍ's positions some forty years later. He first voiced his disapproval in a string of articles published in the journal *Epistle*, and later collected them in a book with the programmatic title *Idle Chatter and Nightly Prattle*.[24] Šākir begins by criticising ʿAwaḍ on the grounds that he relies solely on Ṭahā Ḥusayn's work on al-Maʿarrī and has neglected contemporaneous sources; at times ʿAwaḍ even misunderstands or misrepresents Ḥusayn.[25] Šākir points out that both Ḥusayn and ʿAwaḍ do not always quote their sources faithfully.

Beyond these criticisms, which deal with the use of the sources, Šākir also finds fault with ʿAwaḍ's linguistic abilities.[26] He repeatedly calls him a charlatan, partly because in his view ʿAwaḍ does not really have any knowledge of Greek; and Šākir claims to have discovered this through his own research:

> I thought that he [ʿAwaḍ] had a command of Greek and other languages, and those who follow his scandalous acts believe this. He wanted to apply this command to the tortured and miserable Greek poet Aristophanes [. . .] He approached his play *The Frogs* and translated it. Yet, before I even read any of it, news reached me and I learned that he is now 'in a confused state of translation'. For even if it is easy for some people [. . .] to count this human being among the poets, it is not easy for me to count him among those who understand even the easiest verse, let alone difficult poetry or the composition of odes.
>
> Then this play was performed, and I was surprised as well that some of the 'gang members' described this translation as 'a marvel in the Arabic language' in a place that this intellectual and comic evangelist had under his thumb, namely the newspaper *The Pyramids* (*al-Ahrām*).[27]

Šākir continues with a long tirade against ʿAwaḍ's translation, claiming that it lacks linguistic rigour and is often blatantly wrong. He carefully analyses the beginning of the play (lines 1–56), criticising the quality of the translation, especially as reflected in single words and expressions.[28]

Yet Šākir shows his true colours, so to speak, when he states what he thinks about the Greek heritage as a creative inspiration for Arabic letters. He talks about the 'imbecility of the allusions that this "charlatan" uses in his writings', 'this renewed Greek imbecility', which he cannot endure and with which he does not want to soil the 'honour of the Arabs'.[29] This onslaught culminates in a profession of faith:

> Thanks be to God who freed us from 'the allusions' [*sc.* to Greek mythology], as he freed us from polytheism; who put a distance between us and the 'myths of the Greeks', as he has put a distance between us and the act of taking equals [*sc.* to God: polytheism]; who kept us away from lies, as he kept us away from submission to others than Him – praise be to Him.[30]

In this way, the fight against Louis ʿAwaḍ takes on decidedly religious overtones. The ancient Greeks worshipped many different gods, not just the one God, and therefore were nonbelievers. To use allusions to their pantheon, as Louis ʿAwaḍ was fond of doing, is an act of polytheism and ought to be avoided at all cost according to Šākir. Employing related literary techniques implies that one copies western values, something Šākir opposed valiantly, not only in his refutations of Louis ʿAwaḍ but also in his other publications.

Another critic who accused ʿAwaḍ of 'westernisation' (*taġrīb*) was Muḥammad ʿImāra (1931–2020), a member of Al-Azhar's Islamic Research Academy who generally advocated Islamic modernism. He wrote a book with the programmatic title *Ǧamāl al-Dīn al-Afġānī: Between the Historical Facts and the Lies of Louis ʿAwaḍ*, which is mainly concerned with ʿAwaḍ's portrayal of al-Afġānī as a religious reformer.[31] Leaving this aspect aside, ʿImāra generally contends that ʿAwaḍ belittles the Arabic and Islamic heritage:

> To this attempt to sever the nation [*al-umma*, i.e. Islam] from its cultural heritage also belong the efforts, past and present, of the orientalist movement, especially those sections that doubt the cultural originality of the Arabs. For the aim here is to strip 'the prey' of its historical glory, so that it might surrender to 'westernisation', given that westernisation, as far as the present and the future are concerned, is presented as 'the only choice' as long as our heritage offers us no alternative.[32]

At this point ʿImāra is primarily discussing ʿAwaḍ's position regarding al-Maʿarrī and the Greek influences on the *Epistle of Forgiveness.* ʿImāra accuses ʿAwaḍ of having deprived al-Maʿarrī of his originality and reduced him to being 'but an echo of Byzantine monks, a pupil of their monasteries, an impression of the western cultural heritage, which the Greeks invented'.[33] In ʿImāra's view, ʿAwaḍ reduces al-Maʿarrī's great work to a patchwork of quotations learnt – horror of horrors – from Christians. Such criticism is certainly unfair, and ʿAwaḍ preemptively defended himself against it by stating clearly that imitation, or even inspiration, does not preclude originality; for what is literature, from its very inception, but a constant reengagement with previous authors and poets?

The example of ʿAwaḍ shows that the comparative approach that he used leads to debates about cultural identity. Unlike Ṭāhā Ḥusayn, ʿAwaḍ was not dragged through the courts. The same could not be said for Naṣr Ḥāmid Abū Zayd (1943–2010), once a professor of Arabic language and literature. In 1992 he was denied promotion, then later was forcibly divorced from his wife.[34] He had insisted that the Qur'ān was a text revealed in a context and applied modern literary theory to its interpretation. Fearing for his physical well-being, he fled to the Netherlands, where he found sanctuary at Leiden University.[35]

The continuing interest in Ḥusayn and ʿAwaḍ is visible in the many reprints of their works, and also in the growing number of refutations. One such critique that is particularly popular at the present in the Arab world is Muṣṭafā Ṣādiq al-Rāfiʿī's *Under the Banner of the Qur'ān: The Struggle between the Old and the New*, a work discussed in chapter 5 that has seen a number of different editions. Such debates about cultural and religious identity and how to negotiate modernity matter, as they concern an ever growing number of Arabs and Muslims. After all, the title *Under the Banner of the Qur'ān* echoes *Knights under the Banner of the Prophet*: this was the 'testament' of Ayman al-Ẓawāhirī (1951–2022), Usāma ibn Lādin's (1957–2011) late right-hand man.[36]

Al-Ẓawāhirī saw Islam and the West locked in a historical battle. At the beginning of his work he says:

> The western forces that are hostile to Islam have clearly identified their enemy. They refer to it as Islamic fundamentalism. [. . .] In the face of this alliance [*sc.* of Western forces], a fundamentalist coalition is taking shape. [. . .] It is a growing force that is rallying under the banner of jihad, against the scope of the new world order.[37]

Of course, al-Ẓawāhirī and his companions did not directly engage with Homeric scholarship. But they denied the close ties between 'Islam' and 'the West'; in that, they resemble Ḥusayn's and ʿAwaḍ's detractors. Both al-Rāfiʿī and Šākir were shocked by Ḥusayn's idea that one should apply historical criticism, and notably the techniques of Homeric scholarship, to pre-Islamic poetry. And their criticism of Ḥusayn (as well as that of ʿAwaḍ) finds favour in conservative circles that seek to construct the idea of a pure and unadulterated Islam. Moreover, we have seen that fundamentalist clerics such as Ibn ʿUṯaymīn adhere to the textual positivism formulated in nineteenth-century classical scholarship. In this sense it is possible to say that al-Ẓawāhirī and his henchmen operated in a world of ideas partly shaped by the views of Lachmann, Mommsen, and Wolf. Sadly, then, one can plot a line from Homer to al-Qāʿida.

## Ubiquitous Imitation and Its Rejection

The Islamic fundamentalist movement was thus influenced by Greek thought and classical scholarship, even as it strove for Islamic authenticity and disdained philosophy as a foreign concept. This leads us to an apparent paradox: on the one hand, Islamic culture is deeply indebted to the classical heritage; on the other, when we hear today about Muslims, it is for the most part about fundamentalists and fanatics animated by a desire for authenticity that rejects the imitation of all things non-Muslim.

What does classical culture mean to the man or woman on the terraces? At one level, very little. It does not matter whether you put this question to a computer engineer, a medical doctor, a clerk, a bricklayer, or a plumber, be they Muslim or not; they would probably not be able to furnish many examples of how Plato or Aristotle are relevant to their lives. And yet, whether they live in Birmingham or in Baghdad, Canterbury or Calcutta, Dulwich or Damascus, Manchester or Mecca, whether they are Muslim, Christian, or Jewish, the world they inhabit and the language they speak were profoundly shaped by an engagement with the classics. Islamic theology of any current persuasion is unthinkable without the classical Greek past; and this theology, when translated into normative religious discourse and concrete rules, has a direct daily impact on many Muslims, especially those living in countries that enforce Islamic law in one way or another.

We encountered in the Introduction the Ḥanbalī scholar Ibn Ṭaymīya (1263–1328) as someone who rejected Greek thought. In fact he authored a treatise against the Greek logicians in which he refutes many claims made in Greek philosophy. But in order to do so he employs the same logical apparatus developed by previous philosophers. Ibn Ṭaymīya also penned a work with the title *The Obligation of Following the Straight Path Is to Be Different from Those Damned to Hell*, in which he insists that Muslims need to differentiate themselves from non-Muslims ('those damned to hell').[38] Yet the word 'path' (*ṣirāṭ*) in the title is, as we saw in Chapter 1, a Latin word. There simply is no escaping the classical influences, hard as Ibn Ṭaymīya and others may try.

In his recent study on how Muslims endeavoured to be different from others, Youshaa Patel examined the various ways in which Muslim legal scholars rejected imitation, often quoting the utterance of the Prophet that 'whoever imitates a people becomes one of them'. Yet, as Patel eloquently states,

> because ordinary Muslims across time and place habitually interacted with and emulated Jews, Christians, and other foreigners [. . .] religious authorities from Ibn Ṭaymīya [to modern times . . .] struggled to set them apart. To the chagrin of these intellectuals, the collective body of Muslims never ceased imitating others. Put differently, it is because Muslims share so much in common with others that being different took on so much value.[39]

It is precisely this paradox that we find in relation to the classical heritage, too: Muslims collectively never stopped engaging with it, even if fundamentalists and others now argue against it. These modern fundamentalists could not be more different from the medieval Islamic tradition, which embraced ambiguity and variant readings and considered them part of the rich fabric of the Qur'ān. As the Prophet Muḥammad reportedly said, '[t]he divergent opinions in my Nation are a blessing [from God] [اِخْتِلاف أُمَّتي رَحْمة]', a thought to which we shall return in the Epilogue.[40]

# Epilogue

## Plato's Children

Plato said: 'People do not arrive at the truth in all its aspects, nor do they get it wrong in every aspect. Each person rather hits upon a facet of the truth.'[1] This is illustrated by the example of blind men brought to an elephant. Each one of them grasps a part of its body, palpates it with his hand, and forms a representation of it in his mind. The one who touched the foot informs [the others] that the character of the elephant is long and round, and resembles the trunk of a tree or the stump of a palm. The one who touched the back informs [the others] that its character resembles a high, towering, elevated hill. The one who touched the ear informs [the others] that it is something stretched out and thin that covers it and is spread over it. Each one of them proffers part of what he knows, yet all call their friends liars and claim that they erred, are wrong, and do not know the characteristics of the elephant they describe. Look how truthfulness unites them, but look also how lies and errors came upon them so as to divide them.

Al-Tawḥīdī, *Sparkling Conversations*[2]

Abū Sulaymān al-Siǧistānī (c. 912–85), nicknamed 'the logician' (*al-Mantiqī*) on account of his interest in Aristotelian philosophy, held regular salon meetings at which the political and cultural elite of his time came together to engage in conversation. He himself was deeply religious and believed that philosophical and revealed truths are the same. One of the attendees at his salon was al-Tawḥīdī (c. 923–1023), a man of letters and a philosopher, who worked most of his career as a secretary to members of the ruling dynasty, the Būyids. These salons, called *maǧlis* in Arabic, were part and parcel of court culture, and the topics for debate included questions such as why and how clothing can be used both to stay warm and to stay cool (this drew on the Aristotelian tradition of 'problems' – *problēmata*) or whether one should consume mulberries after watermelons.[3] *Sparkling Conversations* is Al-Tawḥīdī's record of what he witnessed at Abū Sulaymān's salon, and the extract above exemplifies the kind of remark the latter would make, as well as why Joel Kraemer talked about an Islamic Renaissance and humanism during this age.

By way of conclusion, this passage also allows us to highlight three common threads that pervade the arguments I presented throughout this book. The first is the ubiquity of classical ideas in Islamic culture. Abū Sulaymān makes his point by referring to Plato. We have to see his quotation not so much as a verbatim report but rather as a summary of Plato's thought, as expressed for instance in the *Republic*. Think of the allegory of the cave: human beings behold only shadowy reflections of the reality that exists. From its inception, Islam was enmeshed with the Greek culture of the world of Late Antiquity, from which it emerged. It is impossible to imagine the history of the Muslim world without this fruitful engagement with the classical past. This is true of the Qur'ān itself, as well as of whole disciplines such as philosophy, theology, and medicine. Arabic literature, both prose and poetry, drew on Greek myth and legend, and even the Arabic language itself contains a significant number of Greek and Latin loanwords.

This engagement is not limited to a perceived golden age such as the period from the eighth to tenth century; it continues throughout the medieval and early modern period. During the so-called renaissance (*nahḍa*) of Arabic culture in the late nineteenth and twentieth centuries, the engagement with Greek poetry, especially comedy and tragedy, forms the basis for the development of a new genre: drama. And although our focus was on the Arab world, we saw that interest in all things Greek was at a peak in the sixteenth century for instance, at the Ottoman Court, or in twentieth-century Iran, where the constitution of the Islamic Republic was inspired by Plato's *Republic*. The story of Alexander the Great, the 'Two-Horned' mentioned in the Qur'ān, was retold countless times and reached the hidden recesses of the Tartar world, as well as Malaysia and Indonesia. Finally, in the twentieth and twenty-first centuries, Horace's *Art of Poetry* was printed in Egypt in a bilingual edition, many Latin authors such as Virgil were translated from the original into Arabic, and the myths of Pygmalion and Narcissus formed the basis of a famous play produced repeatedly and lavishly on the Egyptian stage. This recent engagement is underpinned by the numerous classics departments that yield graduates able to read Greek and Latin in the original, who can take charge of institutions of cultural heritage such as the Egyptian Supreme Council of Antiquities.

My second thread is this. Abū Sulaymān begins by quoting Plato, but then relates the story of the blind men and the elephant. This animal already provides a good indication as to what its place of origin is: India. The story of the blind men and the elephant is linked to a Buddhist milieu. In other words, Abū Sulaymān combines a Greek idea with material from other cultures and creates something new. We have seen this process at work time and again, when discussing the Greek influence on Muslim civilisation. I am not going to dwell on philosophy and theology, where the case is particularly strong, but rather proceed to the medical tradition that evolved in the lands of Islam. It drew on Greek humoral pathology – that is, on the basic idea that the balance of the four humours (blood, phlegm, yellow bile, black bile) leads to health and their imbalance causes disease. But it also incorporated new medicinal substances from the East – from India, for example. Ibn Serapion (fl. 870s), author of a medical handbook, listed the recipe for an 'Indian pill' that helps against headaches and halitosis while also having an aphrodisiac effect – what Jim al-Khalili once likened to 'toothpaste, viagra, and aspirin'.[4] The topic of sexual intercourse generated a new genre of manuals on sexology. It started with largely Greek-inspired material, but then branched out into erotic literature and Kama Sutra; we thus witness how the Indian heritage gets combined with the Greek. In literature, too, Greek story lines provided a starting point, but authors adapted their subjects in creative ways. Al-Ḥakīm's *Praxa* follows the Greek play relatively closely in Act 1, but then diverges significantly from its model. The same could be said of the five adaptations of Sophocles' *Oedipus King*, or of the reimaginings of Aristophanes' *Lysistrata*, one of which is set in the Oil Ministry in Baghdad. Again and again, in different areas, Graeco-Roman thought is transformed into something new and startling; and this is achieved through a highly creative process. In many cases, the classical heritage thus transformed also impacted European culture: it is impossible to imagine scholastic philosophy without Arabo-Latin translations of such eminent figures as Avicenna (980–1037) or Averroes (1126–98). It is for this reason that John Selden, the English jurist and scholar, could still say in 1642: 'Previously, the liberal and correctly taught sciences were for a long time called by us "the studies of the Arabs" or "Arabic studies", as if they took their name from the only people and places where they were then cultivated in a serious way.'[5]

Al-Kindī insisted that '[w]e must not be ashamed to admire the truth or to acquire it from wherever it comes. [. . .] There is for the student of truth nothing more important than the truth.'[6] This brings me to my third and last thread: the great amount of openness and tolerance for the other that characterised much of this engagement with the classics. Abū Sulayman ponders the human condition and acknowledges that our ability to reach the truth is limited. As humans, we shall never know the whole truth; we can only grasp aspects of it. We see here again the culture of ambiguity: all three blind men are right in their report about the elephant, even if at first glance their descriptions seem to be mutually exclusive. This tale is an indirect warning not to accuse others of mistakes or ignorance because we could all be right. The truth unites, but false accusations divide us. Abū Sulaymān's warnings were prophetic. The Muslim world today is riven not just by conflict between Shiites and Sunnis but also by disputes within various religious groups; at the origin of these conflicts and divisions lie claims about the absolute truth and accusations of apostasy.

Take the examples of Ṭāhā Ḥusayn and Ibn ʿUṯaymīn: both claimed to know the truth. Ḥusayn asserted: '[b]ut *the truth* is this: these seven readings do not belong to the revelation'.[7] Ibn ʿUṯaymīn knew exactly how the Qur'ān was transmitted. While medieval commentators and scholars often finished an argument with the formula 'God knows better' (اللهُ أَعْلَمُ), Ibn ʿUṯaymīn ended his chapter on the history of the Qur'ānic text with the following invocation: 'Therefore praise be to God, Lord of the Heavens and Lord of the Earth, Lord of the universe.'[8] In these words he thanks God for the certain knowledge that God had imparted to him. The way in which both Ṭāhā Ḥusayn and Ibn ʿUṯaymīn laid claim to the truth as their own possession is alien to the modes of discourse we find in medieval Muslim scholarship.[9]

To sum up, Muslim civilisation is characterised by (1) the ubiquitous presence of the Graeco-Roman legacy; (2) an innovative engagement with this heritage and the creation of new genres and disciplines that are of immense importance for intellectual history; and (3) achieving all this in a tolerant way. Therefore the Muslim world is heir to the classical tradition just as much as the West. In fact the western engagement with classical sources often went via Arabic texts translated into Greek, Latin, or even Hebrew. Because of this constant exchange, one could say that the Muslim and Christian worlds belong in the same cultural sphere.[10] Today, when cultural and religious identities and authenticity are often strongly contested, we can learn an important lesson from the arguments presented here. There simply is no pure or unadulterated civilisation, independent of the rest, just as no man is an island, entire of itself. The Greeks drew on the ancient Near Eastern and ancient Egyptian heritage; Greek art even had an 'orientalising' period in the seventh century BC. The Romans famously found inspiration in the literature and philosophy of the Greeks. And Muslim culture in its turn adapted and adopted large parts of the classical legacy.

This process of engagement with the Graeco-Roman heritage is not merely a historical phenomenon, frozen in time and of no relevance today. On the contrary, the classical legacy is at the heart of modern debates about decolonisation, cultural identity, and politics – both in the West and in the Muslim world. The story of the blind men and the elephant teaches us that each one of us finds only some aspects of the truth. Let us therefore seek the truth wherever it comes from; and let us also embrace tolerance and humility. In the end, we are all Plato's children.

# Acknowledgements

*Habent sua fata libelli*. Books have their own stories to tell, and this one has been at least thirty years in the making. It started in 1992, when I went as a volunteer with Aktion Sühnezeichen/ Friedensdienste to work with Holocaust survivors in a geriatric hospital in South Tel-Aviv. It was there that I fell in love with a Palestinian girl, and felt that I needed to learn her mother tongue. On my return to Hamburg, my native city, I enrolled in Arabic at university, and quickly realised that the Arabo-Islamic civilisation is as much heir to the classics as our 'western' culture.

Over the course of my academic career, I focused on the reception of the classics in the Islamic world, not just in the Middle Ages, where my research began, but also in the modern period.[1] In particular, I was fortunate in securing funding from the Leverhulme Trust to work on the Arab Athena project from 2013 to 2015; I would like to record my gratitude to the Trust for its unstinting support as well as its forbearance. Therefore this is, at one level, a very personal book. In large part, it draws on my previous work, published over the past twenty years or so. Critics may take umbrage at the fact that I quote so much of my own scholarship, but this is in part because I had to open new fields of reception studies, and I have dealt with many questions of detail in earlier publications. Here my aim is to tell an engaging story, which will often surprise and astonish; there is no need to be bogged down in the minutiae of recondite arguments, some of which can be found in these earlier publications.

Although I had long thought about writing a book such as this one, it was George B. Owers, my commissioning editor at Polity, who contacted me in late October 2024, suggesting that I write a contribution for the new series 'What the Classics Did for' on the subject of Islam. We entered into an extremely fruitful dialogue, and I am most grateful to him, his board, and the readers for their feedback. Some colleagues and friends were kind enough to read the chapters as I drafted them, and I wish to thank them for their kindness; they include Peter Adamson, Michael Hölzl, Jeremy Kurzyniec, Christian Laes, Lijuan Lin, and Chiara Thumiger. On 10 July 2025, I presented a paper titled 'The Classical Tradition and Islam: An Unknown Encounter' at the Berliner Antike-Kolleg, and am grateful to the audience for their comments and criticism. Likewise, I benefitted greatly from interaction with colleagues at the Humboldt University, where I was a Mercator Fellow in 2025. Here I want to single out Philip J. van der Eijk, who deserves my special gratitude both as principal investigator of the long-term project 'Galen's Commentary on the Hippocratic *Aphorisms*' and as chair of the executive board of the Berliner Antike-Kolleg. I could not have hoped for a better and more diligent copy-editor than Manuela Tecusan, who saved me from many an error. Finally, my production editor at Polity, Rachel Moore, and staff at Cheshire Typesetting handled this difficult manuscript, including the Arabic, Persian, Hebrew and Greek, with poise and precision, and made the whole experience a breeze for the author; they have my thanks.

Over many years, Manchester has provided superb research facilities, especially with its outstanding libraries and congenial research culture. The colleagues from document supply and inter-library loan are true unsung heroes; they provided me with even the most obscure Arabic and Persian publications, and without them I could not have written this book. I would like to thank colleagues in Egypt, Syria, and Lebanon for their hospitality, even if I have not been able to visit them much lately; they include Marīhān Bakr, Našwā Ǧum'a, Īmān Ḥāmid, Šarīf Miṣrī, Iktimāl Raǧab, and Māhir Šafīq. The Avicenna Bookshop (Librairie Avicenne, مَكْتَبة اِبْن سينا) in Paris, formerly (in my view) the best place to find Arabic publications, was a constant source of inspiration for many years. It was there that I first encountered the new *Iliad* translation by Aḥmad 'Etmān (1945–2013), whom I then met in Cairo and who became a good friend.[2] We collaborated intensively together, but he was tragically killed before his time, in a car accident. At the Avicenna Bookshop I also met the Iraqi academic and critic Kāẓim Ǧihād Ḥasan, whose work had inspired me.[3] He then invited me to give a talk on the Arabic Homer in January 2007 at the Institut des Langues et Civilisations Orientales (INALCO), Paris. Finally, my old friends Stefan Buchen and Christoph Hansen helped in ways they cannot even imagine.

I dedicate this book to my daughter Sophie. She and her siblings have given me joy and strength over the years, and I can only hope that the world they inherit will be a better, more peaceful, and more tolerant place. When I think of the conflict and hardship in the Middle East today, two snippets from two of my favourite twentieth-century poets come to mind: *quelle connérie la guerre* ('what a bloody stupid thing is war'), said Jacques Prévert in his poem *Barbara*; and إنَّ اللَيل زائِل ('The night will end'), as Maḥmūd Darwīš put it.[4] Looking at our shared heritage will, I hope, overcome some of these conflicts and make us all realise how much we share with each other.

# Note on transliteration, translations, names, and dates

How to write (or transliterate) words in non-Latin scripts, be they Arabic, Persian, Ottoman Turkish, Hebrew, or Greek, is always somewhat contentious. Here I have opted for a system where I minimise foreign expressions; but, if necessary, I transliterate them according to the rules adopted by Brill's *New Pauly*, a great generalist encyclopaedia for classical studies. For Arabic, the main letters to remember are *ǧ* for the 'j' sound in 'journey' and *š* for the 'sh' sound in 'shout'; *ġ* for a French 'r'; *ḥ*, a strongly aspirated 'h'; ḫ as in the Scottish 'gh' (e.g. in Noughtie); *ḍ*, *ṣ*, *ṭ* are emphatic versions of 'd', 's', and 't'; and *ḏ* and *ṯ* are the voiced and unvoiced 'th', as in 'the' and 'think', respectively.

Orientalists have long favoured transliteration over transcription when it comes to Persian, Ottoman Turkish, Arabic, and other semitic languages. Even today, most western scholars transliterate sources rather than give them in the original spelling. In part, this was necessitated by the high cost of printing non-Latin scripts. But it led to a situation where a work as important as the *Dictionary of Classical Arabic* (*Wörterbuch der Klassischen Arabischen Sprache*), mostly compiled by Manfred Ullmann, is virtually unusable to Arabic native speakers, as all the quotations appear in transliteration.[1] Ullmann himself preferred Arabic in

Arabic script, a preference to which his many handwritten publications testify.[2] In my view, it is intolerable to have significant Arabic quotations in transliteration. Consequently, here I have opted to give the Arabic, Persian, Hebrew, and Greek quotations in their own script; and I always provide an English translation. In this way all readers without knowledge of (any of) these languages can easily follow. These readers would not understand the text in transliteration any more than in the original alphabet – but native speakers or those with some familiarity with the language can read the quotations in the correct alphabet. I mostly limit non-English text to passages from the Qur'ān, poetry, the notes, and the bibliography. In my opinion, transliteration should largely be relegated to the dustbin of history, a relic from a colonial past that is no longer necessary in the age of Unicode, when it is so cheap and easy to print non-European scripts. This said, in a few cases I still had to transliterate – to explain a term or illustrate a rhyme; but I have endeavoured to keep these instances to a minimum.

Most translations are my own and are based on the editions listed in the Bibliography. For the rest, I used (and sometimes modified) the translations cited there.

All dates, unless otherwise indicated, refer to the Christian Era (AD), also known as the Common Era (CE). Only once do I refer to a date according to the Islamic calendar (AH), which begins in the year 622, with the flight (*hiǧra*) of the Prophet Muḥammad. It is a lunar calendar in which the months move backwards in relation to the seasons, so that, for instance, the dates for the month of fasting, Ramaḍān, occur roughly eleven days earlier each year.

Where there is an established English name for a person or place, I favour it: so 'Cairo', not 'al-Qāhira'; 'Mecca', not 'Makka'; 'John', not 'Yuḥannā' or 'Iōhánnēs'; and so on. I also prefer English names for well-known figures from Jewish, Christian, and Muslim scripture – 'Moses' rather than 'Mūsā', or 'Jesus' rather than "Īsā'. In classical Arabic culture there was more than one way to refer to a person. Take Abū Bakr Muḥammad ibn Zakarīyā' al-Rāzī as an example. He can be called 'Abū Bakr', literally 'father of Bakr', his firstborn son; or 'Muḥammad', his name (what one might call his Christian or first name in our tradition); or 'Ibn Zakarīyā'', 'son of Zachariah'; or 'al-Rāzī', a 'relational adjective' (*nisba*) meaning 'from Rayy' (today a suburb of modern Tehran). Here I have generally tried to keep things simple and just give the part of the name by which the individual is best known. If there is an accepted English way of referring to an individual, I adopt it; so 'Avicenna' rather than 'Ibn Sīnā', 'Averroes' rather than 'Ibn Rušd', and 'Maimonides' rather than 'Mūsā ibn 'Ubayd Allāh' or 'Rabbī Mōšēh ben Maymōn' (acronym, 'Rambam'). In many cases, when I first mention a person, I provide the Arabic or Persian form of the name alongside the more usual 'English' term. The situation is different for modern Arab and Persian people, who are generally known by a first and last name, for example Louis 'Awaḍ, Ṭāhā Ḥusayn, or Suhayl Afnān. In such cases I refer to the last name when discussing them. But there sometimes is an established English name such as 'Khomeini', which I favour over the more correctly transliterated 'Ḫumaynī' (which I also provide).

Arabic became a universal language; this can be illustrated here with two complaints, one by a Christian bishop in ninth-century Cordoba and the other by a Karaite Jew in tenth-century Jerusalem, about the fact that their coreligionists neglect their own language – Latin and Hebrew respectively. The Christian exclaims:

> Is it not the case that all Christian young men, who . . . excel in the study of the Gentiles [*sc.* Islamic studies] and reach the outmost height in Arabic linguistic competence, teach the books of the Muslims most eagerly, read them extremely closely, and discuss them with great fervour? How painful it is [to see that] the Christians do not know their language, and Latin speakers pay no attention to their own tongue![3]

And the Jew laments a similar situation, writing in Judaeo-Arabic (Arabic written in Hebrew letters):

> How many sins do we commit each day and how many wrongs are done by us, while we mingle with the Gentiles [*sc.* the Arab Muslims] and imitate their behaviour! We aim at learning their language through grammar, and spend good money on acquiring it, but we omit to learn the Holy Tongue and to seek [to fulfil] God's Commandments.[4]

Christians, Jews, and Muslims alike could use the *basmala*, the invocation 'in the name of God, the Merciful, the Compassionate' (بِاسمِ اللهِ الرَّحمٰنِ الرَّحيم), or talk about 'God's law' (*šarīʿat Allāh*) and thereby understand their own religious law. It is for this reason that I always prefer translation over transliteration when it comes to Arabic technical terms. I know that people sometimes speak of 'Sharia law' when referring to Islamic law, but to me that makes little sense; as I have just said, *šarīʿa* means 'law' and can refer to Jewish, Christian, and Muslim law alike. Moreover, they often use 'Allah' as a translation for Arabic 'Allāh'; but it simply means 'God', and Christians and Jews called their God 'Allāh' as well, as the use of the *basmala* shows. It is precisely this universality of Arabic and the openness of the Muslim civilisation to other cultures that allowed it to thrive so much.

# Notes

## Notes to Introduction

1. Pormann 2015a.
2. Jonge 2023; see also Strohmaier 1998 – an essay programmatically titled 'The Greeks were not Europeans'.
3. Cicero, *On behalf of the Poet Archias* 23, in Watts 1923: 33.
4. West 1997.
5. Ahmed 2016: 174.
6. Brockelmann 1937–49.
7. Von Hees 2017.
8. See e.g. Wisnovsky 2004; Saliba 2007; *contra* Pormann 2010a; Griffel 2021.
9. Montgomery 2007.
10. Montgomery 2013.
11. Hallaq 1993.
12. Goldziher 1916, *pace* Gutas 1997: 198–208.
13. Marquet 2006, *pace* De Smet 2007.
14. Sophocles, Fr. 505 Radt: ὅρκους ἐγὼ γυναικὸς εἰς ὕδωρ γράφω ('The oaths of a woman I write on water'), in Lloyd-Jones 1996: 362–3 (trans. slightly modified); Ullmann 1989.
15. Fraenkel 2015: 3.

## Notes to Chapter 1

1. Ahmed 2016.
2. Goethe 1819: 108, lines 15–16.
3. Halm 2022.
4. Howard-Johnston 2010.
5. In Ullmann 1955–2011, vol. 2: 1313b12–21.
6. Qur'ān 1: 6–7.
7. Crone 1987a.
8. Crone 1987a: 107–9.
9. Cole 2020.
10. Cole 2022.
11. Sozomen 6.38.5; see Bidez and Hansen 1960.
12. Shahîd 1984: 152 n. 54.
13. Shahîd 1995–2010.
14. Nicolle 2007.
15. Crone 2007.
16. Crone 1987b.
17. Donner 2010, *pace* Hoyland 2012.
18. Neuwirth 2019: 379–418.
19. Khorchide and von Stosch 2019: 62–118; see now Reynolds 2025: 42–94.
20. Van der Horst 2015; Jacob of Serugh, trans. in Brock 2007.
21. Neuwirth 2014; 2019.
22. Fowden 2005; 2007.
23. Quoted in Fowden 2007: 36 n. 41.

## Notes to Chapter 2

1. Aly 2023 provides a short survey that largely summarises recent English language scholarship, although it was written without much (if any) knowledge of Greek and ignores seminal publications in German, French, and Italian.
2. Gutas 1997. See now also Gutas 2022 for discourses about translation.
3. Pormann 2024a; 2024b.
4. Ullmann 2002–18, vol. 1; Brentjes 1994.

5. Gutas 1997: 36–41.
6. Gutas and Biesterfeldt 1999.
7. See Adamson 2006; Adamson and Pormann 2012, especially the Introduction, on which what follows is largely based.
8. Adamson and Pormann 2012: 12.
9. Zimmermann 1986: 211–19.
10. Adamson 2002.
11. These examples are taken from Adamson 2002 and Adamson and Pormann 2012.
12. Ed. and trans. Butterworth 2001; trans. Hourani 1961.
13. Izdebska 2022: 198 –200.
14. In Rowson 1988.
15. Mubaššir ibn Fātik, in Badawī 1958, p. 62, lines 7–8.
16. Averroes, in Rosenthal 1956, and see Roth 1958; Lerner 1974.
17. E.g. Plato, *Republic* 466c–d.
18. Cf. Rosenthal 1956, p. 53, lines 24–5 (§ 1.25.7) and p. 58, lines 15–18 (§ 1.28.1); Lerner 1974: 58, 66. Because I found Rosenthal's text and his and Lerner's translations sub-par, I decided to collate the relevant manuscript myself – i.e. Munich, Bayerische Staatsbibliothek, MS Cod. hebr. 308 (henceforth MS M), fol. 17a, lines 22–3 and fol. 19b, lines 5–8 – and offer here a fresh and more idiomatic translation. The manuscript correctly reads והתבונה המשובחות אינו נמנע instead of Rosenthal's והתכונה המשובחת אינו נמצא.
19. Rosenthal 1956, p. 103, lines 6–10 (§§ 3.19.4–5); Lerner 1974: 144–5; MS M, fol. 42, lincs 15–22. The expression ואתה תבאר suggests that the Hebrew translator understood تبين to be a second person singular ('you make clear'), but in the original it must have been a third person, fifth form verb تَبَيَّنَ, meaning 'it is clear'. I also take the phrase 'regime bent on honour' (הַהַנְהָגָה הַכְּבוֹדִיִּית ← مَدينة الكَرامة ← τιμοκρατία) as having a negative connotation in this context.
20. Walzer 1985.
21. Adamson and Pormann 2017.
22. Lamoreaux 2016.

23. Ḥunayn, in Lamoreaux 2016: 8–11.
24. Kessel 2016.
25. Gutas and van Bladel 2009.
26. See e.g. Büttgen et al. 2009.
27. Pormann 2012a; 2021.
28. Lamoreaux 2016: 100–103; Pormann 2008a: 253; and Vagelpohl 2016: 763.
29. Pormann 2008a: 268–9; 2013c; 2019b.
30. Pormann 2008c; see also Pormann 2010b for later developments.
31. Hallum 2012.
32. For Galen's *Commentary on Hippocrates' 'Epidemics'*, see Vagelpohl 2012: 125–130; 2014: 46–7.
33. Pormann 2009b.
34. Ibid.
35. Pormann 2008a; 2012a.
36. Pormann 2021a: 3–5.
37. Gudeman 1929; Bergsträßer 1931.
38. Bergsträßer 1931: 61–2.
39. Tarán and Gutas 2012.
40. Ḥunayn, in Lamoreaux 2016: 38–9.
41. See e.g. Pormann and Savage-Smith 2007: 225–6, under 'innovations'.
42. Pormann 2019a.
43. Kurzyniec 2024.
44. On al-Rāzī, see Pormann 2007b.
45. Kunitzsch and Smart 1986: 45–6, 54.
46. See https://ptolemaeus.badw.de/works_arabic.
47. For the rich history of the astrolabe, visit the dedicated website at Oxford's History of Science Museum: https://www.mhs.ox.ac.uk/astrolabe/index.html.
48. See https://www.mhs.ox.ac.uk/astrolabe/exhibition/index.html.
49. Lin 2024.
50. See https://hunaynnet.oeaw.ac.at.
51. Barry 2017; 2018; Mimura 2017a; 2017b; Karimullah 2021; Pormann 2026.

52. Ullmann 2002–18; Pormann 2012b; Bhayro et al. 2013.
53. Pormann 2011b.
54. Treiger 2015: 189.
55. See 'Forschungsvorhaben "Biblia Arabica" bewilligt' ('Research Project "Arabic Bible" Approved for Funding') at https://aktuelles.uni-frankfurt.de/forschung/forschungsvorhaben-biblia-arabica-bewilligt.
56. Griffith 2013.
57. Griffith 2013: 20.
58. Treiger 2015.
59. Mavroudi 2023.
60. Mavroudi 2002: 395–413.
61. In Oberhelman 1991.
62. Artemidorus, in Harris-McCoy 2012.
63. Mavroudi 2002.
64. Mavroudi 2002: 188–98.
65. Pormann 2015c.
66. Kraemer 1986.
67. Makdisi 1981.
68. Ibid., p. 280.
69. Makdisi 1990; Daiber 2013.
70. Pormann 2015a.
71. Roth 1958: 76.

## Notes to Chapter 3

1. Savage-Smith et al. 2020, vol. 2.1, p. 466, lines 4–6; vol. 3.1, p. 493 (§8.29.2).
2. Ibid., vol. 2.1, p. 466, lines 9–14; vol. 3.1, p. 493 (§8.29.3).
3. I am correcting here my earlier portrayal of this episode in Pormann 2007a: 28.
4. E.g. Lewis 2002: 139.
5. Pormann 2014: 5–6.
6. Quoted in Ullmann 1961: 28 (no. 92), 36 (no. 159), 39 (no. 177), 45 (no. 233), and 56 (no. 325).
7. Ibid.

8. See the rich resources at https://ancientwisdoms.ac.uk.
9. Mubaššir ibn Fātik, translated from Badawī 1958: 29–30.
10. Laes forthcoming.
11. See Rosenthal 1961: 133–4.
12. Lin 2020.
13. In Badawī 1958: 222–42 (life) and 243–51 (utterances).
14. Doufikar-Aerts 2022.
15. For the following sketch, I draw on Doufikar-Aerts 2022: 322–5.
16. Maróth 2006.
17. In Swain 2013: 180–207.
18. Text in Maróth 2006: 27.
19. Doufikar-Aerts 2010.
20. For the following sketch, I draw on Southgate 1977.
21. As quoted in Seyed-Gohrab 2020: 55.
22. Frank 2000.
23. Van Leeuwen 1937.
24. Darke 2002: 61.

## Notes to Chapter 4

1. Al-Bīrūnī, in Zaryāb 1991: 12, lines 10–15; Pormann 2007c: 76.
2. See Ullmann 2009, who completely revolutionised our understanding of how this important text was rendered into Arabic. His findings are summarised in English in Gutas 2012 and Pormann 2011b: 498.
3. Pormann 2018.
4. Pormann and Joosse 2012.
5. See Pormann and Karimullah 2017, on which this sketch is based. Previous literature is also quoted there. The Greek text of books 1–4 is currently being edited and translated into German at the Humboldt University in Berlin; books 5 and 7 are forthcoming in the Corpus Medicorum Graecorum, and an edition and Italian translation of book 6 has appeared (Savino 2020). Pormann et al. 2017a produced a first edition of the Arabic translation, and books 1–4 are currently being reedited by Raphaela Veit on the basis of more manuscripts. See also the discussion in chapter 2.

6. Forcada 2011.
7. Pormann et al. 2017b; van Dalen 2023.
8. Maimonides, in Bos 2019, vol. 1, pp. 38–9.
9. Karimullah 2017a; 2017b; 2019.
10. Vienna, Österreichische Nationalbibliothek, MS Palatinus Mxt. 1408, fol. 57b, lines 7–14; see Pormann and Karimullah 2017: 29.
11. Pormann 2017.
12. Calder 1993.
13. On the treatise *Airs, Waters, Places*, see now Strohmaier 2024.
14. See Adamson 2013, with additional literature.
15. Adamson 2013: 1.
16. See McGinnis 2010 for the natural sciences and Marmura 2005 for metaphysics.
17. Adapted from Pormann 2013a.
18. Robinson 2023.
19. In Bakoš 1956: 159; quoted in Pormann 2013a: 103.
20. In Bakoš 1956: 177; quoted in Pormann 2013a: 104 (slightly modified).
21. Van der Eijk 1997.
22. Pormann 2022: 28.
23. Ibid. (translation slightly modified).
24. Browne 1920: 88–90.
25. Galen, *On Prognosis*, ch. 6, in Nutton 1979: 100–4; see also pp. 194–8 for an extensive and insightful commentary on this story and p. 100 for Nutton's list of parallels.
26. Avicenna 1877, vol. 2, p. 72, lines 13–14.
27. Quoted in Fancy 2013.
28. See Adamson and Di Giovanni 2018.
29. Ben Ahmed 2019; 2020; 2023.
30. Budak 2024.
31. Uslu 2017: 138, 163, fig. 30.
32. Critobulus of Imbros, *History of Mehmed the Conqueror* 4.11.5, in Reinsch 1983: 170; translation from Riggs 1954: 180 (with some modifications).

33. Istanbul, Topkapı Saray, MS Ahmed III 1896; see Mavroudi 2011: 183–6.
34. Trans. in Mavroudi 2011: 185.
35. Morrison 2025.
36. Bachour 2018.
37. Hallum 2008.
38. Vries 2021: 127; Newman 2019: 30.

## Notes to Chapter 5

1. Gelvin 2020; Mitchell 1991.
2. See the highly readable study by Dueck 2010.
3. Ḥusayn 1970–4, vol. 9, p. 24.
4. Pormann 2009a: 202–4; Reid 1996.
5. Ḥusayn, in Glazer 1954: 80–1.
6. Selected papers were published in the proceedings; see أوراق كلاسيكية [*Classical Papers*] 7 (2007), 8 (2008).
7. See Fearn 2010, on which I draw for the following.
8. Budge 1920, vol. 2, pp. 351–5.
9. *The Times*, Thursday 24 December 1896 (issue 35082), p. 7, col. e; quoted in Fearn 2010: 168 (my emphasis).
10. Colomo et al. 2001.
11. Mazza 2024.
12. See Gad 2021 for an Egyptian perspective.
13. Ḥusayn 1970–4, vol. 9, pp. 281–2; trans. in Pormann 2013b: 127.
14. ʿEtmān 2000; Almohanna 2010.
15. ʿEtmān 2000: 13.
16. See Tayib 1983 for a traditional account of its development.
17. Nasser 2025.
18. This is chapter 1.2, titled ‘Research Method’ (منهج البحث).
19. Ḥusayn 1926: 45; trans. in Pormann 2009a: 210 (slightly modified).
20. Ḥusayn 1926: 45–6; trans. in Pormann 2009a: 210–11.
21. Mahmoudi 1998, ch. 3, ‘The Discovery of History’.
22. Šalabī 1972.
23. Al-Rāfiʿī 1926.
24. Al-Rāfiʿī 1954: 6; in Pormann 2009a: 225.

25. Al-Rāfiʿī 1954: 14.
26. Donohue and Tramontini 2004, vol. 1, pp. 153–9.
27. Published later as ʿAwaḍ 1963.
28. ʿAwaḍ 1965a; in the preface (especially pp. 7–10), ʿAwaḍ explains the strange circumstances of its publication and ponders the problem of writing in the dialect rather than the literary register.
29. ʿAwaḍ 1947a.
30. ʿAwaḍ 1965b.
31. In Schoeler and van Gelder 2016.
32. ʿAwaḍ 1966a: 125–6.
33. Trans. Schoeler and van Gelder 2013: 222–3 (§14.2).
34. Ibid.
35. When ʿAwaḍ mentions Ibn ʿAbbās, he does not refer to ʿAbd Allāh ibn al-ʿAbbās (c. 619–688), an important early Qurʾān scholar and ancestor of the ʿAbbāsid dynasty, but rather to an account of the 'journey to heaven' attributed to him, which is almost certainly apocryphal.
36. ʿAwaḍ 1966a: 126.
37. See Pormann 2009a: 217–18.
38. Gavillet 2005.
39. ʿAwaḍ 1966b, 1967, 1969, reprinted in one volume in ʿAwaḍ 1986.
40. ʿAwaḍ 1968.
41. For a more detailed analysis, see Pormann 2009a: 219–24.
42. ʿAwaḍ 1968: 101–2.
43. ʿAwaḍ 1947b: 89.
44. Some scholars have coined the terms 'illuminationist' and 'illuminationism' to refer to this school.
45. Pourjavady 2019.
46. Griffel 2021.
47. Khomeini n.d. I was able to consult the copy from Edinburgh University Library, shelfmark Serj. Coll. 297: 32 Kho [LCN 10961275], which, to my knowledge, is the only exemplar of the original publication present in UK libraries. It was given to the university by Robert B. Serjeant (1915–93), a leading Arabist originally from Edinburgh who worked at SOAS and Cambridge, lately as Sir

Thomas Adams's Professor of Arabic. The full title of this book is as follows:

> The Islamic Government in Iran. The Islamic Government. [By] the highest religious source, the Imām and Muǧāhid, Mr Rūḥullāh al-Ḫumaynī. Lessons on Jurisprudence given by His Eminence, Imām al-Ḫumaynī, the highest source for Shiites to students of religious sciences in Noble Najaf with the title 'Guardianship of the Jurist', 13 Ḏū Qaʿda–1 Ḏū Ḥiǧǧa 1389 [AH, i.e. 20 January–7 February 1970].

It is a small (14 × 20 $cm^2$), unassuming white volume, undated, with a small note at the back that reads: 'Price 50 Lebanese piasters or equivalent'. It must have been printed in Lebanon shortly after the lectures were given. The price corresponds roughly to US$1.50 at the time or something like US$12 or £8 in today's money. Although modestly printed, this book changed the history of the Middle East and beyond, in significant ways.

48. Martin 1996.
49. Ibid., p. 31.
50. Yavari 2013: 296.

## Notes to Chapter 6

1. I take the details of this event, as well as the next two quotations, from an anonymous article titled الإِحْتِفال بِمُتَرْجِم الإِلياذة ['The Celebration of the Translator of the *Iliad*'], which appeared in the journal *The Selection* (المُقتَطَف), in July 1904, at pp. 610–18. See also Hourani 1991: 181–2.
2. The following sketch draws on Pormann 2007a.
3. See Al-Bustānī 1904.
4. Ibid., pp. 77–89.
5. See also DeYoung 2023: 57–8.
6. Al-Bustānī 1904: 47–53.
7. Al-Hāšim 1960; Ṣawāyā n.d.
8. See Pormann 2007a: 30–8, 42–3. They include Dirīnī Ḫašaba (1903–64) in the 1950s; Amīn Salāma (1921–98) in the 1960s; ʿAnbara

Salām al-Ḫālidī (1897–1986) in the 1970s; and Mamdūḥ ʿAdwān (1941–2004), Aḥmad ʿEtmān (1945–2013), and Ayman ʿĀdil in the 2000s.

9. ʿEtmān 2004; al-Bustānī 1904.
10. ʿEtmān 2006.
11. Karawān translated the following Greek plays: *Agamemnon*, *Libation Bearers*, and *Eumenides* by Aeschylus; *Ajax*, *Antigone*, *Oedipus King*, *Oedipus at Colonus*, *Philoctetes*, and *Women of Trachis* by Sophocles; *Electra*, *Hecuba*, *Helen*, *Iphigenia at Aulis*, *Iphigenia at Tauris*, *Medea*, *Phoenician Women*, *Rhesus*, *Suppliants*, and *Trojan Women* by Euripides; and Aristophanes' *Lysistrata*.
12. Šaʿrāwī 2011–16.
13. Al-Ḥaǧǧāǧī 1975: 114.
14. Al-Raʿi 1992: 394.
15. Visit https://www.youtube.com/watch?v=-1P8wkiJFzE&t=7s.
16. Mahfouz 2012. The plays by Tawfīq al-Ḥakīm (*King Oedipus*, 1949), ʿAlī Aḥmad Bākaṯīr (*The Tragedy of Oedipus*, 1949), ʿAlī Sālim (*The Comedy of Oedipus, or You're the One Who Killed the Beast*, 1970), and Walīd Iḫlāṣī (*Oedipus: A Modern Tragedy*, 1981) are available in English translation in Carlson 2005; Fawzī Fahmī's *The Return of the Absent* (1968) has not yet been translated into English. See also Carlson 2024 and the interesting thesis in Cormack 2017; Cormack traces seven different versions of Oedipus.
17. In Hutchins 1981–4, vol. 1, pp. 274–5, 280–81 (translation slightly modified).
18. Al-Raʿi 1992: 375.
19. In Hutchins 1981–4, vol. 1, p. 288; see also Denooz 2003.
20. See Pormann 2010c: 101–5; 2014: 7–12.
21. Al-Ḥakīm 2023: 7.
22. Ibid., p. 11.
23. Al-Ḥakīm 2008: 20; in Khedry and Costandi 1950: 33.
24. Al-Ḥakīm 2008: 58–9; in Khedry and Costandi 1950: 56.
25. Al-Ḥakīm 2008: 9; 2023: 9.
26. Al-Ḥakīm 2008: 114–15; in Khedry and Costandi 1950: 87.

27. Al-Ḥakīm 2008: 116; in Khedry and Costandi 1950: 88.
28 Ibid.
29. ʿEtmān 1978.
30. ʿEtmān 1999; Dessouki 2008; see Pormann 2014: 12–16.
31. Dessouki 2008: 38–42.
32. Basiouny 2009.
33. Ibid.
34. Cortright 2023.
35. Kotzamani 2006b.
36. Kotzamani 2006a.
37. Al-Ramlī 2005a; it is summarised in Kotzamani 2006a: 26–9.
38. This prologue is omitted from the printed version of the play (al-Ramlī 2005a), but included in ʿAzmī 2005.
39. Al-Ramlī 2005b: 175.
40. Ibid., p. 176.
41. Morales 2007: 17–18.
42. DeYoung 1993: 39.
43. Ibid., p. 40.
44. Darwīš 2003; English translations are available in Pormann 2015b: 308–9 and at https://www.best-poems.net/mahmoud_darwish/only_iraq.html.
45. Lucian of Samosata, *A True Story* 2.20.
46. Jonge 2023: 65–8; Zeitlin 2001: 246; and also West 1997 for the general debate about Mesopotamian influences on Greek literature and culture.
47. Aslah and Dorchin 2025.
48. This is a quotation from Darwīš's poem 'I Do Not Know the Desert' (لا أعْرِف الصَحْراء). In the Arabic original, he says: مَنْ يَكْتُبْ حِكايَتَهُ يَرِثْ أرْضَ الكَلام.
49. The Arabic *bayt* has the double meaning of 'poetic unit' or 'verse' and 'house' or 'home', which prompts Darwīš to frame the poem as a place of existential refuge (home).
50. Darwīš 2005.
51. What follows is based on Kraemer 1963: 14–17.
52. Letter dated 4 November 1950, from Carl Rathjens to Israel

Subeiri (Isrā'īl Ṣubayrī, c. 1900–67); Hamburg, Staats- und Universitätsbibliothek, Nachlass Carl Rathjens, Korrespondenzen, Buchstabe S): 'Er ist ein großer Gelehrter und übersetzt die griechischen Klassiker ins Neupersische . . .'; on Rathjens, see now Buchen 2025.

53. Letter dated 2 November 1950 from Rathjens to Emmy Caskel; Hamburg, Staats- und Universitätsbibliothek, Nachlass Carl Rathjens, Korrespondenzen, Buchstabe C): 'Ich bin nach der Marburger Tagung noch mit dem sehr gebildeten Perser, wohl dem intelligentesten Orientalen auch nach europäischem Geschmack, den ich bisher getroffen habe, Soheil Afnan, einen Tag in Frankfurt gewesen'; see also the previous quotation.
54. Afnān 1948; 1952. I was able to consult the latter in the copy now kept at SOAS Library (shelfmark PM 822.93467), which bears his autograph note on the recto of the flyleaf: 'With the compliments of the author'. There is another note on the title page, which reads 'from Mrs Callum'. Although the book was published by Maisonneuve in Paris, it was extremely handsomely printed in Beirut by the Catholic Press (Imprimerie Catholique المَطْبَعَة الكاثوليكيّة).
55. Aeschylus, *Persians*, 918–20, 929–931; in Sommerstein 2008: 114–17 (translation slightly modified).
56. Afnān 1952: 93.
57. Kraemer 1963: 17–24.
58. Ibid., pp. 20–1.
59. Donizeau et al. 2024.
60. Ibid., pp. 6–7.
61. Khajehi 2024; Zandieh 2024.
62. Letailleur 2024.
63. Ovid, *Metamorphoses* 10.243–97 (Pygmalion) and 3.316–510 (Narcissus).
64. Al-Ḥakīm n.d.; Khedry and Costandi 1950: 294–359.
65. Al-Ḥakīm n.d.: 141; Khedry and Costandi 1950: 351.
66. Muṭrān 1948, vol. 3, p. 73 (verses 324–7).
67. Muṭrān 1948, vol. 3, p. 49.
68. Darwīš 1980, vol. 1, pp. 21–2.

**Notes to Chapter 7**

1. For what follows, see Bauer 2021: 37–40.
2. ʿUmar 1982–5 (also visit https://corpuscoranicum.de/en).
3. Marx 2007–24.
4. Nasser 2013; 2020; Melchert 2025.
5. Bauer 2021. In this chapter I often draw on Bauer's work.
6. Quoted in Bauer 2021: 287, n. 1.
7. This is a close paraphrase of Bauer's version of the list: see Bauer 2021: 79.
8. Griffel 2021.
9. Ibn ʿUṯaymīn 2008: 23–7.
10. Ibid., p. 26, my emphasis; I have omitted the pious formula 'may God be pleased with him' (رَضِيَ اللهُ عَنْهُ), which Ibn ʿUṯaymīn inserted after each mention of the caliphs Abū Bakr and ʿUṯmān.
11. Ibn ʿUṯaymīn 2003: 41.
12. On fundamentalism and modernity, see e.g. the now classic Marty and Appleby 1991.
13. Ḥusayn 2017: 78–80.
14. Ibid., p. 80.
15. Ibid., p. 82.
16. Latour 1991.
17. Wolf 1985: 18–26.
18. Timpanaro 2005.
19. Roelli 2020: 74; my emphasis.
20. Ewald 1831: 595.
21. Goodacre 2002; see also the summary of his arguments at https://markgoodacre.org/Q.
22. Ibn ʿUṯaymīn 2008: 27 used the word *mutawātir* ('continuous') to designate this phenomenon; see also Nasser 2013.
23. ʿAwaḍ 1966a: 8.
24. Šākir 1972.
25. Ibid., pp. 27–9.
26. See also Šafīq 2008: 50–2, which indicates that other Egyptian classicists agree with this point.
27. Šākir 1972: 563.

28. Ibid., pp. 566–78.
29. Ibid., p. 428.
30. Ibid., p. 437.
31. ʿImāra 1997.
32. Ibid., pp. 16–17.
33. Ibid., p. 17.
34. Abū Zayd 1995.
35. Abū Zayd with Nelson 2004; Abū Zayd 2006.
36. Al-Ẓawāhirī 2002; Kepel and Milelli 2008: 193–205.
37. Kepel and Milelli 2008: 193–4.
38. Patel 2022: 117–43.
39. Ibid., p. 12.
40. This utterance of the Prophet is reported and discussed by the Shiite scholar Ibn Bābawayh al-Qummī (918/19–991/2), who devotes a whole chapter (*bāb*) to it in his *Meanings of Reports* (مَعاني الأَخْبار), ed. al-Ġaffārī 1959: 157.

## Notes to Epilogue

1. The second *qāla* ('he said') here marks the end of the quotation and I translate it by putting the inverted commas.
2. In Sandūbī 1929: 259–60, no. 64.
3. Pormann and Selove 2017.
4. Pormann 2008b: 352–3; see the BBC documentary 'Science and Islam', Part 1, at c. 30:00. https://www.youtube.com/watch?v=M9eLxDm7mrE.
5. Selden 1642: 156; translation (slightly modified) by Charles Burnett (see Pormann 2012b).
6. Adamson and Pormann 2012: 12.
7. Ḥusayn 2017: 79, my emphasis.
8. Ibn ʿUṯaymīn 2008: 27.
9. See also Bauer 2021: 62.
10. Becker 1922; Kraemer 1959.

## Notes to Acknowledgements

1. I dealt with modern receptions in a series of articles written since the mid-2000s; see Pormann 2006; 2007a; 2009a; 2010c; 2013b; 2014; 2015b.
2. ʿEtmān 2004 described our first encounter in his new preface to the second edition of 2008, p. 9.
3. Jihad 1995; 2007.
4. Darwīš 1980, vol. 1, p. 21.

## Notes to Note on transliteration, translations, names, and dates

1. Ullmann 1955–2011.
2. His last handwritten publication was Ullmann 2021. After that, the then 91-year-old giant of Arabic philology and lexicography put down his pen.
3. *Patrologia Latina*, ed. Migne, vol 121, coll. 555–6; in Pormann 2024b: 45. The expression *Chaldaeorum*, literally 'of the Chaldaeans', clearly refers to Muslims, hence my translation.
4. Abdul-Latif Abul-Karim 1976: 43, lines 20–3; in Pormann 2024b: 44.

# Bibliography

NOTE The Arabic article 'al-' is ignored in alphabetisation.


أوْراق كلاسيكية [*Classical Papers*] 7 (2007). Journal of the Department of Greek and Latin Studies, Faculty of Arts, Cairo University.

— 8 (2008). Journal of the Department of Greek and Latin Studies, Faculty of Arts, Cairo University.

Abdul-Latif Abul-Karim, Mohammed (1976). 'Salmon ben Yeruḥam, Commentary on *Lamentations*: A Critical Edition'. PhD thesis, University of St Andrews.

Abū Zayd, Naṣr Ḥāmid (1995). التّكفير في زَمَن التّفْكير [*Being Declared an Apostate in the Time of Thinking*] (Cairo: Maktabat Madbūlī; 2nd edn. 2003).

— (2006). *Reformation of Islamic Thought: A Critical Historical Analysis* (Amsterdam: Amsterdam University Press).

—, with Esther R. Nelson (2004). *Voice of an Exile: Reflections on Islam* (Westport: Praeger).

Adamson, Peter (2002). *The Arabic Plotinus: A Philosophical Study of the 'Theology of Aristotle'* (London: Duckworth).

— (2006). *Al-Kindī* (Oxford: Oxford University Press).

—, ed. (2013). *Interpreting Avicenna* (Cambridge: Cambridge University Press).

—, and Matteo Di Giovanni, eds (2018). *Interpreting Averroes* (Cambridge: Cambridge University Press).

—, and Peter E. Pormann (2012). *The Philosophical Works of al-Kindī* (Karachi: Oxford University Press).

—, and Peter E. Pormann, eds (2017). *Philosophy and Medicine in the Formative Period of Islam* (London: Warburg Institute).

Afnān, Suhayl, trans. and comm. (1948). نامهٔ أرسطوطاليس دَر بارهٔ هُنَرِ شِعر أز يونانى بِفارِسى گِردانيده سُهَيْل أفْنان [*Aristotle's* Treatise on the Art of Poetry, *Translated from Greek into Persian by Suhayl Afnān*] (London: Luzac).

—, trans. and comm. (1952). اِئسخِلوس. إيرانيان، نَمايِشنامهٔ اِئسخِلوس شاعِر يونان باستان أَز يونانى بفارِسي گِردانيده سُهَيْل أَفنان [*Aeschylus:* Persians, *the Play of Aeschylus, the Poet of Ancient Greece, Translated from Greek into Persian by Suhayl Afnān*] (Paris: Adrien Maisonneuve).

Ahmed, Shahab (2016). *What Is Islam? The Importance of Being Islamic* (Princeton, NJ: Princeton University Press).

Almohanna, Mohammad N. (2010). 'The Reception of the *Ichneutai* in the Modern Arabic World'. *New Voices in Classical Reception Studies* 5. https://fass.open.ac.uk/sites/fass.open.ac.uk/files/files/new-voices-journal/issue5/Almohannafm.pdf.

Aly, El-Hussein A. Y. (2023). *The Graeco-Arabic Translation Movement* (Cambridge: Cambridge University Press).

Aslah, Kawthar, and Haim Dorchin (2025). 'Homeric Memory in Israeli and Palestinian Poetry: Meir Wieseltier and Mahmoud Darwish', in *Classics Transformed in Jewish, Israeli, and Palestinian Receptions*, ed. by Vered L. Kenaan and Patricia A. Rosenmeyer (Oxford: Oxford University Press), 349–78.

Avicenna (Ibn Sīnā) (1877). كِتاب القانون في الطِّبّ [*The Canon of Medicine*] (Cairo: Maṭbaʿat Būlāq).

ʿAwaḍ, Ibrāhīm (1987). مَعْرَكة الشِّعْر الجاهِلي بَين الرافِعي وطَه حُسَين: بَحْث مَوضوعي مُفَصَّل [*The Fight for Pre-Islamic Poetry between Muṣṭafā Ṣādiq al-Rāfiʿī and Ṭāhā Ḥusain: A Detailed Factual Study*] (Cairo: Maṭbaʿat al-fağr al-ğadīd).

ʿAwaḍ, Louis (1947a). هورس. فَنّ الشِّعْر [*Horace: Art of Poetry*] (Cairo:

Maktabat al-Nahḍa al-Miṣrīya; 3rd edn. 1988, Cairo: al-Hay'a al-Miṣrīya al-'Āmma li-l-Kitāb (as vol. 7 of the series الرَوائِع المِئَة, *One Hundred Masterpieces*)).

— (1947b). بلوتولاند وقَصائِد أُخرى [*Plutoland and Other Poems*] (Cairo: Maṭba'at al-Karnak).

— (1963). *The Theme of Prometheus in English and French Literature: A Study in Literary Influences* (Cairo: Ministry of Culture).

— (1965a). مُذَكِّرات طالِب بَعْثة [*Memoirs of a Scholarship Student*] (Cairo: Mu'assasat Rūz al-Yūsuf; reprint 1991, Cairo: al-Hay'a al-Miṣrīya al-'Āmma li-l-Kitāb).

— (1965b). نُصوص النَقْد الأَدَبي اليوناني [*Greek Texts on Literary Criticism*] (Cairo: Dār al-Ma'ārif).

— (1966a). عَلى هامِش الغُفْران [*On the Margins of the Epistle of Forgiveness*] (Cairo: Dār al-Hilāl).

—, trans. (1966b). أجامِمنون لإسخيلوس [*Agamemnon, by Aeschylus*] (Cairo, Dār al-Kitāb al-'Arabī).

—, trans. (1967). حامِلات القَرابين لإِسخيلوس [*Libation Bearers, by Aeschylus*] (Cairo: Dār al-Ma'ārif).

— (1968). أُسْطورة أورست والمَلاحِم العَرَبية [*The Myth of Orestes and Arabic Epic Poetry*] (Cairo: Dār al-Kātib al-'Arabī).

—, trans. (1969). الصافِحات لإِسخيلوس [*Eumenides, by Aeschylus*] (Cairo: Dār al-Ma'ārif).

—, trans. (1986). ثُلاثيّة أوريست [*The Orestes Trilogy*] (Cairo: al-Hay'a al-Miṣrīya li-l-Kitāb).

'Azmī, Ḥāzim (Hazem Azmi) (2005). 'سَلام النِساء للينين الرَّملي: مِن النَصّ المُقْتَبس إلى الواقِع المُلْتَبِس' [*The Peace of Women* by Lenin al-Ramlī: From the Quoted Text to the Ambiguous Reality]. *Al-Masraḥ*, 17 February 2005.

Bachour, Natalia (2018). 'Iatrochemistry and Paracelsism in the Ottoman Empire in the Sixteenth and Seventeenth Centuries'. *Intellectual History of the Islamicate World* 6, 82–116.

Badawī, 'Abd al-Raḥman, ed. (1958). *Mubaššir ibn Fātik:* كِتاب مُخْتار الحِكَم ومَحاسِن الكَلِم [*The Choicest Maxims and Best Sayings*] (Madrid: Maṭba'at al-Ma'had al-Miṣrī li-l-Dirāsāt al-Islāmīya).

Bakoš, Ján, ed. (1956). *Psychologie d'Ibn Sina (Avicenne) d'après son œuvre aš-Šifā'* (Prague: Éditions de l'Académie tchécoslovaque des sciences).

Barry, Samuel C. (2017). 'Comparing the Terminology of the Major Syriac and Arabic Translations of the Hippocratic *Aphorisms* I'. *Semitica et Classica* 10, 103–10.

— (2018). *Syriac Medicine and Ḥunayn ibn Isḥāq's Arabic Translation of the Hippocratic Aphorisms* (Oxford: Oxford University Press on behalf of the University of Manchester). Special issue of *Journal of Semitic Studies* (Supplement 39).

Basiouny, Dalia (2009). 'Millions Wasted on Lavish Reworking of "Praxa"'. *Daily News Egypt*, 24 July 2009.

Bauer, Thomas (2021). *A Culture of Ambiguity: An Alternative History of Islam*, trans. by Hinrich Biesterfeldt and Tricia Tunstall (New York: Columbia University Press).

Becker, Carl H. (1922). 'Der Islam im Rahmen einer allgemeinen Kulturgeschichte'. *Zeitschrift der Deutschen Morgenländischen Gesellschaft* 76, 18–35.

Ben Ahmed, Fouad (2019). 'Ibn Rushd in the Ḥanbali Tradition: Ibn Taymiyya and Ibn Qayyim al-Jawziyya and the Continuity of Philosophy in Muslim Contexts'. *Muslim World* 19, 561–81.

— (2020). 'Re-Writing the History of Philosophy in Sunni Muslim Contexts: Ibn Taymiyyah and the Impact of Ibn Rushd'. *Hespéris-Tamuda* 55, 303–54.

— (2023). 'Ibn Rushd in the Safavid Iran: "En Orient, après Averroès . . ." Revisited', *Intellectual History of the Islamicate World* 11, 302–30.

Bergsträßer, Gotthelf (1931). Review of Tkatsch 1928. *Der Islam* 20, 48–62.

Bhayro, Siam, Robert Hawley, Grigory Kessel, and Peter E. Pormann (2013). 'The Syriac Galen Palimpsest: Progress, Prospects and Problems'. *Journal of Semitic Studies* 58, 131–48.

Bidez, J. and G. C. Hansen, eds (1960). *Sozomenus: Kirchengeschichte* (Berlin: Akademie-Verlag).

Bos, Gerrit, ed. and trans. (2019). *Maimonides: Commentary on Hippocrates' 'Aphorisms'* (Leiden: Brill).

Brentjes, Sonja (1994). 'Textzeugen und Hypothesen zum arabischen Euklid in der Überlieferung von al-Ḥaǧǧāǧ b. Yūsuf b. Maṭar (zwischen 786 und 833)'. *Archive for History of Exact Sciences* 47, 53–92.

Brock, Sebastian P. (2007). 'Jacob of Serugh's Poem on the Sleepers of Ephesus', in *'I Sowed Fruits into Hearts' (Odes Sol. 17:13. Festschrift for Michael Lattke)*, ed. by Majella Franzmann Allen and Rick Strelan (Strathfield: St Pauls Publications), 3–30.

Brockelmann, Carl (1937–49), *Geschichte der arabischen Litteratur*, vol. 1 (1937), vol. 2 (1949), supplement vol. 1 (1938), supplement vol. 2 (1942), supplement vol. 3 (1949) (Leiden: Brill; reprinted in 5 vols, Leiden: Brill, 1996).

Browne, Edward G., trans. (1920). *Revised Translation of the* Chahár maqála *('Four Discourses') of Niẓámí-I-'Arúḍí of Samarqand* (London: Luzac).

Buchen, Stefan (2025). *Carl Rathjens (1887–1966): Geschichte eines Nonkonformisten* (Göttingen: Wallstein Verlag).

Budak, Samet (2024). 'Teaching Greek, Studying Philosophy, and Discovering Ancient Greek Knowledge at the Ottoman Court in the Fifteenth Century'. *Dumbarton Oaks Papers* 78, 355–98.

Budge, Ernest A. W. (1920). *By Nile and Tigris, a Narrative of Journeys in Egypt and Mesopotamia on behalf of the British Museum between the Years 1886 and 1913* (2 vols, London: J. Murray).

Al-Bustānī, Sulaymān, ed. and trans. (1904). إلياذة هوميروس، مُعَرَّبة نَظمًا وعليها شَرْح تَأْريخي أَدَبي وهي مُصَدَّرة بمُقَدِّمة في هوميروس وشِعْرِه وآداب اليونان والعَرَب ومُذَيَّلة بِمُعْجَم عامّ وفهارِس [Homer's *Iliad*, translated into Arabic verse, with a historical and literary commentary; prefaced with an introduction on Homer and his poetry, as well as the literature of the Greeks and the Arabs; and appended to it are a general lexicon and indices] (Cairo: Maṭbaʿat al-Hilāl [Crescent Press]; reprinted Cairo: al-Maǧlis al-aʿlā li-l-ṯaqāfa [Supreme Council for Culture], 2004).

Butterworth, Charles E., ed. and trans. (2001). Averroës: *The Book of the Decisive Treatise Determining the Connection between the Law and Wisdom & Epistle Dedicatory* (Provo, UT: Brigham Young University Press).

Büttgen, Philippe, Alain de Libera, Marwan Rashed, and Irène Rosier-Catach, eds (2009). *Les grecs, les arabes et nous: Enquête sur l'islamophobie savante* (Paris: Fayard).

Calder, Norman (1993). 'Tafsīr from Ṭabarī to Ibn Kathīr: Problems in the Description of a Genre, Illustrated with Reference to the Story of Abraham', in *Approaches to the Qur'ān*, ed. by Gerald R. Hawting and Abdul-Kader A. Shareef (London: Routledge), 101–40.

Carlson, Marvin, ed. (2005). *The Arab Oedipus: Four Plays from Egypt and Syria* (New York: Martin E. Segal Theatre Center Publications).

— (2024). 'Oedipus of Thebes on Arab Stages', in Donizeau et al., 41–52.

Cole, Juan (2020). 'Muhammad and Justinian: Roman Legal Traditions and the Qur'ān'. *Journal of Near Eastern Studies* 79, 183–96.

— (2022). 'Late Roman Law and the Quranic Punishments for Adultery'. *Muslim World* 112, 207–24.

Colomo, Daniella, Agnese Giacomoni, Christian Jung, Alberto Nodar Dominguez, and Peter E. Pormann (2001). '4577. Demosthenes, XIX 154–8, 173–5, 203–5, 211, 231–2, 234–40, 243–5, 293–4', in *Oxyrhynchus Papyri*, vol. 67, ed. by Revel A. Coles (London: Egypt Exploration Society).

Cormack, Raphael C. (2017). 'Oedipus on the Nile: Translations and Adaptations of Sophocles' *Oedipus Tyrannos* in Egypt, 1900–1970'. PhD thesis, University of Edinburgh. http://hdl.handle.net/1842/23624.

Cortright, David (2023). 'The Impact of the Anti-War Movement 20 Years after the US Invaded Iraq'. *The Nation*, 20–27 February 2023.

Crone, Patricia (1987a). *Roman, Provincial, and Islamic Law: The Origins of the Islamic Patronate* (Cambridge: Cambridge University Press).

— (1987b). *Meccan Trade and the Rise of Islam* (Princeton, NJ: Princeton University Press).

— (2007). 'Quraysh and the Roman Army: Making Sense of the Meccan

Leather Trade'. *Bulletin of the School of Oriental and African Studies* 70, 63–88.

Daiber, Hans (2013). 'Humanism: A Tradition Common to both Islam and Europe'. *Filozofija i društvo* 24, 293–310. Reprinted in Hans Daiber (2022), *From the Greeks to the Arabs and Beyond*, vol. 4: *Islam, Europe and Beyond*. Leiden: Brill.

Darke, Hubert (2002). *The Book of Government or Rules for Kings: The Siyar Al Muluk or Siyasat-Nama of Nizam Al-Mulk* (London: Taylor & Francis).

Darwīš, Maḥmūd (1980). ديوان مَحْمود دَرْويش (*Maḥmūd Darwīš's Collected Poems*) (2 vols, Beirut: Dār al-ʿAwda).

— (2003). 'ليس سوى العراق' [There is only Iraq]. *Al-Quds al-ʿArabī*, 29 March 2003, p. 1.

— (2005). كَزَهْرِ اللَّوْز أو أَبْعَد [*Like Almond Blossom or Farther*] (Beirut: Riyāḍ al-Rayyis li-l-Kutub wa-l-Našr).

Denooz, Laurence (2002). *Entre Orient et Occident: Rôles de l'hellénisme et du pharaonisme dans l'œuvre de Tawfiq al-Hakim* (Geneva: Librairie Droz).

— (2003). 'Œdipe-Roi en trompe-l'œil: Étude d'*al-Malik Œdipe* de Tawfīq al-Ḥakīm'. *Kernos*, 16, 211–24.

De Smet, Daniel (2007). 'Yves Marquet, les Iḫwān al-Ṣafā' et le pythagorisme'. *Journal Asiatique* 295, 491–500.

Dessouki, Fatma Khalil M. (2008). *Al-Hakim ne suit pas le cortège*, Publicaciones del Instituto Egipcio de Estudios Islámicos en Madrid (Madrid: Instituto Egipcio de Estudios Islámicos).

DeYoung, Terri L. (1993). 'A New Reading of Badr Shākir al-Sayyāb's "Hymn of the Rain"'. *Journal of Arabic Literature* 24, 39–61.

— (2023). 'On Modern Arabic Poetry and the Graeco-Roman Classical Tradition', in *Brill's Companion to Classical Reception and Modern World Poetry*, ed. by Polina Tambakaki (Leiden: Brill), 47–82.

Donizeau, Pauline, Yassaman Khajehi, and Daniela Potenza, eds (2024). *Greek Tragedy and the Middle East: Chasing the Myth* (London: Bloomsbury Academic).

Donner, Fred (2010). *Muhammad and the Believers: At the Origins of Islam* (Cambridge: Belknap).

Donohue, John J., and Leslie Tramontini (eds) (2004). *Crosshatching in Global Culture: A Dictionary of Modern Arab Writers: An Updated English version of R. B. Campbell's 'Contemporary Arab Writers'* (2 vols, Würzburg: Orient-Institut der Deutschen Morgenländischen Gesellschaft / Ergon in Kommission).

Doufikar-Aerts, Faustina C. W. (2010). *Alexander Magnus Arabicus: A Survey of the Alexander Tradition through Seven Centuries: From Pseudo-Callisthenes to Ṣūrī*, trans. by Ania Lentz-Michaelis (Paris: Peeters).

— (2022). 'Alexander in Medieval Arab Minds: Archetype of Kings, Magnificent Warrior, and Custodian of Philosophy and Divine Principles', in Stoneman, 308–33.

Dueck, Jennifer M. (2010). *The Claims of Culture at Empire's End: Syria and Lebanon under French Rule* (London: British Academy).

'Etmān, Aḥmad (1978). المَصادِر الكلاسيكية لِمَسْرَح تَوْفيق الحَكيم: دِراسة مُقارَنة [*The Classical Sources in Tawfīq al-Ḥakīm's Theatre: A Comparative Study*] (Cairo: Al-Hay'a al-Miṣrīya al-'Āmma li-l-Kitāb; new edition Cairo: al-Šarika al-Miṣrīya al-'ālamīya: Longman, 1993).

— (1999). الحَكيم لا يَمْشي في الزَفّة [*Al-Ḥakīm Does Not Follow the Common Crowd*] (Cairo: Šarikat al-Amal li-l-ṭibā'a wa-l-našr).

— (2000). مَسْرَحية مَعيز البَهنَسا [*The Play 'Goats of Oxyrhynchus'*] (Cairo: al-Markaz al-Handasī li-l-ṭibā'a wa-l-našr).

—, ed. (2004). إلياذة هوميروس [*Homer's* Iliad] (Cairo: al-Mağlis al-a'lā li-l-ṯaqāfa [Supreme Council for Culture]; 2nd edn Cairo: al-Mağlis al-a'lā li-l-ṯaqāfa, 2008; 3rd edn Cairo: al-Mağlis al-a'lā li-l-ṯaqāfa, 2013).

—, ed. (2006). الإلياذة عَبْرَ العُصور : أعمال الحَلقة البَحثية، 29 مايو – 1 يونيو 2004 بِمُناسَبة مِئَوِيّة تَرْجَمة سُلَيمان البُستاني وصُدور تَرْجَمة جَديدة عَن الإغْريقيّة مُباشَرَةً [*The 'Iliad' across the Ages: Proceedings of the Symposium held from 29 May to 1 June 2004 on the Occasion of the Centenary of Sulaymān al-Bustānī's Translation, and the Publication of a New Translation Directly Made from the Greek*] (Cairo: al-Mağlis al-a'lā li-l-ṯaqāfa [Supreme Council for Culture]).

Ewald, Heinrich (1831). Review of Johan J. Stähelin, *Kritische*

*Untersuchungen über die Genesis* (Basle, J. G. Neukirch, 1830). *Theologische Studien und Kritiken* 4, 595–606.

Fancy, Nahyan A. G. (2013). *Science and Religion in Mamluk Egypt: Ibn al-Nafis, Pulmonary Transit and Bodily Resurrection* (London: Routledge).

Fearn, David (2010). 'Imperialist Fragmentation and the Discovery of Bacchylides', in *Classics and Imperialism in the British Empire*, ed. Mark Bradley (Oxford: Oxford University Press), 158–85.

Forcada, Miquel (2011). 'Ibn Bājja on Medicine and Medical Experience'. *Arabic Sciences and Philosophy* 21, 111–48.

Fowden, Garth (2004). *Quṣayr 'Amra: Art and the Umayyad Elite in Late Antique Syria* (Berkeley: University of California Press).

— (2007). 'Greek Myth and Arabic Poetry at Quṣayr 'Amra', in *Islamic Crosspollinations: Interactions in the Medieval Middle East*, ed. Anna A. Akasoy, James E. Montgomery, and Peter E. Pormann (Oxford: Oxbow), 29–45.

Fraenkel, Carlos (2015). 'Teaching Plato in Palestine', in *Teaching Plato in Palestine: Philosophy in a Divided World*, ed. by Carlos Fraenkel (Princeton, NJ: Princeton University Press), 3–29.

Frank, Allen J. (2000). 'Historical Legends of the Volga–Ural Muslims concerning Alexander the Great, the City of Yelabuga, and Bāchmān Khān', *Revue des mondes musulmans et de la Méditerranée* 89–90, 89–107.

Gad, Usama (2021). 'Receptions of Classical Antiquity in Egypt and the Arab World: Parallel Narratives, Invisible Corpora and a Troubled Archive', in *Handbook of Modern Arabic Historical Scholarship on the Ancient and Medieval Periods*, ed. by Amar S. Baadj (Leiden: Brill), 249–93.

al-Ġaffārī, 'Alī Akbar, ed. (1959). مَعاني الأَخْبار لِـ[. . .] بن بابَوَيْه القُمّي [*The Meanings of Reports by . . . Ibn Bābawayh al-Qummī*] (Teheran: Maktabat al-Ṣadūq).

Gavillet, Marguerite (2005). *La geste du Zir Salim d'après un manuscrit syrien* (سيرة الزِّير سالِم حَسْبَ إحدى المَخْطوطات السُّوريّة) (Damascus: Institut français du Proche-Orient).

Gelvin, James L. (2020). *The Modern Middle East: A History* (5th edn, Oxford: Oxford University Press).

Glazer, Sidney, trans. (1954). *Ṭāhā Ḥusayn: The Future of Culture in Egypt* (Washington: American Council of Learned Societies).

Goethe, Johann Wolfgang von (1819). *West-östlicher Divan* (Stuttgart: Cotta).

Goldziher, Ignaz (1916). *Stellung der alten islamischen Orthodoxie zu den antiken Wissenschaften* (Berlin: Verlag der Königlichen Akademie der Wissenschaften).

— (1981). 'The Attitude of Orthodox Islam toward the Ancient Sciences', in *Studies on Islam*, ed. and trans. by Merlin L. Swartz (New York: Oxford University Press), 185–215.

Goodacre, Mark (2002). *The Case against Q: Studies in Markan Priority and the Synoptic Problem* (Harrisburg, PA: Trinity Press International).

Griffel, Frank (2021). *The Formation of Postclassical Philosophy in Arabic* (Oxford: Oxford University Press).

Griffith, Sidney H. (2013). 'When Did the Bible Become an Arabic Scripture?', *Intellectual History of the Islamicate World* 1, 7–23.

Grössing, H. (2014). 'Tkáč (Tkatsch), Jaroslav (Jaroslaus) (1871–1927), Altphilologe, Altertumskundler und Arabist'. *Österreichisches Biographisches Lexikon und biographische Dokumentation 1815–1950*, 14, 359–60.

Gudeman, Alfred (1929). Review of Tkatsch 1928. *Philologische Wochenzeitschrift* 49, 167–78.

Gutas, Dimitri (1975). *Greek Wisdom Literature in Arabic Translation: A Study of the Graeco-Arabic Gnomologia* (New Haven, CT: American Oriental Society).

— (1997). *Greek Thought, Arabic Culture* (London: Routledge).

— (2012). 'The Arabic Transmission of Dioskurides: Philology Triumphant'. *Journal of the American Oriental Society* 132, 457–62.

—, ed. (2022). *Why Translate Science? Documents from Antiquity to the 16th Century in the Historical West (Bactria to the Atlantic)* (Leiden: Brill).

—, and Kevin van Bladel (2009). 'Bayt al-Ḥikma', in *Encyclopaedia of Islam Three Online*, ed. by Kate Fleet, Gudrun Krämer, Denis Matringe, John Nawas, and Devin J. Stewart. https://doi.org/10.1163/1573-3912_ei3_COM_22882.

—, and Hans H. Biesterfeldt (1999). 'The "Alexandria to Baghdad" Complex of Narratives: A Contribution to the Study of Philosophical and Medical Historiography Among the Arabs'. *Documenti e studi sulla tradizione filosofica medievale* 10, 155–93.

Al-Ḥağğāğī, Aḥmad Šams al-Dīn (1975). الأُسطورة في المَسرَح المِصري المُعاصِر ١٩٣٣–١٩٧٠. مجلد ١: مَصادِر الأُسطورة في المَسرَح [*Myth in Contemporary Egyptian Theatre, 1933–1970*, vol. 1: *Mythological Sources in Theatre*] (Cairo: Dār al-Ṯaqāfa li-l-ṭibā'a wa-l-našr).

Al-Ḥakīm, Tawfīk (n.d.). پِجمَليون [*Pygmalion*] (Beirut: Dār al-Kitāb al-Lubnānī).

— (2008). براكسا أو مُشْكِلة الحُكم [*Praxa or the Problem of Government*] (Cairo: Dār al-Šurūq).

— (2023). براكسا أو مُشْكِلة الحُكم [*Praxa or the Problem of Government*] (Windsor: Mu'assasat Hindāwī).

Hallaq, Wael B., trans. and comm. (1993). *Ibn Taymiyya: Against the Greek Logicians* (Oxford: Clarendon).

Hallum, Benjamin C. (2008). 'Zosimus Arabus: The Reception of Zosimos of Panopolis in the Arabic/Islamic World'. PhD, Warburg Institute.

— (2012). 'The Arabic Reception of Galen's *Commentary on Hippocrates' "Epidemics"*', in Pormann 2012a, 185–210.

Halm, Heinz (2022). *Shi'ism* (2nd edn, Edinburgh: Edinburgh University Press).

Hámori, András (1978). 'Reality and Convention in Book Six of Bustani's "Iliad"'. *Journal of Semitic Studies* 23, 95–101.

Harris-McCoy, Daniel E., ed., trans., and comm. (2012). *Artemidorus'* Oneirocritica*: Text, Translation, and Commentary* (Oxford: Oxford University Press).

al-Hāšim, Joseph (1960). سُلَيمان البُستاني والإلياذة [*Sulaymān al-Bustānī and the Iliad*] (2nd edn, Beirut: Dār al-Kitāb al-Lubnānī).

Hourani, Albert (1991). 'Sulaiman al-Bustani and the Iliad', in *Islam in European Thought*, ed. Albert Hourani (Cambridge: Cambridge University Press), 174–87.

Hourani, George F., ed., trans., and comm. (1961). *Averroes: On the Harmony of Religion and Philosophy* (London: Luzac (for the E. J. W. Gibb Memorial)).

Howard-Johnston, James D. (2010). *Witnesses to a World Crisis: Historians and Histories of the Middle East in the Seventh Century* (Oxford: Oxford University Press).

Hoyland, Robert (2012). Review of Donner 2010. *International Journal of Middle East Studies* 44, 573–6.

Ḥusayn, Ṭāhā (1926). في الشِّعْر الجاهِلي [*On Pre-Islamic Poetry*] (Cairo: Maṭbaʿat Dār al-Kutub al-Miṣrīya; reprinted with Preface by ʿAbd al-Munʿim Tulayma, Cairo: Dār al-Nahr li-l-našr wa-l-tawzīʿ, 1996).

— (1970–74), المَجْموعة الكامِلة لمُؤَلَّفات الدُّكتور طَهَ حُسَين [*The Complete Collected Works of Dr Ṭāhā Ḥusayn*] (16 vols, Beirut: Dār al-Kitāb al-Lubnānī).

— (2017). في الأَدَب الجاهِلي [*On Pre-Islamic Literature*] (Windsor: Mu'assasat Hindāwī).

Hutchins, William M., ed. and trans. (1981–4). *Plays, Prefaces & Postscripts of Tawfiq al-Hakim* (2 vols, Washington, DC: Three Continents Press).

Ibn ʿUṯaymīn, Muḥammad (2003). تَفسير جُزء عَمَّ [*Commentary on the Final Section of the Qur'ān*] (3rd edn, Riyad: Dār al-Ṯurayyā li-l-Našr wa-l-Tawzīʿ).

— (2008). في أُصول التَفسير [*On the Foundations of Qur'ānic Exegesis*] (Damām: Dār Ibn al-Ǧawzī li-l-Našr wa-l-Tawzīʿ).

ʿImāra, Muḥammad (1997). جَمال الدّين الأَفْغاني: بَينَ حَقائِق التّأْريخ وأَكاذيب لويس عَوَض [*Ǧamāl al-Dīn al-Afġānī: Between the Historical Facts and the Lies of Louis ʿAwaḍ*] (Cairo: Dār al-Raššād).

Izdebska, Anna (2022). 'Popular Pythagoreanism in the Arabic Tradition: Between Biography and Gnomology', in *Brill's Companion to the Reception of Pythagoras and Pythagoreanism in the Middle Ages and the Renaissance*, ed. Irene Caiazzo, Constantinos Macris, and Aurélien Robert (Leiden: Brill), 193–228.

Jihad, Kadhim [Kāẓim Ǧihād Ḥasan] (1995). 'Al-Bustânî, traducteur de l'Iliade'. *Revue d'Études Palestiniennes* 56, 79–100.

— (2007). La part de l'étranger: La traduction de la poésie dans la culture arabe: Essai critique (Paris/Arles: Sindbad / Actes Sud).

Jonge, Casper C. de (2023). 'Grieks zonder grenzen: Interculturele dialogen in de Griekse literatuur van de Romeinse Keizertijd' [Greek without Borders: Intercultural Dialogues in Imperial Greek Literature]. *Lampas* 56, 55–71. (Reworked version of his inaugural lecture 'Grieks zonder grenzen' at Leiden University, 2022. www.universiteitleiden.nl/medewerkers/casper-de-jonge/publicaties#tab-4.)

Karimullah, Kamran I. (2017a). 'Avicenna and Galen, Philosophy and Medicine: Contextualising Discussions of Medical Experience in Medieval Islamic Physicians and Philosophers'. *Oriens* 45, 105–49.

— (2017b). 'Assessing Avicenna's (d. 428/1037) Medical Influence in Prolegomena to Post-Classical (1100–1900 CE) Medical Commentaries: Ibn Abī Ṣādiq (d. after 460/1067), 'Abd al-Laṭīf al-Baġdādī (d. 629/1231), Faḫr al-Dīn al-Rāzī (d. 606/1210)'. *Mélanges de l'Institut dominicain d'études orientales* 32, 93–134.

— (2019). 'The Emergence of Verification (*taḥqīq*) in Islamic Medicine'. *Oriens* 47, 1–113.

— (2021). 'On the Authorship of the Syriac *Prognostic*', in Pormann, 286–318.

Kepel, Giles, and Jean-Pierre Milelli, eds (2008). *Al Qaeda in Its Own Words* (Cambridge, MA: Belknap Press of Harvard University Press).

Kessel, Grigory (2016). 'Appendix 4: Inventory of Galen's Extant Works in Syriac', in Lamoreaux, 168–92.

Khajehi, Yassaman (2024). 'So Many Medeas!', in Donizeau et al., 93–110.

Khedry, A., and N. Costandi, trans. (1950). *Tewfik el Hakim: Théâtre arabe* (Paris: Nouvelles Éditions Latines).

Khomeini (Ḫumaynī), Rūḥullāh (n.d.). الحُكومة الإسْلاميّة. ولاية الفقيه [*Islamic Government: The Guardianship of the Jurist*] ([probably Beirut, c. 1973]).

Khorchide, Mouhanad, and Klaus von Stosch (2019). *The Other Prophet: Jesus in the Qur'an* (London: Gingko).

Kotzamani, Marina (2006a). 'Lysistrata on the Arabic Stage'. *PAJ: A Journal of Performance and Art*, 83, 13–41.

— (2006b). 'Artist Citizens in the Age of the Web: The Lysistrata Project (2003–present)'. *Theater* 36, 103–10.

Kraemer, Joel L. (1986). *Humanism in the Renaissance of Islam: The Cultural Revival during the Buyid Age* (Leiden: Brill).

Kraemer, Jörg (1959). *Das Problem der islamischen Kulturgeschichte* (Tübingen: Niemeyer).

— (1963). 'Der islamische Modernismus und das griechische Erbe'. *Der Islam* 38, 1–27.

Kunitzsch, Paul, and Tim Smart (1986). *Short Guide to Modern Star Names and Their Derivations* (Wiesbaden: Harrassowitz).

Kurzyniec, Jeremy (2024). "Alī ibn Naṣr's *Jawāmiʿ al-Ladhdha* and the Development of Pre-Modern Arabic Sexology'. PhD thesis, Yale University.

Laes, Christian (forthcoming). 'Close Encounters of the Unexpected Kind: Lifeworlds and Slavery in the *Vita Aesopi*, Version G, (Re) considered', in *Lebenswelt neu gedacht: Ansätze und Konzepte zur Rekonstruktion antiker Lebenswelten von augusteischer Zeit bis in die Spätantike*, ed. by Veronika Egetenmeyr and Susanne Froehlich (Tübingen: Mohr Siebeck).

Lamoreaux, John C., ed. and trans. (2016). *Ḥunayn ibn Isḥāq on His Galen Translations* (Provo, UT: Brigham Young University Press).

Latour, Bruno (1991). *Nous n'avons jamais été modernes* (Paris: La Découverte).

—, (1993). *We Have Never Been Modern*, trans. Catherine Porter (New York: Harvester Wheatsheaf).

Lerner, Ralph (1974). *Averroes on Plato's 'Republic'* (Ithaca, NY: Cornell University Press).

Letailleur, Erica (2024). 'From Ancient Greek Theatre to Turkish Theatre and Back', in Donizeau et al., 53–70.

Lewis, Bernard (2002). *What Went Wrong? The Clash between Islam and Modernity in the Middle East* (London: Weidenfeld & Nicolson).

Lin, Lijuan [林丽娟] (2020). 'A Winged Word on Marriage: Socrates and the Gnomological Tradition'. *Oriens* 48: 251–81.

—, (2024) '元代传入中国的希腊–阿拉伯学知识：再论元〈秘书监志〉中的回回书籍和仪器' ('Graeco-Arabic Knowledge Introduced into China during the Yuan Dynasty: A Re-Examination of the *Huihui Books* and Instruments in Mishujian zhi of the Yuan Dynasty),《文史》146: 154–87.

Lloyd-Jones, Hugh, ed. and trans. (1996). *Sophocles: Fragments* (Cambridge, MA: Harvard University Press).

Mahfouz, Safi Mahmoud (2012). 'The Arab Oedipus: Oriental Perspectives on the Myth'. *Modern Drama*, 55, 171–196.

Mahmoudi, Abdelrashid (1998). *Ṭahā Ḥusain's Education: From the Azhar to the Sorbonne* (Richmond: Curzon).

Makdisi, George A. (1981). *The Rise of the Colleges: Institutions of Learning in Islam and the West* (Edinburgh: Edinburgh University Press).

— (1990). *The Rise of Humanism in Classical Islam and the Christian West* (Edinburgh: Edinburgh University Press).

Maróth, Miklós (2006). *The Correspondence between Aristotle and Alexander the Great: An Anonymous Greek Novel in Letters in Arabic Translation* (Piliscsaba, Hungary: Avicenna Institute of Middle Eastern Studies).

Marquet, Yves (2006). *Les 'frères de la pureté' pythagoriciens de l'Islam: La marque du pythagorisme dans la rédaction des Épîtres des Iḫwan aṣ-Ṣafā'* (Milan: Archè).

Marty, Martin E., and Appleby, R. Scott (eds) (1991). *Fundamentalisms Observed: A Study Conducted by the American Academy of Arts and Sciences* (Chicago, IL: University of Chicago Press).

Mavroudi, Maria V. (2002). *A Byzantine Book on Dream Interpretation: The Oneirocriticon of Achmet and Its Arabic Sources* (Leiden: Brill).

— (2013). 'Pletho as Subversive and His Reception in the Islamic World', in *Power and Subversion in Byzantium: Papers from the 43rd Spring Symposium of Byzantine Studies, Birmingham, March 2010*, ed. by Michael Saxby and Dimiter Angelov (London: Routledge), 177–203.

— (2023). 'Byzantine Translations from Arabic into Greek: Old and New Historiography in Confluence and in Conflict'. *Journal of Late Antique, Islamic and Byzantine Studies* 2, 215–88.

Marmura, Michael E., trans. and comm. (2005). *Avicenna: The Metaphysics of* The Healing (Provo, UT: Brigham Young University Press).

Martin, Vanessa (1996). 'A Comparison between Khumainī's *Government of the Jurist* and the *Commentary on Plato's Republic* of Ibn Rushd'. *Journal of Islamic Studies* 7, 16–31.

Marx, Michael (2007–2024). 'Print Edition: Overview'. *Corpus Coranicum*. Berlin-Brandenburgische Akademie der Wissenschaften. https://corpuscoranicum.de/en/print.

Mazza, Roberta (2024). *Stolen Fragments: Black Markets, Bad Faith, and the Illicit Trade in Ancient Artefacts* (Stanford, CA: Redwood Press).

McGinnis, Jon, ed., trans., and comm. (2010). *The Physics of* The Healing*: Book I & II* (Provo, UT: Brigham Young University Press).

Melchert, Christopher (2025). 'Variant Qur'anic Readings before and after Ibn Mujāhid'. *Journal of the International Qur'anic Studies Association* 10, 173–208.

Mimura, Taro (2017a). 'A Reconsideration of the Authorship of the Syriac Hippocratic *Aphorisms*: The Creation of the Syro-Arabic Bilingual Manuscript of the *Aphorisms* in the Tradition of Ḥunayn ibn Isḥāq's Arabic Translation'. *Oriens* 45, 80–104.

— (2017b). 'Ḥunayn ibn Isḥāq and the Text of the Hippocratic *Aphorisms*'. *Galenos* 10, 67–71.

Mitchell, Timothy (1991). *Colonising Egypt* (Berkeley: University of California Press).

Montgomery, James E. (2007). 'Islamic Crosspollinations', in *Islamic Crosspollinations: Interactions in the Medieval Middle East*, ed. by Anna A. Akasoy, James E. Montgomery, and Peter E. Pormann (Oxford: Oxbow), 148–93.

— (2013). *Al-Jāhiẓ: In Praise of Books* (Edinburgh: Edinburgh University Press).

Morales, Helen (2007). *Classical Mythology: A Very Short Introduction* (Oxford: Oxford University Press).

Morrison, Robert G. (2025). *Merchants of Knowledge: Intellectual Exchange in the Ottoman Empire and Renaissance Europe* (Redwood City, CA: Stanford University Press).

Muṭrān, Ḫalīl (1948). ديوان الخَليل نَظَمَهُ خليل مُطْران [*The Poetry Collection of the Friend (al-ḫalīl), Compiled by Ḫalīl Muṭrān*] (3 vols, Cairo: Dār al-Hilāl).

Nasser, Shady H. (2013). *The Transmission of the Variant Readings of the Qur'ān: The Problem of Tawātur and the Emergence of Shawādhdh* (Leiden: Brill).

— (2020). *The Second Canonization of the Qur'ān (324/936): Ibn Mujāhid and the Founding of the Seven Readings* (Leiden: Brill).

— (2025). *Arabic, Qur'ān, and Poetic License: Reciting the Word of God* (Abington: Routledge).

Neuwirth, Angelika (2014). *Scripture, Poetry and the Making of a Community: Reading the Qur'an as a Literary Text* (Oxford/London: Oxford University Press / Institute of Ismaili Studies).

— (2019). *The Qur'an and Late Antiquity: A Shared Heritage* (Oxford: Oxford University Press).

Newman, William R. (2019). *Newton the Alchemist: Science, Enigma, and the Quest for Nature's 'Secret Fire'* (Princeton, NJ: Princeton University Press).

Nicolle, David (2007). 'Byzantine, Western European, Islamic and Central Asian Influence in the Field of Arms and Armour from the Seventh to Fourteenth Century ad', in *Islamic Crosspollinations: Interactions in the Medieval Middle East*, ed. by Anna A. Akasoy, James E. Montgomery, and Peter E. Pormann (Oxford: Oxbow), 94–118.

Nutton, Vivian, ed., trans., and comm. (1979). *Galen: On Prognosis* (Berlin: Akademie-Verlag).

Oberhelman, Steven M., ed., trans., and comm. (1991). *The Oneirocriticon of Achmet: A Medieval Greek and Arabic Treatise on the Interpretation of Dreams* (Lubbock: Texas Tech University Press).

Parsons, Peter (2007). *The City of the Sharp-Nosed Fish: Greek Lives in Roman Egypt* (London: Weidenfeld & Nicolson).

Patel, Youshaa (2022). *The Muslim Difference: Defining the Line between Believers and Unbelievers from Early Islam to the Present* (New Haven, CT: Yale University Press).

Pormann, Peter E. (2006). 'The Arab "Cultural Awakening" (*Nahḍa*), 1870–1950, and the Classical Tradition'. *International Journal of the Classical Tradition* 13, 3–20.

— (2007a). 'The Arabic Homer: An Untold Story'. *Classical and Modern Literature* 27, 27–44. Reprinted in *Muqāranāt* (*Comparisons*) 3 (2010), 24–43.

— (2007b). 'Al-Rāzī (d. 925) on the Benefits of Sex: A Clinician Caught between Philosophy and Medicine', in *O Ye Gentlemen: Arabic Studies on Science and Literary Culture, in Honour of Remke Kruk*, ed. by Arnoud Vrolijk and Jan P. Hogendijk (Leiden: Brill), 115–27. Reprinted in Pormann (2011a), vol. 2: 134–45.

— (2007c). 'Islamic Medicine Crosspollinated: A Multilingual and Multiconfessional Maze', in *Islamic Crosspollinations: Interactions in the Medieval Middle East*, ed. by Anna A. Akasoy, James E. Montgomery, and Peter E. Pormann (Oxford: Oxbow), 29–45.

— (2008a). 'Case Notes and Clinicians: Galen's Commentary on the Hippocratic *Epidemics* in the Arabic Tradition'. *Arabic Sciences and Philosophy* 18, 247–84.

— (2008b). 'ابن سَرابيون: طَبيب عَلى مُفْتَرَق طُرُق الحَضارات بَيْنَ الشَّرْق والغَرْب' ['Ibn Serapion: A Physician at the Crossroads of Cultures between East and West']. *Al-Mašriq* 82, 343–59.

— (2008c). 'Medical Methodology and Hospital Practice: The Case of Tenth-Century Baghdad', in *In the Age of al-Farabi: Arabic Philosophy in the 4th/10th Century*, ed. by Peter Adamson (London: Warburg Institute), 95–118. Reprinted in Pormann 2011a, vol. 2: 179–206.

— (2009a). 'Classics and Islam: From Homer to al-Qāʿida'. *International Journal of the Classical Tradition* 16, 197–233.

— (2009b). 'Colville, David (c. 1581–1629), Classical and Oriental

Scholar'. In *Oxford Dictionary of National Biography*. https://doi.org/10.1093/ref:odnb/98330.

— (2010a). 'Arabic Astronomy and the Copernican "Revolution" (review article of Saliba 2007). *Annals of Science* 67, 243–8.

— (2010b). 'Islamic Hospitals in the Time of al-Muqtadir', in *Abbasid Studies II: Occasional Papers of the School of 'Abbasid Studies, Leuven, 28 June–1 July 2004*, ed. by John Nawas (Leuven: Peeters), 337–82. Reprinted in Pormann 2011a, vol. 1: 136–78.

— (2010c). 'The Continuing Tradition of Arab Humanism' (review article of Michael Kreutz, *Arabischer Humanismus in der Neuzeit*, Berlin: Lit-Verlag, 2007). *International Journal of the Classical Tradition* 17, 95–106.

—, ed. (2011a). *Islamic Medical and Scientific Tradition* (4 vols, Routledge: London).

— (2011b). 'The Formation of the Arabic Pharmacology: Between Tradition and Innovation'. *Annals of Science* 68, 493–515.

—, ed. (2012a). *Epidemics in Context: Greek Commentaries on Hippocrates in the Arabic Tradition* (Berlin: De Gruyter).

— (2012b). 'The Development of Translation Techniques from Greek into Syriac and Arabic: The Case of Galen's *On the Faculties and Powers of Simple Drugs*, Book Six', in *Medieval Arabic Thought: Essays in Honour of Fritz Zimmermann*, ed. Rotraud Hansberger, M. Afifi al-Akiti, and Charles Burnett (London/Turin: Warburg Institute / Nino Aragno Editore), 143–62.

— (2013a). 'Avicenna on Medical Practice, Epistemology, and the Physiology of the Inner Senses', in Adamson (2013), 91–108.

— (2013b). 'Classical Scholarship and Arab Modernity', in *Modernity's Classics*, ed. Sally Humphreys and Rudolf Wagner (Springer: Heidelberg), 123–41.

— (2013c). 'Qualifying and Quantifying Medical Uncertainty in 10th-Century Baghdad: Abu Bakr al-Razi'. *Journal of the Royal Society of Medicine* 106, 370–72.

— (2014). 'Arabs and Aristophanes, Menander among the Muslims: Greek Humour in the Medieval and Modern Middle East'. *International Journal of the Classical Tradition* 21, 1–29.

— (2015a). 'Abrahamic Religions and the Classical Tradition', in *Oxford Handbook of the Abrahamic Religions*, ed. by Adam Silverstein and Guy G. Stroumsa (Oxford: Oxford University Press), 297–314.

— (2015b). 'Greek Thought, Modern Arabic Culture: Classical Receptions since the *Nahḍa*'. *Intellectual History of the Islamicate World* 3, 291–315.

— (2015c). 'Al-Fārābī: The Melancholic Thinker and Philosopher Poet'. *Journal of the American Oriental Society* 135, 209–24.

— (2017). 'Philosophical Topics in Medieval Arabic Medical Discourse: Problems and Prospects', in Peter Adamson and Peter E. Pormann (eds), *Philosophy and Medicine in the Formative Period of Islam* (London: Warburg Institute), 10–33.

—, ed. (2018). *Cambridge Companion to Hippocrates* (Cambridge: Cambridge University Press).

— (2019a). 'Medical Conceptions of Health from Antiquity to the Renaissance', in *Health: A History*, ed. by Peter Adamson (Oxford: Oxford University Press), 43–74.

— (2019b). 'Concepts of Patient Groups in 10th-Century Iraq and Persia'. *Journal of the Royal Society of Medicine* 112, 160–3.

—, ed. (2021). *Hippocratic Commentaries in the Greek, Latin, Syriac and Arabic Traditions: Selected Papers from the XVth Colloque Hippocratique, Manchester* (Leiden: Brill).

— (2022). 'Medical Epistemology in Arabic Discourse: From Greek Sources to the Arabic Commentary Tradition', in *Islam and Biomedicine*, ed. by Afifi al-Akiti and Aasim I. Padela (Amsterdam: Springer), 17–38.

— (2024a). 'Translation into Syriac, Arabic, and Hebrew', in *Oxford Handbook of Galen*, ed. by Ralph Rosen and Peter N. Singer (Oxford: Oxford University Press), 512–34.

— (2024b). 'The Role of Syriac in the So-Called "First Translation Movement" from Greek into Arabic', in *The Translation Movement between East and West*, ed. by Sharaf Ahmed Zaki Yamani et al. (London: Al-Furqān), 9–46.

—, ed. (2026). *The Syriac Galen Palimpsest* (London: British Academy).

—, and N. Peter Joosse (2012). 'Commentaries on the Hippocratic

Aphorisms in the Arabic Tradition: The Example of Melancholy', in Pormann 2012a: 211–49.

—, and Kamran I. Karimullah (2017). 'The Arabic Commentaries on the Hippocratic *Aphorisms*: Introduction'. *Oriens* 45, 1–52.

—, and Emilie Savage-Smith (2007). *Medieval Islamic Medicine* (Edinburgh / Washington, DC / Cairo: Edinburgh University Press / Georgetown University Press / American University in Cairo Press).

—, and Emily Selove (2017). 'Two New Texts on Medicine and Natural Philosophy by Abū Bakr al-Rāzī'. *Journal of the American Oriental Society* 137, 279–99.

— et al., eds (2017a). *Book 1–7 of Ḥunayn Ibn Isḥāq's Translation of Galen's Commentary on the Hippocratic Aphorisms* (Manchester: University of Manchester). https://doi.org/10.3927/51689293, https://doi.org/10.3927/51689327, https://doi.org/10.3927/51689446, https://doi.org/10.3927/51931732, https://doi.org/10.3927/51931800, https://doi.org/10.3927/51931843, https://doi.org/10.3927/51931881.

— et al. (2017b). 'The Enigma of Arabic and Hebrew Palladius'. *Intellectual History of the Islamicate World* 5, 252–310.

Pourjavady, Reza, ed. (2019). *Philosophy in Qajar Iran* (Leiden: Brill).

Raby, Julian (1983). 'Mehmed the Conqueror's Greek Scriptorium'. *Dumbarton Oaks Papers* 37, 15–62.

Al-Rāfiʿī, Muṣṭafā Ṣādiq (1926). تَحت راية القُرآن: المَعْرَكة بَين القَديم والحَديث [*Under the Banner of the Qur'ān: The Struggle between the Old and the New*] (Cairo: al-Maktaba al-'Ahlīya).

—, (1956). تَحت راية القُرآن: المعركة بَين القَديم والحَديث [*Under the Banner of the Qur'ān: The Struggle between the Old and the New*] (4th edn), ed. by Muḥammad Saʿīd al-ʿIryān (Cairo: al-Maktaba al-Tiǧārīya al-Kubrā).

al-Raʿi, Ali (1992). 'Arabic Drama since the Thirties', in *The Cambridge History of Arabic Literature: Modern Arabic Literature*, ed. by Muḥammad M. Badawī (Cambridge: Cambridge University Press), 358–403.

Al-Ramlī, Lenin [Lenin El-Ramly] (2005a). سَلام النِّساء: عَن مَسْرَحيّة ليزيستراتي لأَريسطوفانيس [*Peace of Women, from the Play* Lysistrata *by Aristophanes*] (Cairo: Dār Miṣr al-Maḥrūsa).

— (2005b). 'Comedy in the East and the Art of Cunning: A Testimony', trans. Ḥāzim 'Azmī, in *The Performance of the Comic in Arabic Theater: Cultural Heritage, Western Models, Postcolonial Hybridity*, ed. Mieke Kolk and Freddy Decreus, special issue of *Documenta: Tijdschrift voor theater; Mededelingen van het documentatiecentrum voor dramatische kunst Gent* 23.3, 166–180. Reprinted in *Ecumenica* (2008) 1.2, 75–86.

Reid, Donald M. (1996). 'Cromer and the Classics: Imperialism, Nationalism and the Greco-Roman Past in modern Egypt'. *Middle Eastern Studies* 32, 1–29.

Reinsch, Diether R., ed. (1983). *Critobuli Imbriotae Historiae* (Berlin: de Gruyter).

Reynolds, Gabriel S. (2025). *Christianity and the Qur'ān: The Rise of Islam in Christian Arabia* (New Haven, CT: Yale University Press).

Riggs, Charles T., trans. (1954). *Kritovoulos: History of Mehmed the Conqueror* (Princeton, NJ: Princeton University Press).

Robinson, Howard (2023). 'Dualism', in *The Stanford Encyclopedia of Philosophy* (2023 edn), ed. by Edward N. Zalta and Uri Nodelman. https://plato.stanford.edu/archives/spr2023/entries/dualism.

Roelli, Philipp, ed. (2020). *Handbook of Stemmatology: History, Methodology, Digital Approaches* (Berlin: De Gruyter).

Rosenthal, Erwin I. J., ed. and trans. (1956). *Averroes' Commentary on Plato's Republic* (Cambridge: Cambridge University Press).

Rosenthal, Franz (1961). 'Al-Mubashshir ibn Fātik: Prolegomena to an Abortive Edition'. *Oriens* 13–14, 132–58.

Roth, Leon (1958). Review of Rosenthal (1956). *Philosophy* 33, 76–77.

Rowson, Everett K. (1988). *A Muslim Philosopher on the Soul and Its Fate: Al-'Amirī's 'Kitāb al-Amad 'alā l-abad'* (New Haven, CT: American Oriental Society).

Šafīq Farīd, Māhir (2008). 'أَثَر الكلاسيكيات في ثَقافَتِنا العَرَبيّة المُعاصِرة: لويس عَوَض مَثَلًا' ['The Influence of Classics on Our Contemporary Arabic Culture: The Example of Louis 'Awaḍ']. أوْراق كلاسيكية [*Classical Papers*] 8 (2008), 49–58.

Šākir, Maḥmūd Muḥammad (1972). أباطيل وأسْمار [*Idle Chatter and Nightly Prattle*] (2nd edn, Cairo: Maṭba'at al-Madanī).

Šalabī, Ḫayrī, ed. (1972). مُحاكَمة طَهَ حُسَيْن: نَصّ قَرار الاتِّهام ضِدَّ طَهَ حُسَيْن سَنة ١٩٢٧ حَوْلَ كِتابِهِ في الشِّعْر الجاهِلي [*The Trial of Ṭāhā Ḥusayn: The Text of the Charge against Ṭāhā Ḥusayn in the Year 1927 regarding His Book 'On Pre-Islamic Poetry'*] (Beirut: al-Mu'assasa al-ʿArabīya li-l-dirāsāt wa-l-našr).

Saliba, George (2007). *Islamic Science and the Making of the European Renaissance* (Cambridge, MA: MIT Press).

Sandūbī, Ḥasan, ed. (1929). أبو حَيّان التَّوحيدي. المُقابَسات [*Abū Ḥayyān al-Tawḥīdī: Sparkling Conversations*] (Cairo: al-Maṭbaʿa al-Raḥmānīya).

Šaʿrāwī, ʿAbd al-Muʿṭī, ed. and trans. (2011–16), الإنيادة [*The Aeneid*] (2 parts, Cairo: al-Mağlis al-aʿlā li-l-ṯaqafa [Supreme Council for Culture]).

Savage-Smith, Emily et al. (2020). *A Literary History of Medicine* (5 vols, Leiden: Brill).

Savino, Christina, ed. (2020). *Galeni In Hippocratis Aphorismorum librum VI commentarium* (Berlin: De Gruyter).

Ṣawāyā, Miḫā'īl (n.d.). سُلَيمان البُسْتاني: إلياذة هوميروس [*Sulaymān al-Bustānī: The* Iliad *of Homer*] (Beirut: Maktabat Ṣādir).

Schoeler, Gregor, and Geert Jan van Gelder, eds and trans. (2013). *Abū l-ʿAlā' al-Maʿarrī: The Epistle of Forgiveness*, vol. 1: *A Vision of Heaven and Hell* (New York: NYU Press).

—, eds and trans. (2016). *The Epistle of Forgiveness by Abū l-ʿAlā' al-Maʿarrī* (New York: NYU Press).

Selden, John, ed., trans., and comm. (1642). *Eutychii Aegyptii, patriarchæ orthodoxorum Alexandrini, scriptoris, ut in Oriente admodùm vetusti ac illustris, ita in Occidente tum paucissimis visi tum perrarò auditi, Ecclesiæ suae origines* [*'The Origins' of His Own Church by Eutychius, the Orthodox Patriarch of Alexandria in Egypt, a Quite Ancient Author Famous in the East, yet Known in the West to Very Few People and Hardly Ever Read*] (London: Richard Bishop).

Seyed-Gohrab, Asghar (2020). 'A Persian Alexander Romance: The Cupbearer's Functions in Niẓāmī's Sharafnāma'. *International Journal of Persian Literature* 5, 40–62.

Shahîd, Irfan (1984). *Byzantium and the Arabs in the Fourth Century* (Washington, DC: Dumbarton Oaks Research Library and Collection; reprinted in 2006).

— (1995–2010). *Byzantium and the Arabs in the Sixth Century* (2 vols, Washington, DC: Dumbarton Oaks Research Library and Collection).

Sommerstein, Alan H., ed. and trans. (2008). *Aeschylus: Persians. Seven against Thebes. Suppliants. Prometheus Bound* (Cambridge, MA: Harvard University Press).

Southgate, Minoo S. (1977). 'Portrait of Alexander in Persian Alexander-Romances of the Islamic Era'. *Journal of the American Oriental Society* 97, 278–284.

Stoneman, Richard, ed. (2022). *A History of Alexander the Great in World Culture* (Cambridge: Cambridge University Press).

Strohmaier, Gotthard, (1998). 'Die Griechen waren keine Europäer', in *Politia Litteraria. Festschrift für Horst Heintze zum 75. Geburtstag*, ed. by Eckhart Höfner and Falk P. Weber (Glienicke: Galda + Wilch), 198–206.

—, ed. and trans. (2024). *Galeni in Hippocratis De aere aquis locis commentariorum I–IV versio Arabica* [*The Arabic Translation of Galen's Commentary in Four Books on Hippocrates'* Airs, Waters, Places] (Berlin: Walter de Gruyter).

Swain, Simon, ed. and trans. (2013). *Themistius, Julian and Greek Political Theory under Rome: Texts, Translations, and Studies of Four Key Works* (Cambridge: Cambridge University Press).

Tarán, Leonardo, and Dimitri Gutas, eds and trans. (2012). *Aristotle Poetics: Editio maior of the Greek Text, with Historial Introductions and Philological Commentaries* (Leiden: Brill).

Tayib, Abdulla El (1983). 'Pre-Islamic Poetry', in *Arabic Literature to the End of the Umayyad Period*, ed. by Alfred F. L. Beeston et al. (Cambridge: Cambridge University Press), 27–113.

Timpanaro, Sebastiano (2005). *The Genesis of Lachmann's Method*, ed. and trans. by Glenn W. Most (Chicago, IL: University of Chicago Press).

Tkatsch, Jaroslaus [Tkáč, Jaroslav] (1928). *Die arabische Übersetzung der Poetik des Aristoteles und die Grundlage der Kritik des griechischen Textes*, vol. 1 (Vienna: Hölder-Pichler-Tempsky).

Treiger, Alexander (2015). 'Christian Graeco-Arabica: Prolegomena to a History of the Arabic Translations of the Greek Church Fathers'. *Intellectual History of the Islamicate World* 3, 188–227.

Ullmann, Manfred (1955–2011). *Wörterbuch der Klassischen Arabischen Sprache* (Wiesbaden: Harrassowitz).

— (1961). *Die arabische Überlieferung der sogenannten Menandersentenzen* (Wiesbaden: Franz Steiner).

— (1989). *Aufs Wasser schreiben*, Beiträge zur Lexikographie des klassischen Arabisch 7 (Munich: Verlag der Bayerischen Akademie der Wissenschaften).

— (2002–18). *Wörterbuch der griechisch-arabischen Übersetzungen des 9. Jahrhunderts* (1 vol. and 3 supplement vols, Wiesbaden: Harrassowitz).

— (2009). *Untersuchungen zur arabischen Überlieferung der Materia medica des Dioskurides* (Wiesbaden: Harrassowitz).

— (2021). *Die arabischen Partikeln* hā *'da',* hāka *'nimm' und* hāti *'gib'* (Tübingen: privately printed).

ʿUmar, Aḥmad M. (1982–5). مُعْجَم القِراءات القرآنيّة [*Lexicon of Variant Qurʾānic Readings*] (8 vols, Kuwait: Ḏāt al-Salāsil; reprinted Tehrān: Intišārāt-i Usvah, 1991–2).

Uslu, Günay (2017). *Homer, Troy and the Turks: Heritage and Identity in the Late Ottoman Empire, 1870–1915* (Amsterdam: Amsterdam University Press).

Vagelpohl, Uwe (2012). 'Galen, *Epidemics*, Book One: Text, Transmission, Translation', in Pormann 2012a: 125–50.

—, ed. and trans. (2014). *Galen: Commentary on Hippocrates' Epidemics Book I, Parts I–III* (Berlin: De Gruyter).

—, ed. and trans. (2016). *Galen: Commentary on Hippocrates' Epidemics Book II, Parts I–VI* (2 vols, Berlin: De Gruyter).

Van Dalen, Elaine (2023). 'The Medieval Hebrew Witnesses of Pseudo-Palladius's Commentary on the Hippocratic *Aphorisms*'. *Aleph* 23, 51–109.

Van der Eijk, Philip J. (1997). 'Galen's Use of the Concept of "Qualified

Experience" in His Dietetic and Pharmacological Works', in *Galen on Pharmacology: Philosophy, History and Medicine*, ed. by A. Debru (Leiden: Brill), 35–57. Reprinted in Van der Eijk, *Medicine and Philosophy in Classical Antiquity: Doctors and Philosophers on Nature, Soul, Health and Disease* (Cambridge: Cambridge University Press, 2005), 279–98.

Van der Horst, Pieter W. (2015). 'Pious Long-Sleepers in Greek, Jewish, and Christian Antiquity', in *Tradition, Transmission, and Transformation from Second Temple Literature through Judaism and Christianity in Late Antiquity*, ed. by Menahem Kister et al. (Leiden: Brill), 93–111.

Van Leeuwen, Pieter J. (1937). 'De Maleische Alexanderroman'. PhD, University of Utrecht.

Venetis, Evangelos, trans. and comm. (2018). *The Persian Alexander: The First Complete Translation of the Iskandarnāma* (London: I. B. Tauris).

Von Hees, Syrinx (2017). *'Inḥiṭāṭ': The Decline Paradigm, Its Influence and Persistence in the Writing of Arab Cultural History* (Würzburg: Ergon).

Vries, Lyke de (2021). *Reformation, Revolution, Renovation: The Roots and Reception of the Rosicrucian Call for General Reform* (Leiden: Brill).

Walzer, Richard, ed., trans., and comm. (1985). *Al-Farabī on the Perfect State: Abū Naṣr al-Fārābīs 'Mabādi' ārā' ahl al-madīna al-fāḍila'* (Oxford: Clarendon).

Watts, Neville H., ed. and trans. (1923). *Cicero: Pro Archia. Post reditum in senatu. Post reditum ad quirites. De domo sua. De haruspicum responsis. Pro Plancio* (Cambridge, MA: Harvard University Press).

West, Martin L. (1997). *The East Face of Helicon: West Asiatic Elements in Greek Poetry and Myth* (Oxford: Clarendon).

Wisnovsky, Robert (2004). 'The Nature and Scope of Arabic Philosophical Commentary in Post-Classical (ca. 1100–1900 AD) Islamic Intellectual History: Some Preliminary Observations', in *Philosophy, Science and Exegesis in Greek, Arabic and Latin Commentaries*, ed. by Peter Adamson, Han Baltussen and Michael

W. F. Stone (2 vols, London: Institute of Classical Studies), vol. 2: 149–91.

Wolf, Friedrich A. (1884). *Prolegomena ad Homerum* (3rd edn), ed. by Rudolf Peppmüller (Halle: Libraria Orphanotrophei).

—, (1985). *Prolegomena to Homer*, ed. and trans. with introduction and notes by Anthony Grafton, Glenn W. Most and James E. G. Zetzel (Princeton, NJ: Princeton University Press).

Yavari, Neguin (2013). 'Khomeini, Ayatollah (1902–89)', in *The Princeton Encyclopedia of Islamic Political Thought*, ed. by Bowering, Gerhard, Patricia Crone, Wadad Kadi, Devin J. Stewart, and Muhammad Q. Zaman (Princeton: Princeton University Press), 296–7.

Zandieh, Rezvan (2024). 'Antigone in Iran', in Donizeau et al., 111–25.

Zaryāb, 'Abbās, ed. (1991). البيروني، كِتاب الصَيْدَنَة في الطِّبِّ [*Al-Bīrūnī: The Book of Medical Pharmacology*] (Tehran: Markaz-i Našr-i Dānišgāhī).

Al-Ẓawāhirī, Ayman (2002). فُرْسان تَحْتَ راية النَّبي [*Knights under the Banner of the Prophet*] (Cairo: al-Maktaba al-Islamīya).

Zeitlin, Froma I. (2001). 'Visions and Revisions of Homer', in *Being Greek under Rome: Cultural Identity, the Second Sophistic and the Development of Empire*, ed. by Simon Goldhill (Cambridge: Cambridge University Press), 195–266.

Zimmermann, Fritz W. (1986). 'The Origins of the So-Called *Theology of Aristotle*', in *Pseudo-Aristotle in the Middle Ages: The 'Theology' and Other Texts*, ed. by Jill Kraye, William F. Ryan, and Charles Schmitt (London: Warburg Institute), 110–240.

# Index